HIDDEN
in PLAIN
VIEW

PAUL IRISH is a Sydneysider who works as a historian and archaeologist with heritage consultancy MDCA. For over ten years, Paul has been piecing together the Aboriginal history of coastal Sydney with researchers from the La Perouse Aboriginal community. It was the subject of his 2015 PhD, and the 2016 exhibition *This Is Where They Travelled: Historical Aboriginal Lives in Sydney*, completed as the recipient of the 2015 NSW History Fellowship. He has published several academic papers, has contributed to the Dictionary of Sydney and City of Sydney Barani websites, and regularly gives public talks and university guest lectures. This is his first book.

For Dad

and his enduring

gift of curiosity

HIDDEN in PLAIN VIEW

The ABORIGINAL PEOPLE of COASTAL SYDNEY

PAUL IRISH

NEWSOUTH

A NewSouth book

Published by
NewSouth Publishing
University of New South Wales Press Ltd
University of New South Wales
Sydney NSW 2052
AUSTRALIA
newsouthpublishing.com

© Paul Irish 2017
First published 2017

10 9 8 7 6 5 4 3 2 1

This book is copyright. Apart from any fair dealing for the purpose of private study, research, criticism or review, as permitted under the *Copyright Act*, no part of this book may be reproduced by any process without written permission. Inquiries should be addressed to the publisher.

National Library of Australia
Cataloguing-in-Publication entry
Creator: Irish, Paul, author.
Title: Hidden in Plain View: The Aboriginal people of coastal Sydney /
 Paul Irish.
ISBN: 9781742235110 (paperback)
ISBN: 9781742242774 (ebook)
ISBN: 9781742248240 (ePDF)
Notes: Includes bibliographical references and index.
Subjects: Aboriginal Australians – New South Wales – Sydney – History.
 Sydney (N.S.W.) – History – 1788-1900.
 Sydney (N.S.W.) – Social conditions – 1788–1900.
 Sydney (N.S.W.) – Colonisation – History.

Design and maps Josephine Pajor-Markus
Cover design Nada Backovic
Cover image GE Peacock 1847, *Port Jackson N.S.W. View in Double Bay S. Side Middle Head in the distance (near sunset)*, State Library of New South Wales DG 37.

COVER IMAGE: The Aboriginal people featured in paintings like this 1847 depiction of Double Bay by George Peacock have literally been hidden in plain view. Aboriginal figures were often viewed as fictional inclusions to romanticise the image on the basis that they were no longer present around Sydney Harbour by the 1840s. A range of historical records now clearly show however that Aboriginal people were still living in places like Double Bay at the time the image was made.

All reasonable efforts were taken to obtain permission to use copyright material reproduced in this book, but in some cases copyright could not be traced. The author welcomes information in this regard.

Contents

Maps	vi
Foreword by Stan Grant	viii
Acknowledgments	xi
INTRODUCTION A gap in place and time	1
CHAPTER 1 Surviving the early colony (1788–1820s)	12
CHAPTER 2 Living to fish (1830s–1840s)	32
CHAPTER 3 Cross-cultural relationships (1790s–1840s)	51
CHAPTER 4 Entangled lives (1850s–1870s)	66
CHAPTER 5 Strangers in their own land (1850s–1870s)	86
CHAPTER 6 Intervention (1870s–1880s)	106
CHAPTER 7 New links and old ways (1890s–1930s)	124
EPILOGUE In plain view	144
Further reading	150
Image references	152
Abbreviations	164
Notes	165
Index	198

Map of Coastal Sydney and Sydney Harbour/Eastern Suburbs

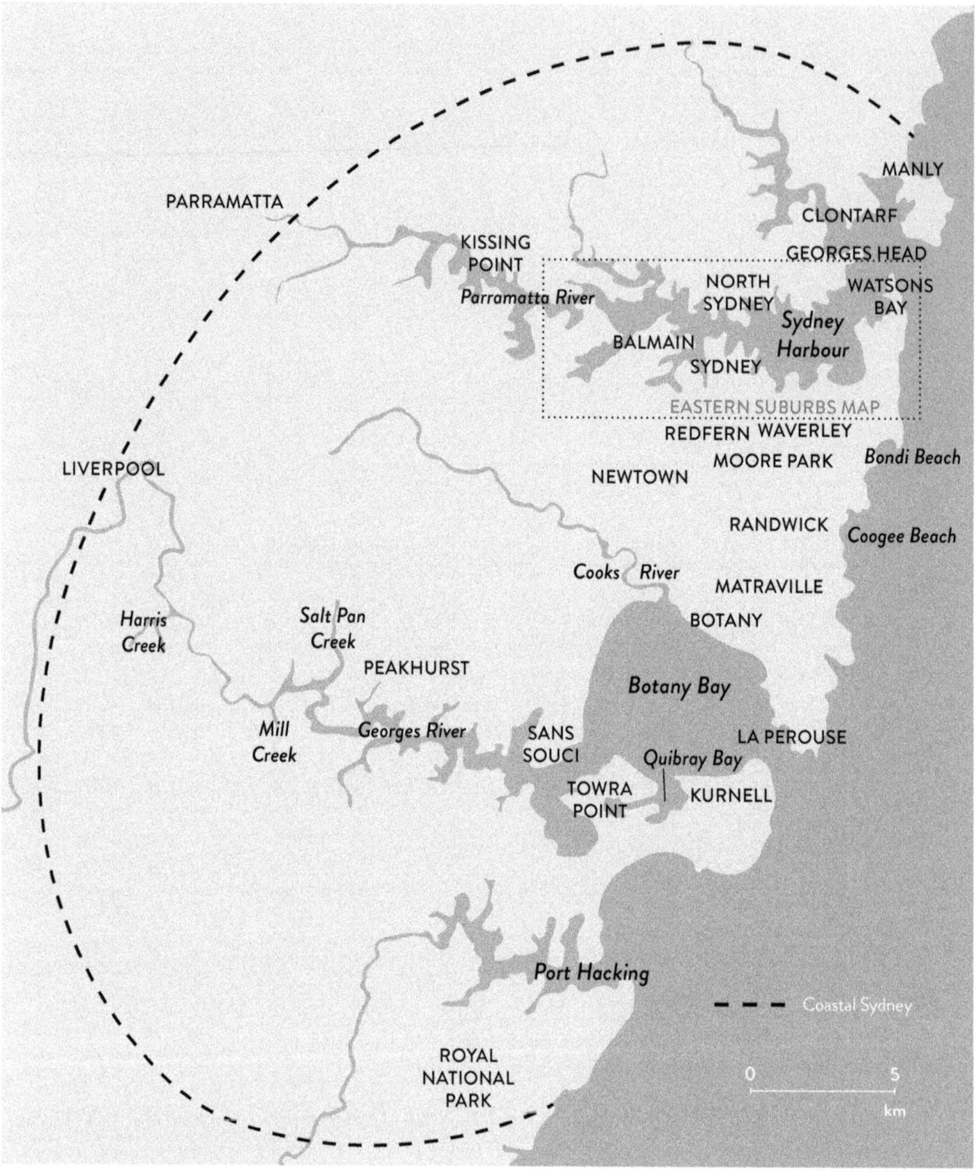

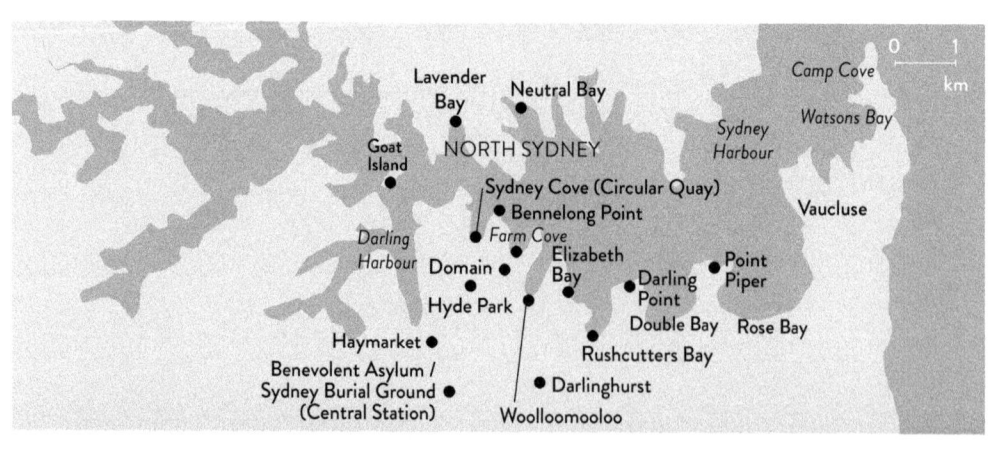

Map of Sydney Region and New South Wales

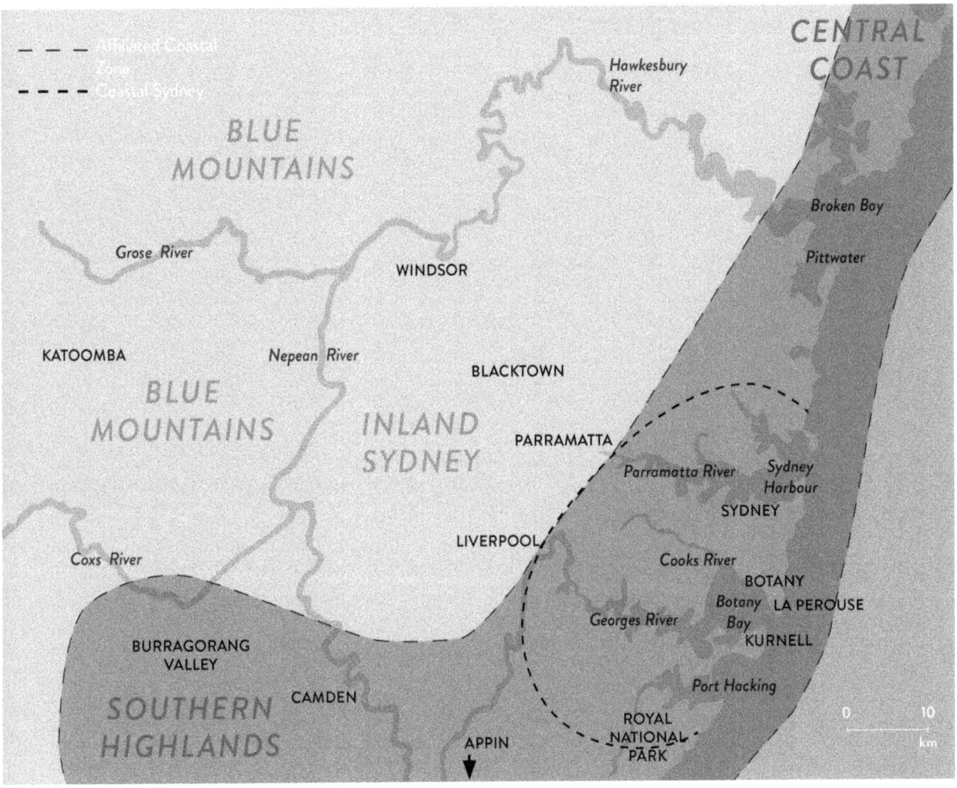

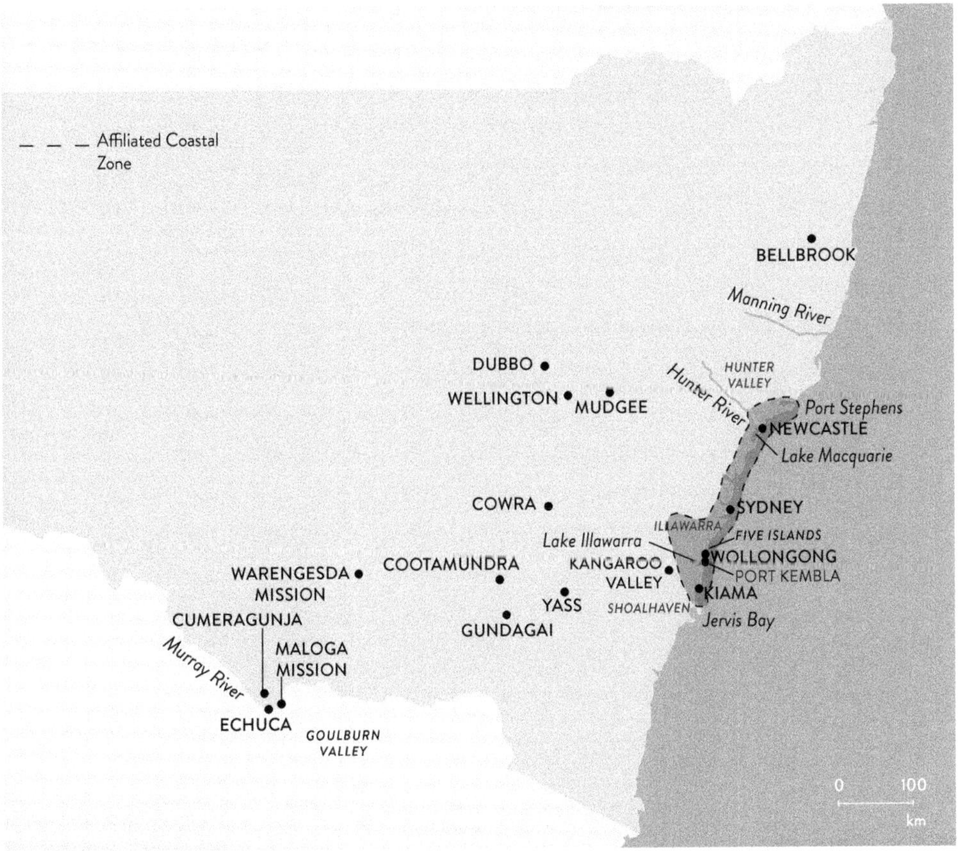

Foreword

I have been trying to find Frank Foster for most of my life – not anymore. Frank is alive to me; a man who existed only as a name buried in my family's past is now flesh and blood. I know where he came from, I know who his parents were, I know what he looked like; the missing pages in his story are now filled with adventure and love and loss.

Frank Foster was my great-great-grandfather. His name appeared fleetingly in Aboriginal mission records and sketches of his story were passed down through our oral tradition. We knew him as 'The Schoolteacher'; it always struck me as odd, this Aboriginal man of the 19th century, a schoolteacher? Yes, indeed he was.

A chance meeting with a young man from La Perouse, who was working with Paul Irish to develop a historical exhibition, unlocked the secrets of Frank's past. It did so much more too; it opened the world that Frank came from. Like so many others, Frank was hidden in plain view. You can find Frank's story in the pages of this book. Paul Irish has breathed new life into people written out of history. These were the people lost to the 'Great Australian Silence'. Paul asks us to look again at Sydney, to see beyond the towers and concrete, the maze of roads and sprawling suburbs to glimpse what is eternal. Everywhere, he says, there are reminders – the rock engravings, shelters, middens that tell us Sydney has an Aboriginal past.

This book tells the story of entangled lives – when white met black – and how a new nation was formed. This is a tale of resilience and ingenuity; a people rendered strangers in their own land, adapted and embraced the ways of the whites while holding to their own traditions. In these pages we meet people like Jack Harris – one of the so-called 'lasts of his tribe' – who engaged with Europeans while never missing a chance to remind them 'this is my country'.

There are others like Jack Harris: Bennelong and Mahroot and Thomas Tamara, William Warrell and Biddy Giles. These people lived, and they lived here in what we now call Sydney. Their roots go back to before the coming of the whites. These people and their ancestors saw those white sails coming through the heads at Botany Bay. This indeed, was not *terra nullius* – an empty land. These were people of culture and language and law and politics and trade and ceremony.

They did not vanish, as popular history has had us believe. In the century after colonisation as Sydney took shape around them, the children, and grandchildren of these First Peoples remained. They continued their traditions, they lived on country and they kept kinship alive. These were people of the coast; they were mobile, setting up new camps as the dispossession continued apace. As Paul points out, despite European occupation there were 'gaps in the grid', and Aboriginal people filled them. They camped in the Domain and Double Bay and Camp Cove. They engaged with the social and economic life of the colony. They navigated this new world; they formed friendships and had children with the newcomers. Bennelong called Governor Phillip *Beanna* (father). Aboriginal people in turn took the names of prominent whites.

Of course, this was an often violent and cruel time. Paul talks about the conflict that rose as cultures and civilisations clashed. He chronicles the devastating impact of smallpox and other disease and how the people regrouped as their numbers were depleted. Amidst this, personal cross-cultural relationships continued to form. As Paul points out this was not the action of a 'defeated people…Aboriginal people in coastal Sydney actively engaged with Europeans to shape their futures as much as possible on their own terms'. This is important. Too often we can see the First Peoples as victims, inheriting a legacy of suffering and injustice – yes, we cannot overlook the darkness of our past, but here is a story of dynamism and creativity; people shaping their destinies in the face of devastation.

Paul chronicles the encroaching heavy hand of authority and control; the missionaries and the government Protectors of Aborigines, a legacy of intervention met with the perseverance of a people. This is the story of Frank Foster – to call him a victim demeans his memory. I found Frank Foster in the boatshed at Circular Quay. In the 1870s he lived there with his parents and siblings among the other huddled remnants of the people of Sydney. It was a brutal place; there was violence and alcohol and sexual exploitation. They lived at the whim of the police. Eventually Frank, along with his family, was moved out to new missions in New South Wales. Here he met and married a Wiradjuri woman and had my great grandmother. Frank was bright and studious; eventually he did in fact become a school teacher in a school set up for Aboriginal kids on the New South Wales south coast. He died in 1941, a long and extraordinary life that lives on still in me.

Frank was not unique or unusual. His story is the story of so many people in this book. They were resilient; they were survivors. They too live on in their descendants who still call Sydney home. I have met cousins of mine whose ancestry reaches back to old times. They live here in this massive metropolis hidden in plain view. But they are here – they have never left.

Stan Grant

Acknowledgments

This book could not have come into being without the Aboriginal people I have had the great privilege of working with, and getting to know, over the past fifteen years. In particular I would like to offer my profound and deepest thanks to Dr Shayne Williams and Michael Ingrey, of the La Perouse Aboriginal community, for sharing their knowledge and friendship over many years, for their ongoing support of my work, and for many enriching and thought-provoking discussions. More recently, as recipient of the 2015 NSW History Fellowship, I have had the pleasure of working with the descendants of some of the Aboriginal people featured in this book to develop the historical exhibition and tour *This Is Where They Travelled: Historical Aboriginal Lives in Sydney*. It provided me not only with the chance to collaboratively research and learn about ten fascinating Aboriginal men and women who lived in coastal Sydney in the 19th century, but also a timely reminder that the history in this book is more than words on a page; it has a continuing, direct and personal importance to many Aboriginal people today. I am thankful to everyone involved in that project, and to Arts NSW for making it possible.

Over the past five years I have learnt much about the craft of history research and writing while completing the PhD that forms the backbone of this book. I owe a large debt of gratitude to Dr Maria Nugent, Professor Tom Griffiths and Dr Sam Furphy at the Australian National University for helping to mould a new recruit with no formal background in history, and to Associate Professor Grace Karskens and Dr Lisa Ford at the University of New South Wales for helping to shape my ideas and words into something worthy of a

PhD. I have also been particularly inspired by Grace's relentless and successful drive to bring history to the public, something which is very much at the heart of *Hidden in Plain View*.

Many colleagues have supported the production of this book by their assistance with historical questions, by holding the fort at work, through valuable discussions about the book and Aboriginal issues more generally, and via their constant encouragement. In particular, I would like to thank Val Attenbrow, Michael Bennett, Mary Dallas, Mark Dunn, Laila Ellmoos, Tamika Goward, Beth Hise, Suzanne Ingram, Lisa Murray, Dom Steele, Dan Tuck and Richard Wright. I am also indebted to many librarians, archivists and local historians who have gone above and beyond the call in searching for answers to my many questions, drawing new information to my attention, and helping me to understand the details. I am particularly grateful to Ronald Briggs and Melissa Jackson at the State Library of New South Wales, to John Ruffels for his eastern suburbs expertise, and to the Woollahra Local History Centre and the Randwick & District Historical Society.

I would especially like to thank Phillipa McGuinness and Kathy Bail of NewSouth Publishing for encouraging me to put this story in print, Paul O'Beirne, Jocelyn Hungerford and Jo Pajor-Markus for helping to make that happen, and the Australian Academy of the Humanities for funding the reproduction of images that form such an essential part of the story. I also greatly appreciate Shayne Williams, Michael Ingrey, Ray Ingrey, Chris Ingrey, Kirsty Beller, Kerri-Ann Youngberry and Michael Bennett taking the time to read and comment on a work in progress.

And finally, to my family. I thank my parents for helping to turn a childhood interest in the past into this book through their constant encouragement to learn. To my beautiful wife, Rowena, I thank you with all my heart for your unwavering support of my work through difficult times, and for the countless times I have leaned on you, often without realising it. I truly could not have done this without you. To my children James, Thomas and Ella, thank you mainly for

Acknowledgments

just being there as a reminder of what's important, and also for your great patience with my fourth child – this book. *Hidden in Plain View* is about your city, and I hope that when you get older, it will have helped to make it a more interesting place for you.

INTRODUCTION

A gap in place and time

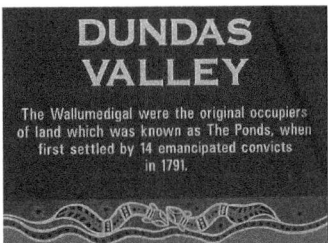
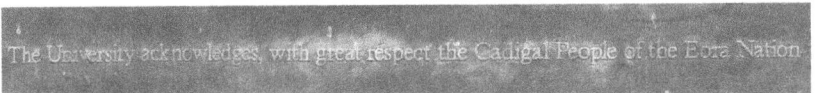

Sprinkled between Sydney's concrete castles and across its sprawling brick and bitumen suburbs are signs like these, erected over the last decade or so, and representing some of the few visible reminders of an Aboriginal presence in the city. In bushland and some backyards, more tangible traces may be encountered in the evocative form of rock engravings, or rock shelters intimately adorned with hand stencils. These sites and signs are effective reminders that Sydney has an Aboriginal *past*. But they are typically encountered without a living Aboriginal presence, giving the impression that Aboriginal Sydney is *a thing of the past*, something that was, but is no more, a people and past deserving of respect and remembrance, but nonetheless ancient, disconnected from modern life, and utterly replaced by the city. For many, these brief encounters mark the beginning and end of their curiosity about Aboriginal Sydney.

Happily, there is a growing number of people who wish to know more, and they can easily find information on websites, in history books, and at museums. They will read descriptions of traditional Aboriginal culture, view its artefacts, learn about the devastating impact of the first decades of the Sydney colony from 1788, and be introduced to some key Aboriginal figures from that time. Then they will skip forward nearly a century to read about the era of government 'protection' from the late 19th century, the pioneering Aboriginal rights movement in Sydney from the 1920s, and the communities and cultural institutions created by Aboriginal migrants from country New South Wales after the Second World War. They will be left in no doubt that Sydney has an ancient Aboriginal past and tragic early colonial history, as well as an equally tragic later history of government control, from which the vibrant Aboriginal present has developed. However, it will be much less clear how, or if, these two ends of the historical spectrum are linked.

This gap in time is even more obvious on the ground. Readers of valuable guidebooks such as Melinda Hinkson's *Aboriginal Sydney: A Guide to Important Places of the Past and Present*, and the City of Sydney's *Barani Barrabugu: Yesterday Tomorrow: Sydney's Aboriginal Journey*, will certainly expand their awareness and experience of Sydney's Aboriginal heritage beyond pre-colonial Aboriginal sites, but what else will they encounter?[1] People using these guides, or participating in Aboriginal cultural tours, are usually shown campsites, rock art and places of early colonial interactions, before leaping forward to 20th-century places associated with the Aboriginal civil rights movement and resettled Aboriginal people from outside of Sydney. They will realise that Aboriginal Sydney did not end in 1788, but they will find virtually nothing to represent the Aboriginal experience between the mid-19th and early 20th centuries.[2] The cultural tourism landscape reflects the dominant interests and findings of the historical and archaeological research on which it is based, but it raises the central question of this book – what happened to Aboriginal people in Sydney in the 19th century?

The answer is hidden in plain view. Sydney's Aboriginal people did not disappear from Sydney in the mid-19th century to be replaced by Aboriginal migrants in the 20th century. But evidence of their ongoing presence in Sydney is less obvious than the vast galleries of rock engravings, the early colonial descriptions and drawings of their ancestors, or the activities of contemporary Aboriginal communities that catch the public's eye. On the ground, little appears to remain of the continuing Aboriginal use of Sydney after the arrival of Europeans, but evidence has survived in other forms, nevertheless. It is scattered lightly across museums, libraries and archives as words, images, maps and artefacts, and in the family histories of some Aboriginal people. It has remained hidden mainly because of a widespread belief that Aboriginal people died out or disappeared from Sydney by the mid-19th century, and that any Aboriginal people in Sydney after this time were either from somewhere else or had lost any cultural attachment to the area.

Like most Sydneysiders, I grew up with this belief of Aboriginal absence. The only time local Aboriginal people featured in my schooling during the 1980s was in a brief cameo in relation to the First Fleet – something about Bennelong, Manly, spearings and smallpox. Then it was all Macquarie, convicts, goldrushes and harbour bridges. I was very interested in the past, but it never occurred to me to study the Aboriginal history of my own country, let alone my city. By the early 1990s, I was studying archaeology at university, walking past the Aboriginal settlement known as The Block each day, but I made no connection between the people there and the archaeological past. I was studying 'real' Aboriginal culture, and like most people, I assumed that this was only found in the distant past or the remote outback. This belief would probably have continued but for a fortunate encounter. While working at the St George Regional Museum in southern Sydney in 2000, I saw a wooden Aboriginal club studded with metal horseshoe nails in the collections. It was a 'real' Aboriginal object but also a cultural hybrid, and it had come from nearby Salt Pan Creek, not the outback.[3] At the same time I met Shayne Williams, a senior Aboriginal man from the La Perouse Aboriginal community, whose father and extended family had lived at

Salt Pan Creek until at least the late 1930s. These encounters made me realise that my home town had a more recent Aboriginal history as well as the ancient past that I had studied; a history grounded in places and objects and still carried in living memory.

From that time on I began researching this hidden history, and found that other historians were grappling with the same puzzle. In particular, Grace Karskens' landmark 2009 book *The Colony: A History of Early Sydney* demonstrates that enduring beliefs about Sydney, such as the idea 'that Aboriginal people simply faded out of the picture and off the "stage" of history', are among the many simplifications and myths of colonial Australia.[4] Karskens devotes a significant portion of her account of Sydney's first half-century to the presence, activities and interactions of Aboriginal people with the city, not to redress a previous absence, but because 'it reflects historical reality'.[5] Heather Goodall and Allison Cadzow's 2009 book *Rivers and Resilience: Aboriginal People on Sydney's Georges River*, explores how different Aboriginal people have been associated with southern Sydney in various ways throughout its entire European history.[6] Like historian Maria Nugent's perceptive study of the many pasts of Botany Bay, it draws on the knowledge of Aboriginal Elders from the La Perouse–based *Individual Heritage Group* in the 1980s and 1990s.[7]

The valuable and ongoing research of these and many other people continues to raise awareness of Sydney's fascinating and nuanced Aboriginal past, but what is still missing is an overarching account of what happened to Aboriginal people across Sydney throughout the 19th century; a history that connects the urban Aboriginal present to the ancient Aboriginal past; a history that explains when and how the cross-cultural interactions so vividly brought to life by Grace Karskens in the 19th century turned into the segregation and brutalisation of Aboriginal communities in the 20th; a history that weaves Aboriginal people and places back into Sydney's past two centuries. This book aims to provide that broader story.

Piecing this history together has involved patient research, often in collaboration with the descendants of coastal Sydney people from

A gap in place and time

the La Perouse Aboriginal community. Michael Ingrey, in particular, has helped trawl vast archives to recover fragments of information – no matter how tiny – from newspaper reports, the reminiscences and papers of residents and visitors, government correspondence, the records of charitable organisations, police and school records, council minutes, parliamentary records, blanket returns, land records, census data, electoral roles, maps, paintings and sketches. These fragments were then painstakingly assembled on a framework of repeatedly mentioned people and places to build up a picture of who lived where and when. Michael and others, including his uncle Dr Shayne Williams, have helped to make sense of this information, and to make sure that Aboriginal ancestors were correctly identified.

Many conversations over a number of years with Michael, Shayne and other Aboriginal people have helped me to unthink what I thought I knew about Aboriginal culture and history. They have made me aware of just how remarkable it was for their ancestors to have navigated a path through the relentless expansion of Sydney. I have also realised that while Aboriginal people strategically chose their responses, they did not do it all on their own – they often interacted with Europeans who were sympathetic to their desire for ongoing access to land and resources. This does not in any way diminish the achievements of Aboriginal people, but it has made me deeply suspicious of histories claiming that Europeans always sought to evict Aboriginal people from cities and other colonial settlements.[8] There needs to be room for the nuance and complex relationships that often ensue when two cultures meet and interact; the story of violence and Aboriginal dispossession certainly needs to be told, but so does that of the friendships and attempts to work things out.

As I pulled the threads of this story together, I became aware that focussing on the whole Sydney region was too complex, as it was essentially the story of two groups of people – one living along the coast and the other in the west of Sydney. When I looked in detail at the movements of Aboriginal people in and around the town of Sydney, I saw that they were mostly contained within the coastal area south from Sydney Harbour to Port Hacking, and inland from Botany Bay to the tidal limits of the Georges River at Liverpool. Throughout the 19th century, Aboriginal people moved around this area and up and down the coast beyond Sydney, but rarely (if at all) moved into western Sydney, or interacted with the other Aboriginal people who lived there. The repeated patterns of movement by different individuals, and through several generations, suggested that the area which I have termed 'coastal Sydney' had some significance for Aboriginal people in this period. Coastal Sydney also includes the residential, business and government centre of Sydney, allowing me to explore in detail the effects of its expansion on local Aboriginal people.

The extent of coastal Sydney is shown in the maps at the start of the book. Its conspicuously regular shape is intended to stress that it is neither precise, nor representative of a cultural boundary. I am acutely aware of ongoing debates about clan and language boundaries among Aboriginal people and academic researchers, the diverse meanings that language and clan names have to different people today, and how easily a line on a map can be misinterpreted. The coastal Sydney area represents the lived reality of Aboriginal people throughout the 19th century. It encompasses the estates of several clans documented in the early years of the colony, and the people who moved and lived within it also travelled into areas north and south of Sydney in which different languages were spoken. Aboriginal people always had complex and long-distance webs of connection and I believe that their historical movements grew out of patterns that operated before the arrival of Europeans – but that does not mean that coastal Sydney can be simply equated with something pre-existing.

Coastal Sydney is the main backdrop of the book, but sometimes it is necessary to discuss the greater Sydney area that extends west to the Blue Mountains. To distinguish this from the city of Sydney, from this point forward I will use the term 'Sydney region', or the more specific term 'inland Sydney' for the area west from Parramatta.

Aboriginal people, and particularly those with mixed ancestry, were labelled in many different ways throughout Sydney's history, most now considered offensive. Aboriginal readers should be aware that I have retained original terminology in historical quotes for authenticity, but in my own discussions I have tried to use less offensive terms such as part-Aboriginal where it is necessary to make this distinction, though I acknowledge that these may not please all readers. Aboriginal readers should also be aware that this book contains images of deceased Aboriginal people, mainly from the 19th century. Throughout the book I use the word 'Europeans' as a way of differentiating non-Aboriginal from Aboriginal people living in Sydney, while recognising that this is a simplification of a relatively diverse group of people. Where it is important to distinguish between new migrants or visitors and those who were living permanently in Sydney, I have used the term Sydneysiders. This is not to suggest that Aboriginal people were not also Sydneysiders, but as their connections are more than just historical, I refer to them as 'coastal Sydney people'.

The seven chapters of this book are ordered chronologically, but also thematically. The book begins by challenging an enduring myth – that Aboriginal culture has never changed and cannot change without ceasing to be 'authentic'. This pervasive and popular perception is responsible for fuelling the belief that Aboriginal people were unable to cope when Europeans arrived; that they quickly lost their traditional ways, and that adopting any European foods, vices or devices indicated a step further away from their authentic former lives. It is an idea that must be abandoned if we are to make sense of the complex and changing lives of Aboriginal people in coastal Sydney during this period. Chapter 1 ('Surviving the early colony') then shows how Aboriginal people drew on a long history of dealing with change, and their extensive webs of connection, to regroup after the arrival of Europeans with their deadly muskets and diseases. The Aboriginal use of old ways to respond to new realities formed one of three foundations of their survival of the early colony. Chapters 2 and 3 ('Living to fish' and 'Cross-cultural relationships') reveal the other two; the ongoing ability of Aboriginal people to fish for survival and trade, and their cultivation of relationships with the first generations of Europeans to be born in Sydney.

As these locally born Sydneysiders grew to become influential members of society, Aboriginal people found that they had a small but powerful group of sympathisers to whom they could turn when needed. These relationships became of great importance when the government withdrew its interest in local Aboriginal affairs in the 1840s, and as Sydney grew rapidly with the goldrush boom of the 1850s. As Chapter 4 ('Entangled lives') explores, Aboriginal people used their connections to remain living in suburban areas, where they also became more deeply entwined with the European economy. Despite these personal cross-cultural relationships, most Europeans neither knew nor cared about the ongoing local connections of Aboriginal people to coastal Sydney. Chapter 5 ('Strangers in their own land') discusses how they came to forget and ignore the local links of Aboriginal people over the first half of the 19th century, including those who knew them best. The result was that by the 1860s and 1870s Aboriginal people in coastal Sydney were either regarded as being from somewhere else, or were no longer considered 'authentically' Aboriginal.

Chapter 6 ('Intervention') and Chapter 7 ('New links and old ways') discuss what happened when the government, urged by a resurgent missionary movement, re-engaged with Aboriginal affairs in the early 1880s after several decades of indifference. Coastal Sydney people were misidentified as migrants, and this fact is central to how the New South Wales Aborigines Protection Board was established; a development that came to affect all Aboriginal people across the state. For those in coastal Sydney, the increasing interventions of government and missionaries led to the biggest changes since the arrival of Europeans a century before. By the early 1900s, the network of Aboriginal settlements that had characterised 19th-century Sydney was largely gone, and most people had come to live at the managed mission at La Perouse. By this time they were outnumbered by other

Aboriginal people arriving from more distant areas, forming Sydney's first urban Aboriginal communities.

Throughout this book, I pay close attention to where things happened. Knowing the locations of Aboriginal settlements near fishing grounds or on the properties of sympathetic Europeans does more than help us to understand why they were there. As the epilogue ('In plain view') considers, if we are made aware of the many places used by Aboriginal people across coastal Sydney, we can begin to fundamentally rethink how most of us view the layers of Sydney's history. There is not just a pre-colonial layer of engravings, middens and rock shelters overlaid by a European layer of buildings and roads. Many of those apparently 'European' structures were also used by Aboriginal people. They represent the culturally entangled reality of Sydney in the 19th century that has for too long been hidden between the brutality of the late 18th century as the colony was being established, and the equally brutal government intrusions into the lives of Aboriginal people in the 20th.

In this book I aim to provide a readable narrative for people with no prior knowledge of Sydney's Aboriginal history. I hope though that Aboriginal people, historians and others already familiar with this history will also find much to confirm or expand their thinking about Sydney's past. While the ideas in this book are extensively referenced, those wanting more expanded considerations of academic arguments, and those who enjoy foraging among forests of footnotes, will find more in the PhD thesis from which this book emerged, which is available online through the University of New South Wales Library.[9] I have referenced Aboriginal community knowledge where I have drawn upon this, but I take full responsibility for my interpretation of others' ideas and words, including the written sources that I have consulted.

I have focussed most attention on the least documented period of Sydney's Aboriginal history, from the 1830s to the early 1900s. References to the detailed and excellent research that others have undertaken into the pre-European and early colonial Aboriginal past of

Sydney are contained in Chapter 1 in particular, and those wanting to know more about these and other aspects of Sydney's Aboriginal past can also consult the 'Further reading' section on page 150. Better still, get to know your Aboriginal neighbours at any one of a growing number of Aboriginal community events across Sydney and (respectfully) ask for yourself. If this book inspires others to make a rich and rewarding personal journey of discovery into Sydney's Aboriginal past, then it will have served its purpose well.

Triumph or tragedy?

In the following chapters I sketch out a history of coastal Sydney that focuses on the ongoing presence of Aboriginal people throughout the 19th century. I am acutely conscious that it is a story of both survival and sorrow, but also that life is always a complex mixture of both of these things and much more. My intention is not to downplay the suffering of Aboriginal people, to make out that their lives were easy and harmonious, or to suggest that all Europeans welcomed their presence, but some balance is required. Contemporary sources either ignored Aboriginal people or portrayed them in a highly negative light, focussing only on their perceived deficiencies, and we should not assume that this accurately represents their lives. It is hard to gauge, for example, just how widespread alcohol consumption was among Aboriginal people, and how they viewed and experienced its use. Drinking was a fact of life for most 19th-century Sydneysiders, but knowing this brings us no closer to actually understanding Aboriginal experiences. Similarly, we do not know how Aboriginal people viewed the supposedly squalid conditions of some of their settlements, or whether indeed such descriptions are accurate. There are no easy answers to these questions, and I have focussed instead on what I can say with some certainty about what Aboriginal people were doing. At the very least, this demonstrates that there was more to life than most contemporary sources acknowledged, and if it proves a springboard for future research into these trickier questions, all the better. By no means do I consider this history to be a definitive account of the Aboriginal experience of this period, not least because it is written from a non-Aboriginal perspective.

I have consciously chosen to focus on the dozens of Aboriginal people who continued to live in coastal Sydney throughout the 19th century. I cannot write of the many more who were never born, due to the cataclysmic effects of introduced diseases and violence, or of the survivors who moved away from Sydney, never to return. These tragic endings should be acknowledged, but they do not diminish the endurance through considerable adversity of the people who stayed. They survived the establishment and expansion of Sydney by engaging strategically with the city and its occupants. Doing so ultimately led to greater government intervention in their lives, but had they shunned the city completely, Sydney might indeed have suffered the Aboriginal absence that haunts so many histories of the city.

Fortunately, they stayed, and their legacy is a strong and proud community of descendants, and a much richer history for Sydney. For all the tragedy of poverty, ill health and ill treatment, we should not overlook the very human story of daily life, of friendships within and across cultures, and the fact that laughter also echoed around the glowing hearths of Aboriginal settlements. If we see the women, men and children who sat around these fires merely as miserable victims or outcasts, we lose sight of the dignity, humanity and purpose that I hope is conveyed by the sketch of their lives that now follows.

1

Surviving the early colony (1788–1820s)

Timing is everything. When Lieutenant Cook sailed into Botany Bay in 1770, followed eighteen years later by Governor Phillip and the First Fleet, they gave the rest of the world its first glimpses of Sydney's Aboriginal people. They described and drew settlements of bark huts with oysters cooking on fires at their entrance; women fishing with hook and line in bark canoes; men poised on the rocky shore with pronged fishing spears. Though they had never seen Aboriginal people before, they were certain of two things: that the history of human life on earth was only short – perhaps a few thousand years, and that the Aboriginal way of life had not changed over that time.

They were wrong on both counts. Had they arrived ten thousand years earlier, they could not have sailed into Botany Bay – it did not yet exist. But they would still have encountered Aboriginal people, who had already been living in the Sydney region for many thousands of years. Had the First Fleet arrived just two thousand years ago, we would have none of their many illustrations of Aboriginal women fishing with *burra* (shell fish hooks) and line from flotillas of bark *nowie* (canoes). *Burra* had not been invented, and all of the social and economic changes that came with the rise of women's line fishing were yet to unfold.

Why is this important? Because these early historical snapshots of Aboriginal life are often regarded as depictions of *real* or *authentic* Aboriginal culture, timeless and unchanging, before it was shattered by the destructive impacts of colonialism. The idea of Aboriginal people as the world's oldest continuous culture is routinely misunderstood to mean that this way of life has never changed, and cannot change. This makes it very hard to understand how the Aboriginal hunters and fishers of coastal Sydney in the late 18th century became the mission dwellers of the late 19th, and the civil rights campaigners of the early 20th, all the while retaining a distinct Aboriginal identity. At the heart of the Aboriginal response to colonialism was a long-honed ability to adapt to change, but it has been hard to recognise with these assumptions clouding our vision. So before we see what happened to Aboriginal people in Sydney after 1788, let's turn back the clock a little further and see how Aboriginal people dealt with change before then.

A culture of change and connection

Traditional Aboriginal life is often imagined as a repeating cycle of movement, food gathering and ceremony around defined 'territories' in the landscape. Whatever kernel of reality this captures, it obscures the environmental and technological changes experienced by Aboriginal people over vast periods of time, and it ignores their complex, widespread and ever-shifting webs of connection that pushed far beyond tribal lands. It also hides the fact that Aboriginal people experienced the dramas of daily life and were players in events now long forgotten that had great importance at the time. In other words, like people everywhere, they too had history.

Aboriginal people have lived in the Sydney region for more than one thousand generations, and have witnessed the formation of the landscape Sydneysiders know today.[1] Twenty thousand years ago, the world was in the midst of a glacial period or ice age. Though there was no ice in the Sydney region (or across most of Australia), the climate was cooler and drier, and sea levels were much lower. Today's great inlets of Sydney Harbour, Broken Bay and Port Hacking were rivers winding through deep sandstone valleys and across a vast coastal plain between six and twenty kilometres further east of the current shoreline. Botany Bay was no bay at all, but consisted of a swampy sand plain where the Cooks and Georges Rivers met, before flowing through what is now the Kurnell Peninsula. From around eighteen thousand years ago, warming global temperatures caused the sea to rise rapidly. For nearly ten thousand years it devoured the coastal plain at an average rate of two metres per year. Aboriginal people perceived this change, and though we can only guess what they made of it, the social impacts must have been profound. The flooding of the coastal plain probably forced some groups to realign or amalgamate.[2] For hundreds of generations of Aboriginal people along the coast, constant environmental change was normal; the ground literally shifted beneath their feet.

The changing climate and landscape brought opportunity as well as challenges for Aboriginal people. By around seven thousand years ago, rising seas had flooded the sandstone river valleys and swampy sand plains of what is now coastal Sydney. Sydney Harbour, Broken Bay and Port Hacking were created, while vast quantities of sand accumulated on the new shoreline to form the Kurnell Peninsula, giving birth to Botany Bay.[3] Many hundreds of kilometres of new coastline provided greater access to rich marine resources. Warmer sea temperatures brought creatures most likely never seen by Sydney's Aboriginal people before. The butchered remains of a six-thousand-year-old dugong found near Botany Bay show that Aboriginal people quickly learnt to exploit them.[4] Likewise, the arrival of the dingo into Australia from south-east Asia around three thousand years ago gave Aboriginal people both a source of food and a valuable companion animal.

Until the past few thousand years, sea levels continued to fluctuate slightly, moving the shoreline to and fro. Large wetland complexes such as Towra Point and Quibray Bay on the southern shore of Botany Bay formed in the past thousand years or so, after sea levels had stabilised. The apparently timeless land that Cook and

Phillip encountered as they sailed through the heads of Botany Bay in the late 18th century had only existed for a fraction of the period in which Aboriginal people had occupied Sydney. While Europeans were oblivious to these developments, Aboriginal people had always lived with change in coastal Sydney. They had forged their intimate familiarity and deep connection with its lands and waters through their accumulated ancestral experience of the diverse and shifting moods of their surroundings.

They met the challenges of a changing environment by developing or adopting new technologies. Most evidence of this comes from stone implements, because those made of organic materials like bark, wood, bone and shell do not normally survive for great lengths of time buried in the soil. Even using this small sample of the Aboriginal toolkit, archaeologists have shown that many elements of the supposedly timeless way of life encountered by early Europeans in Sydney are in fact relatively recent. Until around four thousand years ago, for example, Sydney's Aboriginal people did not have the *mogo* (ground-stone hatchet). This meant that they could not cut toe-holds in trees and race up them to catch possums or gather native honey, as impressed Europeans noted in the late 18th century. Without a *mogo* to help remove large slabs of tree bark, it is also possible that the type of bark *nowie* which dotted Sydney waterways in the late 19th century were not being made at that time.

The *mogo* was just one of many stone implements that found their way into the coastal toolkit over the past five thousand years. Others included a range of cutting, incising and drilling implements and wood-working tools that continually changed the ways Aboriginal people carried out their subsistence activities (see Figure 1.1). Over the past three thousand years Aboriginal people began to use animal and fish bone to fashion deadly barbs for their *garrara* (fishing spears) as well as needles and awls to make and decorate skin cloaks. They also began to use tools made of shell, most notably the *burra* from around a thousand years ago.[5]

Inventing and adopting these new technologies influenced the way Aboriginal people lived. As vast middens and engraved fish motifs near waterways remind us, coastal Sydney people revolved their lives around the sea and its resources, so the introduction of *burra* around one thousand years ago was a major innovation. They were primarily used by women, who fixed them to lines of twine and cast them from their bark *nowie*, giving them greater self-sufficiency. *Burra* also influenced daily life and cultural practices.[6] They began to be used as personal adornments, along with other shells and fish jaws, while the ceremonial practice of *malgun*, in which a ligature was used to remove two joints of young girls' left little finger, was said to better allow fishing line to be wound around the hand.[7] All of these practices, eagerly recorded by early Europeans as timeless tradition, flowed instead from Aboriginal people incorporating new technologies into their way of life. Their subsequent adoption of metal axes, metal fish hooks and other European technologies had a long pedigree, and did not signify the end of their Aboriginal identity.

Technology influenced the way coastal Sydney people interacted with other Aboriginal groups. Because the coast lacks most of the stone types needed to make hatchets, points and chisels, Aboriginal people had to develop extensive trade networks to source tools or the raw materials to make their own. Hatchets were obtained from up to several hundred kilometres away, while cobbles for flaking stone were sourced from inland Sydney and the Illawarra. The discovery that a bark shield collected by Cook from Botany Bay in 1770 was made of mangrove wood growing along the coast at least five hundred kilometres north of Sydney demonstrates that even more distant trade connections existed.[8] When different Aboriginal groups met to trade, the transactions were not just technological. Knowledge also flowed to and fro along these networks, as well as ceremony and marriage partners. So when technologies changed, many other things changed along with them.

In Sydney, a major social shift occurred around fifteen hundred years ago. Aboriginal people from the coast began to make most of their implements from locally available materials, changing from inland Sydney river cobbles to locally available quartz for their flaked stone implements, and making tools of bone and shell. Whether this caused, or was caused by, changing social organisation or the closure of trade networks is not clear, but there was a marked decrease in interaction between the two areas from that time on. By the time Europeans arrived, coastal Sydney people drew a clear distinction between themselves and inland Aboriginal groups, and oriented their relationships along the coast to the north and south of Sydney.[9]

These observations from the archaeological past alert us to the fact that Sydney's Aboriginal people related to places and to each other in more complex and dynamic ways than early European descriptions suggest. The First Fleet naval officers who wrote most of these accounts had stowed some powerful assumptions on their tall ships from past experiences elsewhere in the colonial world. When Aboriginal people (mostly men) in Sydney described belonging to particular clans with defined estates, this chimed with what the Europeans had observed of the tribal territories of Native American groups, and some even referred to Aboriginal people as 'Indians'.[10] They assumed that Aboriginal people lived their lives primarily within their clan estates and, combined with a belief that this way of life was unchanging, these early accounts created a misleading but enduring picture of timeless territorial identity.

The reality was very different. Like other groups across Australia, the relationships between Sydney's Aboriginal people and land gave them both stability *and* mobility.[11] They related most directly to land through their clans, whose members shared totems and descent from a common ancestor, and retained primary rights to their clan estates. Across the Sydney region in 1788 there were at least two dozen clans, each containing perhaps twenty-five to sixty people, ancestrally related through their fathers. Clans were named after their estate, such that *Cadi* along the southern side of the harbour was the estate of the *Cadigal*, *Gwea* south of Botany Bay was that of the *Gweagal*, and so on.[12] But these clans did not live in isolation. They intermarried; the children of these relationships gained connections to two different clan estates, and perhaps to even more areas through their grandparents and other extended family. These inherited rights and responsibilities varied in strength according to the directness of each person's ancestral connection. They existed in a hierarchy that had to be constantly negotiated as senior people died, or as different groups were united by marriage. The result was that at any one time, there were a number of Aboriginal people from a range of clan groups who held connections and ceremonial obligations to particular areas, including people who lived some distance away.

Adding further dynamism to these relationships was the fact that Aboriginal people lived on a daily basis in groups known as bands, which were made up of the male members of a clan, their wives (married in from other clans) and children, and unmarried female clan members.[13] As such, they were multilingual groups comprising members of different clans, giving them connections and rights to much broader areas than single-clan estates. We do not know the names of the land-using bands in Sydney, if indeed they had names, but they contained up to fifty people, and fragmented at times into smaller nuclear family groups.

The lives of Aboriginal people were very different from the cycle of movement around relatively small clan estates that early European descriptions conjure up. Throughout their lives, individuals retained primary rights and links to their clan estate, but also held secondary rights to other areas inherited from parents and grandparents, enacted through marriage, or because life events such as birth, conception, or death (of parents and grandparents) had occurred there. They travelled across clan estates in their bands on the basis of these rights and responsibilities, which were continually changing in prominence with the birth or death of others with greater rights. It created complex and shifting webs of connection to land and other people that linked bands across and beyond coastal Sydney.

The enduring perception of timeless territoriality has imagined Aboriginal culture as a sheet of glass, strong and cohesive in isolation but highly vulnerable to the hammer blow of colonial impact. The reality could not be more different. The intimate Aboriginal familiarity with land was hard won by living through shifting seasons, droughts, floods and longer-term environmental changes, and finding new opportunities. Connections to land were inherited through clan ancestors, but individuals also retained varying rights of access to areas far more distant through their extended family affiliations. Regular movement and shifting webs of connection may appear incompatible with a strong culture, but as historian Grace Karskens has neatly expressed, they operated around a 'stable core, a sense of rightness in one's skin'.[14] No amount of past exposure to change could inoculate the people of coastal Sydney from the ravages of introduced disease they were to face, but the Aboriginal logic of connection through movement shaped the way that the survivors regrouped in its aftermath.

Devastation

There may have been as many as fifteen hundred Aboriginal people living in coastal Sydney in January 1788 when the ships of the First Fleet disgorged a similar number of Europeans onto the shores of Sydney Cove, known to Aboriginal people at the time as Warrane.[15] The new arrivals quickly realised that they were strangers in someone else's land. They were tentative and restricted in their movements, venturing out in armed parties beyond their tent town in the Tank Stream valley to explore, to search for food and resources around the harbour, or to tend their crops at nearby Farm Cove. Their forays brought about conflicts with Aboriginal people; some caused unwittingly by unsanctioned use of Aboriginal resources; others caused by open acts of violence towards, and theft from, Aboriginal people. In that first year, Europeans became increasingly desperate to understand the Aboriginal people who dominated the landscape but shunned their fledgling settlement. By the end of 1788, they resorted to kidnapping local man Arabanoo from the beach at Manly Cove in a desperate but misguided attempt to establish contact with Sydney's Aboriginal people.[16]

Five months later Arabanoo was dead, one of the many victims of the smallpox epidemic that raged among the Aboriginal people of the harbour. First Fleet officer David Collins recorded Aboriginal bodies strewn and abandoned around the harbour 'as if, flying from the contagion, they had left the dead to bury the dead'.[17] Those who fled from the devastation spread the disease further, as Europeans realised years later when they saw signs of smallpox far beyond this area.[18] Another local man, Bennelong (c.1764–1813), who was kidnapped a few months later and went on to become the colony's key Aboriginal informant, told them more about the impact of the epidemic. Though mortality rates probably varied markedly across the Sydney region, Bennelong estimated that smallpox had claimed the lives of 'one-half of those who inhabit this part of the country'.[19] Never again did the Aboriginal population of coastal Sydney come close to the number of Europeans.

The devastating human impact of the smallpox epidemic can scarcely be exaggerated, and coastal Sydney was ground zero. Hundreds upon hundreds of Aboriginal people perished in a matter of months. All families lost loved ones, and some entire families were swept away. It was not the end of Aboriginal Sydney but its legacy was immense. Throughout the 19th century we can speak of just *dozens* of Aboriginal people in coastal Sydney at a time rather than the many hundreds that there could have been. We can only imagine the thousands upon thousands of Aboriginal children who would never feel the soft sands of Sydney's beaches under their feet over the next two centuries.

While we will never know the full effect of smallpox on Sydney's Aboriginal people, many historians have equated the loss of life with a broader loss of connection to land. This does not take into account the webs and hierarchies of connection that linked Aboriginal people from a wide area to particular places, and it has made it difficult to recognise how Aboriginal people regrouped along old lines in the years that followed. The most commonly quoted example concerns the fate of the Cadigal, whose clan estate ran along the southern side of the harbour and included the fledgling colony at Warrane (Sydney Cove). Bennelong stated that his Cadigal friend Colebee's 'tribe [was] reduced by its effects to three persons'.[20] Many scholars have assumed that by 'tribe', Bennelong meant Colebee's clan, and because clans were thought to have a bounded territorial identity, they have concluded that this left just three Cadigal (the men Colebee, Nanbaree and Caruey) with rights to the Cadigal estate.[21] Yet several decades later Governor Macquarie established a fishing village for several dozen Aboriginal people of the 'Sydney tribe' at Gurrajin (Elizabeth Bay), which was recognised as 'a place much frequented and delighted in by the Sydney blacks, to a family of whom indeed it belonged'.[22] These people, and the many others who were recognised by Europeans as having ties to the Cadigal estate in later decades, were not all descendants of Colebee, Nanbaree and Caruey, so what was going on?

It is most likely that Bennelong was referring to Colebee's band, a mixture of fellow clansmen and others. Even if he was referring to Colebee's *clan*, he was discussing the loss of human life, not connection to land. Cadigal women were married into a number of other clans, and both they and their children retained rights to the Cadigal estate. Other people also retained connections to the area by marriage or through more distant relationships. It was this broader group of survivors with connections to Cadi and other clan lands who not only lived in coastal Sydney in later years, but regarded it as their own. We can only guess at the survivors' trauma, compounded by the simultaneous loss of land and status. That they found the strength to carry on, rebuild and find a place for themselves in the growing colony is nothing short of incredible.

Regrouping

The Aboriginal survivors of the devastating smallpox epidemic had to regroup in a period of rapid change. By the early 1790s, Europeans had explored extensively in all directions from Sydney Cove, and had begun carving a patchwork of small farm clearings out of the forests around Parramatta at the head of the harbour, and near what became Windsor on the Hawkesbury River. Sydney town remained within the Tank Stream valley but had sprouted sown fields at the head of the adjacent bays, while an increasing number of tracks probed further into the bush from its margins. Aboriginal people began to frequent Sydney town and the other settlements, establishing relationships with Europeans that sometimes unravelled into violent conflict. At the same time, a sustained guerrilla war was being waged across the region under the leadership of the Aboriginal warrior Pemulwuy (c.1750–1802). But nothing could halt the expansion of the colony, fed a few times a year by more convicts and free settlers arriving from England.[23]

Too much had been lost for Aboriginal people to reconstruct what had gone before. Many senior people with ceremonial knowledge and primary connections to land were gone; as existing customs for dealing with 'unnatural' deaths were rendered irrelevant by the speed and scale of the smallpox epidemic, their core beliefs were shaken; and all was compounded by the relentless European appropriation of Aboriginal land.[24] The deaths of so many women was an ongoing crisis, not just in terms of producing children. Women bound Aboriginal groups together through marriage, and this meant that new bands had to draw people from broader areas than before.[25] This in turn led to more women being abducted, and ensuing cycles of payback through ritual combat.[26] Despite these new realities and chaotic times, the new bands were not formed randomly. As historian Daniel Richter has observed in relation to a similar post-epidemic regrouping of Native Americans, the survivors drew on existing familial connections and other relationships to create 'new peoples [...] from pieces of the old'.[27]

The links between the old and new Aboriginal groups in Sydney have been hard to trace, because we do not know a lot about most individuals, including the extensive webs of connection that linked each one to distant places and people. But we can get a sense of this by mapping the movements of well-documented Aboriginal people (all men in this period) who lived before and after the epidemic. If we compare this to their known connections through birth or marriage, we can detect patterns that tell us about how they related to other Aboriginal people and to the land. These patterns are what anthropologists have defined elsewhere in Australia as *beats* or *runs*, which Aboriginal people used to maintain their family connections.[28] Not only do early colonial Aboriginal beats give us a way to examine continuity before and after the arrival of Europeans, they can also be compared to those of successive generations over the next century to see what changed as the colony grew.

The beat of early colonial go-between Bennelong, shown in Figure 1.2, is a good place to start. He was born to a Wanngal father and appears to have inherited rights to Goat Island within his clan lands on the southern shore of the Parramatta River.[29] We do not know the affiliations of his mother and grandparents, but through his wives he was also linked to Botany Bay, the north shore of the harbour and the northern side of the Parramatta River. After Governor Phillip ordered his abduction from Manly in 1789, the two men developed a relationship, and Phillip built him a hut on the eastern point of Sydney Cove.[30] When Bennelong returned from a trip to England with Phillip, he lived for a decade or so on his last wife Boorong's clan estate at Kissing Point, in a band formed from the amalgamation of their extended families. He died there in 1813 and was buried in a local orchard.

Bennelong's activities blended old and new ways. He maintained the pre-existing practice of polygamy, but he also participated in the increased violence towards women of the 1790s when he abducted his Botany Bay wife Goroobooroballo.[31] He developed new links to Sydney Cove through his relationship with the European settlement and the governors resident there, but he spent the rest of his time in Sydney living in areas to which he was connected by birth or marriage. Bennelong's time on his wife Boorong's lands at Kissing Point also illustrates how the shortage of women seems to have instigated, or at least made more common, the practice of husbands coming to live with their wives' families rather than the reverse.

Despite the need for Aboriginal bands to be drawn from larger areas, the pre-existing divide between coast and inland groups remained. Bennelong's movements and connections, like those of his contemporaries Colebee and Caruey, were entirely contained within the coastal zone, except for occasional trips on ceremonial business or European expeditions.[32] The divide was also passed onto the generations born after European arrival. Mahroot (1790s–1850) was born to Botany Bay parents in the midst of the regrouping, and like many of his contemporaries, was not initiated. As Figure 1.3 shows, he lived with Europeans in Sydney for a time and participated in a number of whaling voyages, but he remained well aware of his traditional connections to coastal Sydney. He moved only within this area when not at sea, living with his wife and sister at Botany, which he described as 'all my country […] water all pretty – sun make it light'.[33] His continuing connections laid the foundations for the ongoing use of this area for generations to come, as we will see in later chapters.

The beats of Bennelong and Mahroot reflected their family connections within coastal Sydney, but others had more distant affiliations, and hence wider beats. Thomas Tamara (1800s–c.1860s) was recognised in both coastal Sydney and the Illawarra as a leader, and married Nanny Nellola (1800s–c.1860s), a Botany Bay woman (see Figure 1.4). He lived in, and travelled regularly between Sydney Harbour, Botany Bay and the Illawarra, but always within the coastal strip where he had connections. William Warrell (1790s–1863), a child of Botany Bay and Illawarra parents, also lived his life within the coastal zone, as did Biddy Giles (1810s–1888), a Botany Bay woman who married an Illawarra man, and a number of others. In fact, if we add together the overlapping beats of virtually every Aboriginal person with some family affiliation to coastal Sydney throughout the entire 19th century, a very consistent pattern emerges. They are all contained within the coastal strip around 140 kilometres north and south of coastal Sydney (between Port Stephens and the Shoalhaven region). I have called this area the *affiliated coastal zone*, to acknowledge its coastal orientation and the family ties and cultural connections it contains (see Figure 1.5).

The affiliated coastal zone did not function as a single social or cultural entity and its edges were fuzzy. Aboriginal people had always maintained marriage and cultural connections between language groups, and several different languages were spoken across the zone. Most Aboriginal people did not have connections across the entire zone though, and those who lived largely at either end of the zone also had connections extending further along the coast. But for Aboriginal people who had some personal connection to coastal Sydney, the affiliated coastal zone was the world in which they lived, travelled and married. Throughout the 19th century most Aboriginal people entering coastal Sydney were from within the affiliated coastal zone. They stayed in one of the established settlements while they were there, and rarely travelled inland to western Sydney. Those entering from outside the zone were far less likely to have come for cultural reasons or kinship, and most did not mix with locally connected people.

The strength and longevity of this pattern suggests that the affiliated coastal zone continued a prior cultural practice rather than being a historical creation, but it was also influenced by new realities. There is no doubt that as Aboriginal people regrouped and formed relationships with Europeans, their mobility increased, but the consistency and uniformity of the resulting movement patterns cannot be coincidental. I am certainly not suggesting that the affiliated coastal zone represented a cultural boundary, but there are clues that it had existed in some form before Europeans arrived. Coastal Sydney people shared cultural practices such as *malgun* (female finger joint removal) with Aboriginal groups north to Port Stephens, for example, and well into the 19th century, their ceremonial gatherings continued to involve people from across the affiliated coastal zone.[34] Aboriginal people living south of the affiliated coastal zone regarded those within the zone to their north as a separate social group, despite sharing some cultural practices with them like the *bunan* (initiation) ceremony. They also recognised a distinction between coastal Katungal (fishermen), and inland Paiendra ('axe people').[35]

The affiliated coastal zone was a lived reality for Aboriginal people, and gave them multiple places of connection. Europeans were aware that Aboriginal people travelled, but assumed that they had one 'home', and so thought something was wrong if Aboriginal people disappeared for any length of time. For example in 1846, some concerned Europeans in Sydney raised the alarm when a fishing party led by Sydney/Illawarra man Thomas Tamara appeared to have been blown out to sea from Botany Bay. It transpired that they were instead fishing their way along the familiar coast to Wollongong, and could not understand why they were presumed lost.[36]

Given that Europeans did not comprehend the extent and complexity of Aboriginal movement and connections, we can question their assumptions about who was an outsider and who was a local in colonial Sydney. The most famous 'outsider' in early colonial Sydney was Broken Bay man Bungaree (1770s–1830, Figure 1.6). Bungaree moved with his family to Sydney in the 1810s and is often portrayed as having taken over a leadership role among the depleted Aboriginal population of coastal Sydney despite having no local connection.[37] But other possibilities emerge when we consider the far-reaching networks of the affiliated coastal zone.

Bungaree grew up at Broken Bay to the north of Sydney before Europeans arrived in Australia, and seems to have had family connections oriented northwards of there, judging by the amount of time he spent in Newcastle and the lower Hunter area.[38] He had been to Sydney first in the late 1790s and early 1800s, and was already well known to the colonial establishment through his participation on maritime exploratory expeditions, but did not move permanently to Sydney at that time. Judging by the ages of his eldest children, what changed in the years between this first visit and his eventual move was that he became affiliated with Sydney through his marriage to one or perhaps two coastal Sydney women, Matora (c.1770s–c.1828) and Cora Gooseberry (1770s–1852, Figure 2.4). Cora Gooseberry was an acknowledged 'queen' of coastal Sydney and spent much of her life in this area.[39] Matora's origins are not known, but she was only recorded living in Sydney, was buried on the harbour at Rose Bay, and her eldest child Bowen Bungaree also spent most of his life (when not sailing the oceans like his father) around Sydney Harbour and Pittwater, and does not appear to have had relatives in other areas.[40]

When Bungaree moved to Sydney Harbour with his family then, he was not recolonising a vacated Aboriginal landscape, but was entering an area to which his wives and children were already connected. Though the move might also have been influenced by his relationship with Sydney town and its governors, the other regrouped Sydney bands would have contested his presence if he had simply tried to occupy land to which he had no claim. The networks of connection across the affiliated coastal zone provided Bungaree with that connection, and his celebrated statement to visiting Russians in 1820 that 'these are my people [...] this is my shore' therefore had some literal basis.[41] The Aboriginal people from within the affiliated coastal zone who lived in Sydney over the next century could have made a similar claim.

Recognition

The deep Aboriginal connections to land, and their ability to blend old and new ways, gave the regrouped bands the stability to exist as social entities for many decades. But their longevity also required recognition from the Europeans who surrounded and outnumbered them. To understand how Aboriginal people obtained this recognition, we need to look at the specific dynamics of expanding settlement in coastal Sydney. Prior to a series of actions initiated in the mid-1810s, there was no overall policy regarding Aboriginal people, and governors generally intervened only in response to particular situations. Aboriginal people and Europeans were largely left to work things out for themselves, and the degree of violence that this involved varied in line with how suitable the land was for cropping and grazing. Outside the Tank Stream valley, coastal Sydney was known as 'rocky, sandy and barren' land and was far less intensively used by Europeans than the undulating plains and river flats to the west.[42] As a consequence, violence in coastal Sydney between Aboriginal people and Europeans had become rare by the early 1810s, even though it raged elsewhere in the Sydney region, particularly to the south-west.[43]

The regrouped coastal Sydney 'tribes' (as Europeans called them) were often living on granted lands with the endorsement of the Europeans who now occupied them. Some of them, like Captain John Piper at Point Piper, and John Connell at Kurnell, advocated on their behalf to the colonial government.[44] For these and other Europeans living close to Aboriginal settlements, Aboriginal people were a fact of life. Growing up near the Kissing Point tribe on the Parramatta River in the early 1800s, William Small recalled much later that he had 'learned all sorts of things from the blackfellows [...] I had many playmates amongst them, and I haven't forgotten the principal words of the tribes round here yet'.[45]

Aboriginal people were also a familiar sight on the streets of Sydney town, which by the 1810s packed around ten thousand Europeans into the Tank Stream valley (today's CBD). They had been frequent visitors to Sydney for two decades, calling on the governor, sleeping in dwellings with convicts, and doing odd jobs around town, and many European residents knew them by name. Aboriginal people also laid claim to spaces in the town such as Hyde Park to hold ritual combats.⁴⁶ Historian Lisa Ford has written about how traditional practices like payback were able to operate in parallel with European law until the 1830s.⁴⁷ European acceptance of Aboriginal violence, whether as spectacle or as justice, undermined government attempts to discourage or ban traditional contests and nakedness on the streets of Sydney town. As a result Aboriginal people were still very much part of Sydney life when Governor Lachlan Macquarie arrived in Sydney at the end of 1809.

Macquarie's first task was to impose order on the colony after the chaos of the so-called Rum Rebellion that had overthrown his predecessor. Macquarie and his wife Elizabeth sought to remake the town, renaming and straightening streets, demolishing old buildings, and as historian Grace Karskens describes, 'issuing endless orders and regulations for moral and civic improvement, security and control'.⁴⁸ The same desire for order was later brought to bear on his administration of Aboriginal groups around the Sydney region. Initially, Macquarie had little interest in Aboriginal people, but when violence erupted to the south-west of Sydney in 1814 he was persuaded that steps should be taken to 'civilise' Sydney's Aboriginal people through 'Christianisation, education and small farming'.⁴⁹

His first action was to establish an Aboriginal boarding school or 'Native Institution' at Parramatta to try to integrate Aboriginal children into European society. To encourage parents to enrol their children, he instigated what became an annual feast and distribution of supplies for Aboriginal people in the Parramatta marketplace at the end of 1814.⁵⁰ In applying his ordered mind to administering these initiatives, Macquarie had to decide whether to impose his own system or accept the entrenched reality of the regrouped bands. He explained his intended approach on the eve of the first feast, stating that:

> the Natives should be Divided into <u>Distinct Tribes</u>, according to the Several Districts they usually reside in: – and that each Tribe should elect its own <u>Chief</u>, who the Governor will Distinguish

> by some honorary Badge [...] That the Chief of each Tribe is to adjust all Differences that may arise between the Individuals of his own Tribe; and that he shall also be held accountable to the Governor for their general conduct, and that through him all the grievances of his Tribe shall be redressed.[51]

On the face of it, this might appear to be an attempt to impose a new social order on Aboriginal people, but in reality Macquarie was describing a system for delineating the existing Aboriginal bands on paper. He was not seeking to dislodge them from where 'they usually reside', but he wanted to know who was who. Aboriginal groups did not have chiefs, but there was already a history of individuals (mostly men) like Bungaree and Bennelong engaging as envoys with Europeans on behalf of their group. It is not possible to determine how the use of chiefs affected social relations among Aboriginal people, but the continued cohesion of the different bands suggests that it was minimal. The idea became incorporated in Aboriginal dealings with Europeans, and in subsequent years Aboriginal chiefs used their perceived status as leverage when they applied for government boats and other assistance on behalf of their groups rather than themselves.

Macquarie recognised that he had more chance of enticing Aboriginal people into a European way of life and removing their unruly presence from Sydney town by going to them. He encouraged Bungaree's band to settle into a life of farming and fishing by giving them land and a boat at Georges Head in 1815, near where they were already living on the north side of the harbour.[52] A similar settlement was established in 1820 for the 'Sydney tribe' at Gurrajin (Elizabeth Bay) in recognition of their existing connections there.[53] The exception was the tragic failure of the Native Institution (1815–1833), where the deaths of a number of Aboriginal children contributed to fluctuating Aboriginal support and its eventual abandonment.[54] The most important legacy of Macquarie's actions was to codify the existing social reality of the regrouped bands on paper, weaving them into colonial administration. When Macquarie's successors began distributing blankets annually to Aboriginal people in 1826, they did not pick a central point like Sydney town or Parramatta and make all Aboriginal people come to them. Instead, they recognised the distinct affiliations of the different 'tribes' and handed out the blankets at a number of centres across Sydney.[55]

SEVERAL DECADES AFTER UNINVITED STRANGERS SET UP PERMANENT camp on their lands, the Aboriginal people of coastal Sydney had developed a place for themselves in this new colonial reality. They had been decimated by disease and dispossessed by musket and pen, but the survivors regrouped and created new bands along old lines. Their past experiences of change and their extensive networks of affiliation sowed the seeds of their survival, and they were able to gain official recognition of their ongoing connections to Sydney. As the colony continued to grow this would not have been enough to ensure their ongoing survival, but as the next two chapters explore, Aboriginal people did two other important and contrasting things. One was to actively engage with the residents and economy of Sydney. The other was to continue a central facet of their lives over thousands of years – fishing.

2

Living to fish (1830s–1840s)

Early on a summer's morning in 1834, visiting Englishman William Proctor and three friends were being rowed down the harbour from Sydney for a day's fishing by local Aboriginal man Salamander and a European companion. Proctor had heard from some Sydney 'gentlemen' that Aboriginal people were 'very expert fishermen and well acquainted with the best fishing grounds round about', and he had decided to experience it for himself. Cicadas serenaded the party as they rowed past the forested and largely uninhabited headlands of today's eastern suburbs, before pulling in to Camp Cove, just inside the southern entrance to the harbour. Salamander went ashore and brought back three other Aboriginal men, and soon the group were out between the harbour heads, catching snapper, kingfish, a small shark and dozens of red bream. They returned to Camp Cove to cook their catch for breakfast, and Proctor went to investigate the 'blue smoke' that he had seen 'curled up at several different points' behind the beach. He found the smoke emanating from the fires of a settlement of around a hundred Aboriginal men, women and children, next to a large lagoon tethered to the cove by a small tidal creek. They were living as family groups, each in their own *gunyah* (bough shelter) with a fire at the entrance, surrounded by their dogs.[1]

William Proctor quickly learnt that Aboriginal people were still a very real part of Sydney life half a century after Europeans arrived.

Living to fish (1830s–1840s)

After his visit to Camp Cove, some local Aboriginal people came to know him, and rowed out regularly to visit him aboard his anchored passenger ship.[2] Many other residents and visitors had similar experiences. In fact encounters with Aboriginal people were so routine at this time that Sydneysiders rarely wrote about them in their journals; that was left to wide-eyed visitors like Proctor. The Sydney newspapers knew, though, that their readers were still interested in the exploits of the Aboriginal people many knew by name, and often included short items about them. For their part, Aboriginal people were used to interacting with Europeans by this time, and knew who to favour and who to avoid. When Proctor and his friends walked into the Camp Cove settlement carrying their hunting rifles, the Aboriginal people did not scatter in fear; they already knew Proctor's friends and that they were the paying customers of fishing guides from their group.

By the 1840s, there were between fifty and one hundred Aboriginal people living across coastal Sydney at any one time, in a number of settlements like the one at Camp Cove. We cannot be more precise about the population because there were no censuses of Aboriginal people in this period and because they were often on the move, but these numbers figure consistently in historical records. In the winter of 1845, for example, documents show that there were a dozen Aboriginal people living at Camp Cove, about twenty at Double Bay, around fifty at La Perouse, and others at Kurnell and along the Georges River. Depending on who was in Sydney at the time, settlements could contain anything from small family groups to several dozen people. They lived in a range of accommodation including *gunyahs*, rock overhangs, wooden huts, tents and other shelters, depending on need and the availability of buildings or building materials.

The Aboriginal people who lived around the coast were bound up in webs of connection across the affiliated coastal zone, around 140 kilometres north and south of Sydney. They travelled in beats across those parts of the zone to which they were personally connected, maintaining their family connections and meeting other obligations. Accordingly, some people spent most of their time within coastal Sydney, while others passed through on broader beats. A detailed list from 1850 of the more than sixty recipients of government blankets distributed in Sydney town gives a good demonstration of these movement patterns. The recipients hailed from the regrouped Sydney, Botany, Georges River and Port Hacking bands of coastal Sydney, as well as the Five Islands, Port Stephens, Wollongong and Burragorang bands from elsewhere within the coastal zone.[3] The government also distributed blankets in these other places outside Sydney, and most people affiliated with these areas were receiving them there. The rest had not travelled all the way to Sydney town merely for a hand-out. They may have given their affiliation as outside of Sydney, but they were in town because they were connected to the area, and after conducting their business often moved on again.

The fifty to one hundred Aboriginal people living across coastal Sydney were still a significant and visible minority, comprising up to a tenth of the population outside of Sydney town. While thirty thousand Europeans were packed into the town by the 1840s, only around a thousand (less than one per square kilometre) lived across the remainder of coastal Sydney.[4] Most of this area comprised rocky, sandy and swampy ground, which Europeans concluded very early on was of little practical use to them (see Figure 2.1). Consequently, food production was focussed further west along the fertile creeks and rivers of inland Sydney, with the exception of a few pockets of land along the Parramatta, Cooks and Georges rivers. Across the rest of coastal Sydney, Europeans made attempts at farming and industry earlier in the 19th century by cutting scrub, draining swamps and damming creeks, but these activities had unpleasant side effects. Blinding 'brickfielder' sandstorms which blew north across the Botany dunes and into Sydney town grew worse as dunes were cleared of vegetation, burying houses on its southern outskirts at Surry Hills up to their chimneys by the mid-19th century (see Figure 2.2).⁵ The vast sandhills, swamps and steep rocky ground of coastal Sydney remained sparsely peopled by Europeans in fishing villages, isolated estates and industry. For Aboriginal people, this meant they had room to live, and crucially, to continue accessing the precious resources of the sea.

Fishing to live

The broad circumference of Botany Bay and the jagged, drowned river valleys of Sydney Harbour and the Georges River created hundreds of kilometres of coastline and a diverse range of habitats for many different species of fish. As vast, ancient heaps of discarded shells and fish bones demonstrate, Aboriginal people had learnt over many years how to read the waters, and knew when the various fishing grounds were well stocked. Fishing was an intrinsic part of their connection to the coast – they literally lived to fish. Men and women fished all day and sometimes into the night by flaming torchlight. Women used their bark *nowie* (canoes) as mobile kitchens. They fished with *burra* (shell fish hooks) and line, cooking on small fires atop clay pads on the canoe floor, and breastfeeding children as they went. Men used their *garrara* (fishing spears) to skewer fish from canoes, from the rocky shore or by wading out off the beach. Their children grew up in and around the water.⁶ As we saw in the last chapter, fishing wound its way into cultural life through the *malgun* ceremony with young girls. Coastal people carved fish motifs into expanses of sandstone near waterways, many of which can still be seen in National Parks across the coast.⁷ They also fixed *burra* and pierced shells on necklaces and used fish jaws as hair ornaments.

Fishing was of course also about food – Aboriginal people fished to live as well as lived to fish. Half a century after Europeans arrived, fishing was still a key activity for men and women at virtually every Aboriginal settlement around coastal Sydney. In fact, it had probably become even more important to Aboriginal people as land animal populations declined around Sydney due to colonial land clearing and hunting. These activities removed not only a food source, but raw materials such as possum skins for cloaks and belts, and bone needles and sinew to bind skins together. Government blankets replaced skin cloaks and partly offset this loss, but in turn Aboriginal people became more reliant on them as a source of winter warmth. Fishing on the other hand fostered self-sufficiency. It gave Aboriginal people food, and they also traded their surplus fish and expert fishing knowledge with Europeans to purchase clothing and other foods and goods that they desired. By the 1840s, traditional *nowie* and *burra* had been replaced by wooden fishing boats and metal hooks, but the techniques of fishing with line and spear continued. The boats were mostly cast-off European rowing boats, which colonial authorities provided to promote self-sufficiency, in response to petitions by Aboriginal people.

Because Europeans occupied the lengthy coastline so sparsely, this meant that Aboriginal people could do more than just access the water; they could set up camp next to prime fishing grounds around the heads of Sydney Harbour and Botany Bay.[8] That does not mean that they had these areas all to themselves. Europeans had also learnt where the best fishing grounds were, and while agriculture was largely focussed on inland Sydney, fishing was a major colonial economic activity around the harbours and bays of the coast. At Camp Cove for example, where William Proctor had visited an Aboriginal settlement in the 1830s, Europeans also took advantage of the rich fishing grounds adjacent inside the southern harbour mouth. European fishermen often set up tent camps along the beach, and a permanent fishing village was laid out at Watsons Bay immediately to the south. In the early 1840s, the Water Police Superintendent had a cottage constructed at the eastern end of Camp Cove beach to keep watch down the length of the harbour. Furthermore, Europeans now considered the land around Camp Cove lagoon private property. It had been granted to Edward Laing in 1793, and though he left Sydney the following year, the land was still technically his.[9]

Living to fish (1830s–1840s)

What Aboriginal people made of the asserted ownership and occupation of their lands is not clear, but it did not keep them away from areas like Camp Cove. The tidal lagoon just behind the beach was a good spot to set up camp (see Figure 2.3), and gave them access to the harbour waters. Later Camp Cove resident Aubrey Murray recalled his neighbour telling him that in the 1830s the beach was 'black with canoes', which the men and women of the settlement also used to fish the cove, floating them at high tide 'in and out of the lagoon […] through an opening at the south end of the beach' (the lagoon is now filled in but was about 200 metres by 60 metres in size and is today marked by the park at Cove Street and surrounding streets).[10] In the winter of 1845, artist George French Angas visited the settlement with his Police Superintendent friend WA Miles, who lived in the police cottage on the beach and was very interested in Aboriginal culture. At this time there were around a dozen people living there, presided over by Cora Gooseberry (1770s–1852), the so-called 'Queen of Sydney and Botany' and widow of Bungaree. Angas sketched Cora (see Figure 2.4), and watched with fascination in the evenings as Aboriginal men waded off the beach into knee-deep water, each 'brandishing a flaming torch, made of inflammable bark' to attract the fish. He saw them move about after their prey, torchlight dancing on the waves, 'and with their four-pronged spears [striking] them with wonderful dexterity'.[11] They were fishing to feed themselves, to fill their fishing boat to take down the harbour to the Sydney Markets, and to earn extra money when guiding tour groups like William Proctor's. Its high visibility meant that Europeans recorded fishing more frequently and in greater detail than most other activities, but there is no doubt that it really was a major focus of life at the Camp Cove settlement.

Apart from the excellent fishing and relative seclusion of Camp Cove, Aboriginal people may have had other reasons for living there. It is safe to assume that they *chose* Camp Cove specifically, because images like Figure 2.3 show that there were many other areas nearby that were still accessible to Aboriginal people in the 1840s and for some decades after. Residents like Cora Gooseberry had a cultural affiliation to the area, and she retained detailed cultural knowledge. The main reason Miles and Angas visited her in 1845 was to ask her about the meaning of the rock engravings found around the harbour, and she told them that they were culturally significant places that she had learnt about from her father.[12] So it is likely that if Camp Cove had a particular cultural significance, Cora and others would have known of it, and this may have influenced their choice of location. Its relative seclusion and plentiful food resources may also have enabled ceremonial activities to take place. The unusually large gathering of around a hundred people there when William Proctor visited in 1834 suggests that several groups had converged on the area, perhaps for this purpose.

We know more about Botany Bay man Mahroot's (1790s–1850) reasons for coming to live on the shores of that bay in the 1830s, and these provide a means of examining the scope of the choices available to other Aboriginal people at this time. As we have seen in the last chapter (and in Figure 1.3), Mahroot was born to Botany Bay parents, but had spent much of his early life living and working with Europeans. He had been on a number of sealing and whaling voyages in the early 19th century, but by the 1830s he had decided that he wished to 'have a fixed residence and [...] support himself by fishing and selling fish'.[13] He wanted a grant of land from Governor Bourke, and found that there was still a great deal of unoccupied land within his area of affiliation around Botany Bay. Rather than leaving the choice of land to the governor, he chose a section of uninhabited beachfront near Bunnerong Creek, adjacent to the rich fishing grounds of Botany Heads, which partly survives today as a piece of land between a bus depot and an electrical substation south of Botany Road at Matraville. He staked his claim by constructing two small wooden slab huts and applied to the governor, who gave him a lease rather than a grant over ten acres of land surrounding these huts (see Figure 2.5). Mahroot fenced off one of the huts and lived in it with his wife, and occasionally his sister Maria and others, planting a patch of cabbages and pumpkins for additional self-sufficiency.[14]

Mahroot and his wife fished for subsistence and cash from their wooden boat, selling their catch to the Sydney Markets via a middle man. He testified to a government select committee on Aborigines in 1845 that their earnings varied 'according how the weather is and the luck', but had previously been up to four to six pounds in some weeks, which was more than enough to live on. They used the money to buy 'clothes, and meat, and flour, and sugar' for themselves and other relatives in the area.[15] By the time of Mahroot's testimony, their income had decreased to 'hardly [...] four shillings a week', but whether this was a seasonal dip in revenue due to the poor fishing conditions of winter or a more sustained decline in fish stocks is not clear.[16] Perhaps to make up the shortfall, Mahroot and his wife found other ways to earn money. They rented out several of the fishing huts and adjacent land on the property to Europeans to fish and graze their cattle.[17] As we will see in Chapter 4, Mahroot also earned money by working as a boatman and guide on fishing and hunting expeditions.

Both Mahroot's land and the Camp Cove settlement were in relatively remote areas that were sparsely occupied by Europeans, but Aboriginal people were also able to live and fish much closer to Sydney town. Just three kilometres east of the town at Double Bay, a group of around twenty Aboriginal men, women and children, led by Sydney/Illawarra man Thomas Tamara and his Botany Bay wife Nanny Nellola, were living in a large sandstone overhang above the western end of the beach nearest to Darling Point in the 1840s.[18] Much of the surrounding area had technically been granted to Europeans, but the land was still largely uncleared and unoccupied, providing space for Aboriginal people to set up camp. We know about the Double Bay settlement from the writings of Leopold Verguet, a young French missionary and keen artist who visited Sydney in the winter of 1845. He had met and sketched one of Tamara's group outside his lodgings at Woolloomooloo and went to Double Bay with a colleague to draw others. Arriving at the bay he met a group stewing 'grass' in a sugary liquid, which young and old residents of the settlement would smoke when dried. When he asked after Tamara, they pointed him up the slope to the shelter, where Verguet found Tamara's group sleeping around a fire on its bare earth floor, wrapped in blankets and surrounded by their dogs. Verguet sketched away, while his colleague discussed the concept of the afterlife with Tamara, who was already acquainted with Christianity (and indeed had baptised his daughter Gertrude in St Mary's Cathedral eighteen years before).[19]

Fishing was also a major activity at Double Bay. Although the inner harbour bays did not have the same extensive fishing grounds as the heads of Sydney Harbour and Botany Bay, and European overfishing had depleted fish stocks, relatively small groups like Tamara's could use their intimate local knowledge to feed themselves and make a living. Like Camp Cove residents, Tamara's group speared fish in the adjacent bay using their *garrara* (see Figure 2.6). They also had a boat which they used to fish the harbour and bring their catch to town.[20] Tamara's group followed the fish. In 1846, the year after Verguet visited them at Double Bay, they took their boat to Botany Heads and fished their way down the coast to the Illawarra, before returning to the harbour to set up a fishing camp at Vaucluse.[21] In addition to their earnings from fishing, women from the settlement harvested eucalyptus gum from the extensive surviving forests in the area, and sold it at the Sydney Markets. Tamara was known as an expert craftsman, and he also sold his returning boomerangs in town.[22]

Knowing what we now know about the survival of Aboriginal people in Sydney more than half a century after Europeans arrived, it is interesting to take a closer look at images from the time, such as Figure 2.6 and the Front Cover. Until recently, images like these have not been considered realistic depictions of Aboriginal life. When art historians wrote key works about colonial art in the 1970s and 1980s, they drew on the common assumption that Aboriginal people had well and truly disappeared from Sydney by the 1840s. They concluded that the

Aboriginal people depicted in later pictures were therefore imagined, and included for exotic effect.[23] The Peacock image of Double Bay in 1847 shown on the Front Cover was described in this way, but we now know that Aboriginal people were still fishing the bay and living on its shores at the time and that few Europeans had permanently settled there.[24] It is even possible that the boat in Peacock's scene is that of Tamara's group. It may not be an exact depiction of what Double Bay was like in the 1840s, but other sources show that it is pretty close. In fact, I now think that if Aboriginal people were not actually captured standing there in pictures like this, then the artist probably observed them somewhere close by. Perhaps they were even looking over his shoulder as he worked, and asked to be put in the picture.[25]

Forcing out?

This picture of 19th-century Aboriginal life is quite different from what most people imagine. It is often assumed that Aboriginal people were pushed further and further from Sydney Cove since the day the English planted a flag there in 1788. In one sense this is true, as they had clearly been dispossessed and no longer had unfettered access to coastal Sydney. The intimate Aboriginal sense of belonging and custodianship was not recognised by Europeans, who considered the land to be theirs to carve up and parcel out. But lines on maps and title deeds were different from practical reality. We need to look at the timing and scale of what was happening on the ground to understand the actual limitations on Aboriginal access to land. The relatively sparse European use of coastal Sydney does not mean there were no constraints to where Aboriginal people could set up camp. Expanding European settlement was closing off some areas, and their lives were also increasingly subject to European laws from the 1830s onwards, where previously their traditional practices had coexisted with the Europeans'. These measures did not automatically push Aboriginal people out of the way however, or enforce particular behaviour.

The most significant limitation on Aboriginal settlement in Sydney was that Europeans were physically appropriating and transforming Aboriginal land into urban space. In the early decades of the colony, Aboriginal people had continued to camp in Sydney town, and to undertake ceremonial activities. They held bloody ritual contests in public spaces such as Hyde Park, and while many Europeans found these violent scenes disturbing, there was an official acceptance of what was perceived as 'tribal' law existing in parallel with European law. By the 1830s, several high-profile cases led the authorities to grow intolerant of these activities, and they began to treat 'payback' and other traditional legal remedies as crimes.[26] At the same time, Sydney town had grown to the point where there were few spaces within the Tank Stream valley for Aboriginal people to set up camp. As a result, they moved their settlements and ceremonies to places outside of Sydney town.[27] Importantly though, while urbanisation may have forced Aboriginal *settlement* out of the town, it did not banish Aboriginal *people*. They continued to enter the town on a regular basis despite no longer living there.

Two laws came into effect in the 1830s that potentially could have restricted Aboriginal visits to Sydney town. The most important was the 1838 *Licensed Publicans Act*. The town was awash with small drinking establishments, and Aboriginal people were among the many customers. The misuse of alcohol was a major issue across all classes in Sydney, and by the 1820s and 1830s, the sight of drunken Aboriginal people on the streets of Sydney was increasingly considered an affront to the decency of the town. Critics complained that alcohol made Aboriginal people 'very quarrelsome and noisy', but their solution was to attempt to prevent them obtaining alcohol, rather than banning them from visiting the town (a stark contrast to the segregationist laws of the twentieth century).[28] The *Licensed Publicans Act* introduced fines for licensed or unlicensed Europeans who supplied alcohol to Aboriginal people, but it did not criminalise the *consumption* of alcohol by Aboriginal people. If it was intended to discourage Aboriginal people from coming into town to obtain liquor, it was a wholly ineffective measure.[29] In practice it meant that the Aboriginal people routinely arrested along with Europeans for drunkenness had to be treated as victims rather than offenders. They were often the only ones to escape a fine or gaol sentence, unless they had committed additional crimes such as offensive behaviour or assault.[30]

Prohibition also ignored the cross-cultural relationships that existed around some Sydney hotels, making it difficult to secure convictions. Not only could Aboriginal people choose from a wide array of hotels across the city, in some cases they were valued customers or personal friends of the owners. Cora Gooseberry and her cousin William Warrell were regularly hosted by publican Edward Borton in the 1840s and 1850s. Prosecution was not in the interests of hotel owners like Borton or their Aboriginal and non-Aboriginal customers, and they often subverted attempts to do so. In 1860 for example, a police constable saw several Aboriginal men served rum at the Plough Inn on George Street and attempted to bring a prosecution, but the hotel's loyal customers contradicted his testimony by denying that the Aboriginal people were ever there, and the charges had to be dismissed.[31] As a result of these relationships, Aboriginal people continued to have easy access to alcohol, and prohibition provided no real disincentive to them entering the town.

Prohibition was based on an idealised view of Aboriginal people as innocent children of nature. They had already been extensively corrupted by European vices, and needed to be protected from further harm. For this reason, the most common complaint in letters to the newspaper about drunken Aboriginal people on Sydney streets was not that they were there, but that Europeans persisted in supplying them with alcohol, and that the authorities continually failed to prevent it.[32] Neither the authorities nor the general public argued that Aboriginal people should be prevented from coming to town, or be corralled into living in one place. If they had desired this outcome, then Aboriginal settlements could have been banned from particular areas in the 1835 *Vagrancy Act*. Instead, the Act was framed to protect

Aboriginal people from the negative influences of European society. It specifically excluded from prosecution any 'black native or the child of any black native [...] found lodging or wandering in company with any of the black natives of this Colony'.[33] In other words, Aboriginal settlements were exempted from the only legal provision that could have allowed authorities to close them down. Though the law mistook Aboriginal travelling as aimless wandering (vagrancy), it was implicit recognition of the Aboriginal beats in, around and beyond coastal Sydney, and reflected a broader acceptance of Aboriginal movement through town, despite its occasionally offensive and unsightly consequences to European eyes.

If the urban consolidation of Sydney town had eventually prevented Aboriginal people from setting up camp there, what was the effect of Sydney's growing suburbs on Aboriginal settlement? In the 1830s, the first Sydney suburbs were created to the east of the town at Woolloomooloo and Elizabeth Bay.[34] They were home to stately villas with gardens, occupied by wealthy new arrivals in the colony like Alexander Macleay and his family, who were keen to cultivate the respectability that they believed came with their real estate. Macleay began building his grand house and gardens in the late 1820s, on fifty acres of land at Elizabeth Bay. Macleay's land included the site of the abandoned Gurrajin (Elizabeth Bay) Aboriginal village (around today's Beare Park) that Governor Macquarie had established in 1820 in an attempt to encourage the 'Sydney tribe' into a settled farmer-fisher lifestyle.[35] This had proved incompatible with the ongoing momentum of coastal Aboriginal beats, and the settlement had closed several years before Macleay arrived.

Unlike many locally born Sydneysiders, the Macleays had no pre-existing relationships with local Aboriginal people, but they soon came into contact with them. As colonial secretary in the late 1820s and 1830s, Alexander Macleay attended the annual Aboriginal feasts instigated at Parramatta in the 1810s, meeting Bungaree in 1829, and assisting him the following year when he became seriously ill.[36] Macleay's son George distributed blankets to Aboriginal people in the 1830s from the family's Brownlow Hill property in south-western Sydney, where local Aboriginal man Werriberri (William Russell) later recalled that he was 'kind to the Aboriginals and took a great interest in their korroberry' (ceremony).[37] Despite these other relationships, the Macleays do not appear to have interacted with the Aboriginal people living around their Elizabeth Bay residence after the death of Bungaree in 1830. Whether the Macleays actively tried to keep Aboriginal people out, or whether the cleared and manicured suburban space they created did it for them, is unclear. But after the 1830s, there is no known evidence that Aboriginal people set up camp at Elizabeth Bay.[38]

While Aboriginal people may have been effectively locked out of one small pocket of coastal Sydney, we need to look at the bigger picture to see the actual long-term effects of the expansion of the city. Suburban expansion was not a bulldozer, forcing Aboriginal people ever outward beyond its margins. It spread unevenly, leaving what archaeologist Denis Byrne has described as 'gaps in the grid'; crucial spaces in the settler landscape that gave Aboriginal people continued access to land.[39] The first Sydney suburbs leapfrogged the large, open public space of the Domain, above the former ceremonial grounds of Farm Cove. Though Aboriginal people no longer used the Domain for initiations, a number had inhabited various parts of it since the early 1800s, such as Bungaree, members of Cora Gooseberry's family, and others visiting from areas to the south and north of Sydney.[40] By the 1840s, Europeans were increasingly using the Domain as a leisure space, but Aboriginal people maintained a presence in the timbered areas of the so-called 'Outer Domain' above Woolloomooloo Bay. There, they occupied a wooden hut, and perhaps some of the sandstone overhangs of the area (see Figure 2.7).[41] The bay provided them with fish (see Figure 2.8), and allowed them to use the Domain as a base for trips into the town. While the urbanisation of Elizabeth Bay shut off one piece of land to Aboriginal people, their use of the Domain, Double Bay, Camp Cove and a number of other settlements show that they continued to be present in coastal Sydney.

Some may be sceptical at the degree of apparent acceptance of Aboriginal settlements, at least where they did not directly collide with European interests. There were no legal mechanisms for shutting Aboriginal settlements down, but we know from example after terrible example that violent means were used across Australia to do just this, regardless of what the law said. It is not possible to say categorically that such extra-legal means were never employed after the end of the initial armed conflicts across coastal Sydney, but the historical record is sufficiently detailed to be able to conclude that it was not common practice. The ongoing presence of a number of such settlements is evidence of this, as is the backing and support their residents often had from some of their European neighbours. The dynamics of Aboriginal and European relations is further revealed by the few documented instances where Europeans attempted to evict Aboriginal people.

In the 1830s and 1840s, Mahroot's European tenants and neighbours made at least two clumsy attempts to evict him from his lease on Botany Bay. While he was absent on a whaling trip in 1837, his tenants broke down the fences between their grazing lands and Mahroot's hut, letting their cattle trample his garden and refusing to pay their rent to his sister Maria, insisting that they did not recognise her right to Mahroot's lease. Mahroot had never been given official papers to document his lease, and so Maria wrote to the governor requesting them, clearly showing her knowledge of the system.[42] The governor unhelpfully told her she would have to wait until Mahroot's return, but it appears that things went back to normal once he did. In 1843, some of Mahroot's neighbours made a farcical attempt, in conjunction with a government surveyor, to authorise the subdivision of Mahroot's land on the basis that he had died (seven years before the fact). However, this plan ran afoul of the personal relationships between colonial governors and Aboriginal leaders, which they had maintained since the time of Bennelong and Phillip.[43] When Mahroot's apparent demise came to the attention of Governor George Gipps, he expressed surprise that he had not heard of the death of such a 'well known and intelligent aboriginal', and one of his staff confirmed that he had seen Mahroot alive and well just a day or two before.[44] Gipps issued a stern rebuke to the surveyor general and Mahroot retained his land up to his death in 1850.

Although Mahroot held onto his land on these occasions, in reality it provided no long-term stability for his family and others. He had been given a lease rather than a grant and in the 1840s, when he began to think about what would happen to the land when he could no longer support himself through fishing, or what security there would be if he died, he found out that the land would resume to the government on his death.[45] Dismayed, Mahroot wrote directly to the governor to ask if he could purchase the land, but received a short, curt reply simply stating it would not be permitted. He could not understand why this was so, when he had lived there and worked as hard or harder than his neighbours, but notes on the correspondence show that the authorities assumed that he did not have means to do so.[46] Mahroot's experience was a reminder that, although there were a number of areas available for Aboriginal settlements in this period, there was no guarantee that they would continue to be available. It was something that Aboriginal people had to bear in mind when they left particular settlements to continue their movements up or down the coast.

Strategic distance

Aboriginal people clearly had a degree of choice in where they located their settlements in the first half of the 19th century. By looking at their movements and settlements as a whole, we can detect an overall pattern to these choices. Aboriginal people tried as much as possible to engage with European Sydney on their own terms, maintaining what could be called a *strategic distance* to the town. We can see this at work by compiling a snapshot of the Aboriginal use of coastal Sydney in the mid-1840s, as shown in Figure 2.9. Even allowing for the bias of reporting towards the heavily populated town centre, it was clearly a focal point for Aboriginal people. Newspaper accounts in particular give a sense that Aboriginal people were visiting Sydney town on a regular basis, yet we do not find most Aboriginal people clinging to its fringes.

Though all Aboriginal people had some European neighbours, they preferred to live away from the town and engage with it on their own terms. Some fishermen like Mahroot at Botany kept their distance, selling their fish to the Sydney Markets via a middle man. Aboriginal people at Camp Cove actively sought customers for fishing trips in town, but this also allowed them to control when Europeans had access to their settlement. When Aboriginal people wanted to access the town and its markets for more than a quick visit, they set up camp in one of an inner ring of settlements at the Domain, Woolloomooloo and Double Bay.[47] Sydney town was within what archaeologist Denis Byrne and historian Maria Nugent have called the 'backyard zone' of these settlements, a radius of around five kilometres within which Aboriginal people could 'walk away from home and back in one day'.[48] These settlements became staging posts for forays into Sydney by the residents of more distant settlements such as Camp Cove, or those entering Sydney from further afield across the coastal zone.

Looking at Figure 2.9, we can see that in 1846, the year after Cora Gooseberry had been living at Camp Cove, she had moved to the staging post settlement in the Domain, on the eastern edge of Sydney. Together with other Aboriginal people including her son-in-law Bowen Bungaree (whose father was the late Bungaree) and her cousin William Warrell, they 'roamed about the city during the day, and [...] often gave exhibitions of boomerang-throwing from Hyde Park', before returning home in the night.[49] A few years later, Bob Chit-Chat, Thomas Potallick and others used the Domain as their base to enter the town and conduct their business after arriving by boat from the Illawarra.[50] Thomas Tamara's group fished their way around the harbour, Botany Bay and down the coast, but it was when they were living at Double Bay that they walked in to the Sydney Markets to sell their fish, gum and artefacts. And when Aboriginal people attended a Christmas feast in town in 1844, they came from the Woolloomooloo settlement and returned there after the event.

Although we can trace these overall patterns, Aboriginal people varied their approaches depending on their particular situations and wants. For this reason we need to be careful about assuming general explanations for their behaviour. It might be true in one sense to say that some Aboriginal people lived on the margins of the Sydney colony, but this was often part of a deliberate strategy. Historians Heather Goodall and Allison Cadzow have described this preference for remoteness in relation to the Aboriginal use of the Georges River to the south of Sydney. They argue that waterways created breaks in European settlement, giving Aboriginal people a kind of safe haven away from settler space to regroup and 'choose their ways to interact with the new economy and society'.[51] This is very similar to what I have described across the remainder of coastal Sydney, but with one important difference. Goodall and Cadzow assume that Aboriginal people needed to use these spaces because they were being forced out of areas closer to town, whereas we have clearly seen that they did not require remoteness to survive, or to strategically engage with Sydney. People like Thomas Tamara and his group at Double Bay were deeply entwined in the social and economic life of the colony.

If any general conclusions can be drawn about the way Aboriginal people were living in coastal Sydney in the first half of the 19th century, it is that fishing provided them with a crucial means of survival, and that they strategically interacted with Europeans rather than seeking refuge from them. Aboriginal people at Camp Cove had nothing to fear from their neighbour, Police Superintendent William Miles. He was far more likely to visit them wielding a pen and sketchbook than a baton. Banishing his friends and ethnological subjects could not have been further from his mind, and the actions of his contemporaries show that he was far from alone in this view. Although Aboriginal people were not uniformly welcome everywhere they went, the broad European acceptance of their presence allowed them to regroup and develop the blended existence of new and old ways that was so characteristic of their way of life by the 1840s. In particular, it was the willingness of a critical group of Sydneysiders to accept their presence that meant Aboriginal people could leave settlements on their broader travels, safe in the knowledge that they could return to rekindle family hearths and re-erect their *gunyahs*.

Cutting, incising and drilling tools (backed artefacts)

Stone adzes (elouera)

Edge ground hatchet

Shell fish hooks

Bone awls and spear points (bone points)

Cockle shell scraper

1.1 New technologies adopted by coastal Sydney people. Scales are in cm.
The Australian Museum

BENNELONG

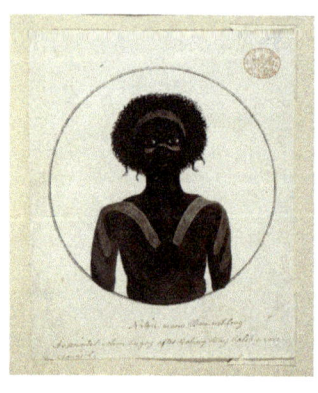

Born c.1764

1. **1789**: Bennelong and Colebee kidnapped at Manly
2. **1790**: 'guest' of Governor Phillip
3. **1790**: at Rose Bay
4. **1790**: attending whale feast at Manly
5. **1790**: participating in ritual combat at Kurnell (abducts Gorooboorooballo)
6. **Early 1790s**: living in brick hut at Bennelong Point
7. **1792–1795**: away in England with Governor Phillip
8. **1795**: participating in ritual combat at Pannerong (Rose Bay)
9. **1790s–1800s**: a number of visits to Sydney town
10. **1790s–1800s**: a number of visits to Parramatta
11. **1800s–1813**: living at Kissing Point with extended family
12. **1805**: participating in ritual combat at Prospect
13. **1813**: death of Bennelong

1.2 The recorded movements and connections of Bennelong (c.1764–1813). *Bennelong image* – © The Trustees of the Natural History Museum, London. See Image References on page 152 for all sources

MAHROOT

1	1790s: born on Cooks River	
2	1798: probably with parents at Kurnell	
3	1809–11: on sealing voyage	
4	1813: living with David Allen at Woolloomooloo	
5	1820s: living at Gurrajin Aboriginal fishing village	
6	1822–23: on whaling voyage	
7	1830–1850: living on lease at Banksmeadow with his wife and sister, fishing	
8	1832–1833/4: on whaling voyage	
9	1836: met Governor Bourke at Botany	
10	1836–37: on whaling voyage	
11	1844: attending Christmas feast at Charles Smith's house	
12	1845: giving evidence to government enquiry	
13	1849: leader of group receiving blankets in Sydney	
14	Late 1840s: working as boatman and fishing guide on Botany Bay	
15	Late 1840s: living in gunyah at Sir Joseph Banks Hotel	
16	1850: dies at Botany	

1.3 The recorded movements and connections of Mahroot (1790s–1850). *Mahroot image – © State Russian Museum, St. Petersburg. See Image References on page 153 for all sources*

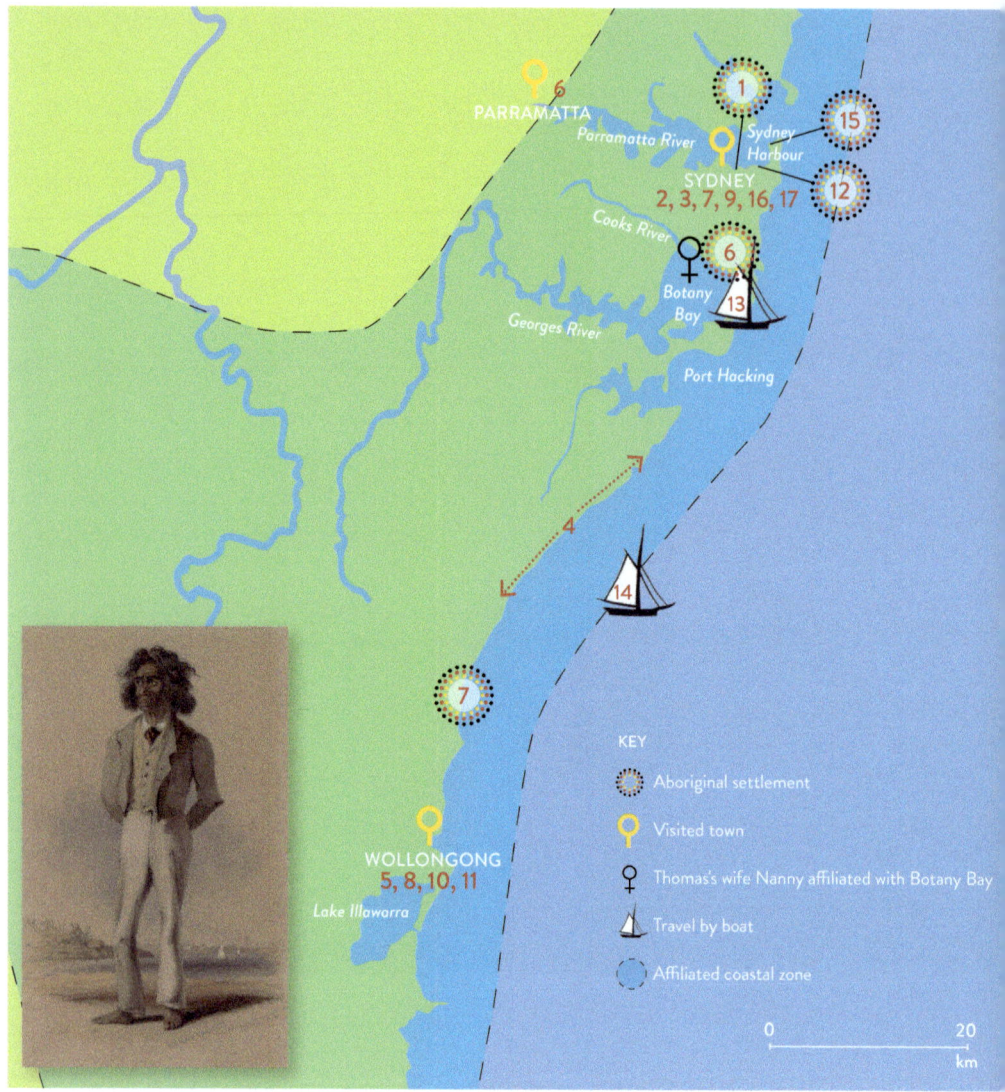

THOMAS TAMARA

Born 1800s (based on age in later records)

1. **1820s**: living at Gurrajin Aboriginal fishing village
2. **1827**: in Sydney to receive blanket and to baptise daughter Gertrude at St Mary's Cathedral
3. **1828**: receiving a blanket in Sydney as leader of a group of eight people
4. **1830s**: travelling frequently between Sydney and the Illawarra by boat or on foot
5. **1830**: receiving a blanket in Wollongong
6. **1836**: receiving a blanket at Parramatta (living at Botany)
7. **1836**: receiving a blanket at Sydney (living at Bulli)
8. **1836**: receiving a blanket at Wollongong
9. **1837**: signs declaration of allegiance to Queen Victoria
10. **1838**: receiving a blanket in Wollongong
11. **1842**: receiving a blanket in Wollongong
12. **1845**: Thomas and Nanny leading group of twenty Aboriginal people living in a rock shelter at Double Bay
13. **1846**: fishing at Botany Heads
14. **1846**: fishing with his group down the coast to the Illawarra
15. **1846**: living and fishing at Vaucluse with a boat given to him by a group of Sydneysiders the previous year
16. **1846**: selling fish to the Sydney Markets
17. **1846**: Thomas and Nanny spend a week at the Benevolent Asylum (refuge)
?   no further records of Thomas and Nanny known

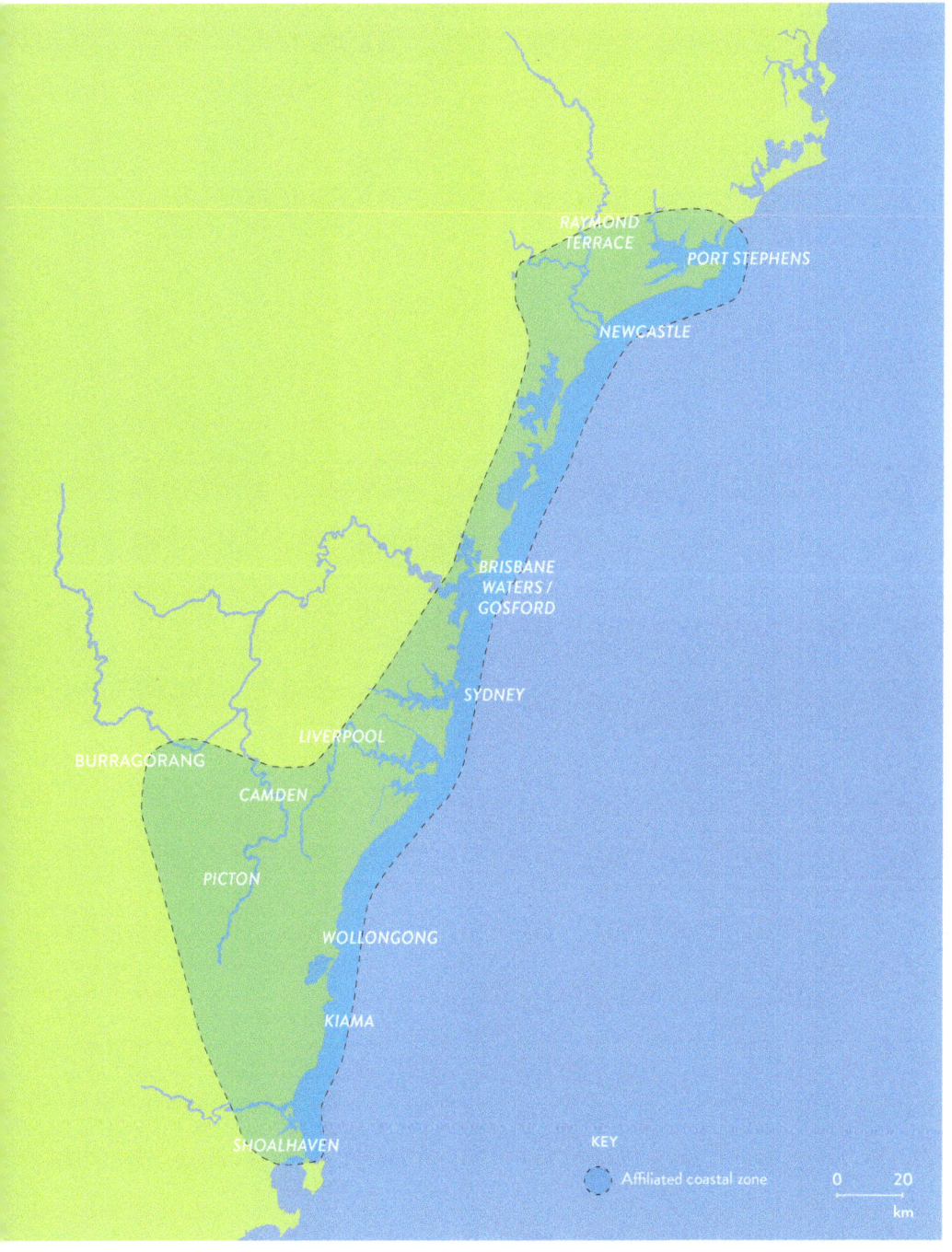

1.5 *Above* The affiliated coastal zone of the 19th century. Areas used for blanket distributions in the 1850s and 1860s are shown in italics. Not all were in use each year.

1.4 *Left* The recorded movements and connections of Thomas Tamara (1800s–c.1860s).
Tamara image – South Australian Museum. See Image References on page 154 for all sources

1.6   *Right* Bungaree in Sydney in 1826. *National Library of Australia*

2.1   *Top right* Much of coastal Sydney was sparsely inhabited by Europeans in the 1840s, as this view over the Cooks River and Botany Bay from around Newtown shows. *National Library of Australia*

2.2   *Middle right* As this view south from Moore Park to Surry Hills shows, the boundaries of Sydney were still sharp and clear in the 1870s. Beyond Surry Hills were vast dunes that regularly blew sand into the city. *State Library of NSW*

2.3   *Below right* Looking west from Camp Cove along the harbour to the uncleared scrub of Vaucluse in the 1870s. The lagoon is the small body of water at centre left, which was still surrounded by bush in the 1840s when Aboriginal people were living there. *State Library of NSW*

2.4   *Left* Cora Gooseberry at Camp Cove in 1845. *South Australian Museum*

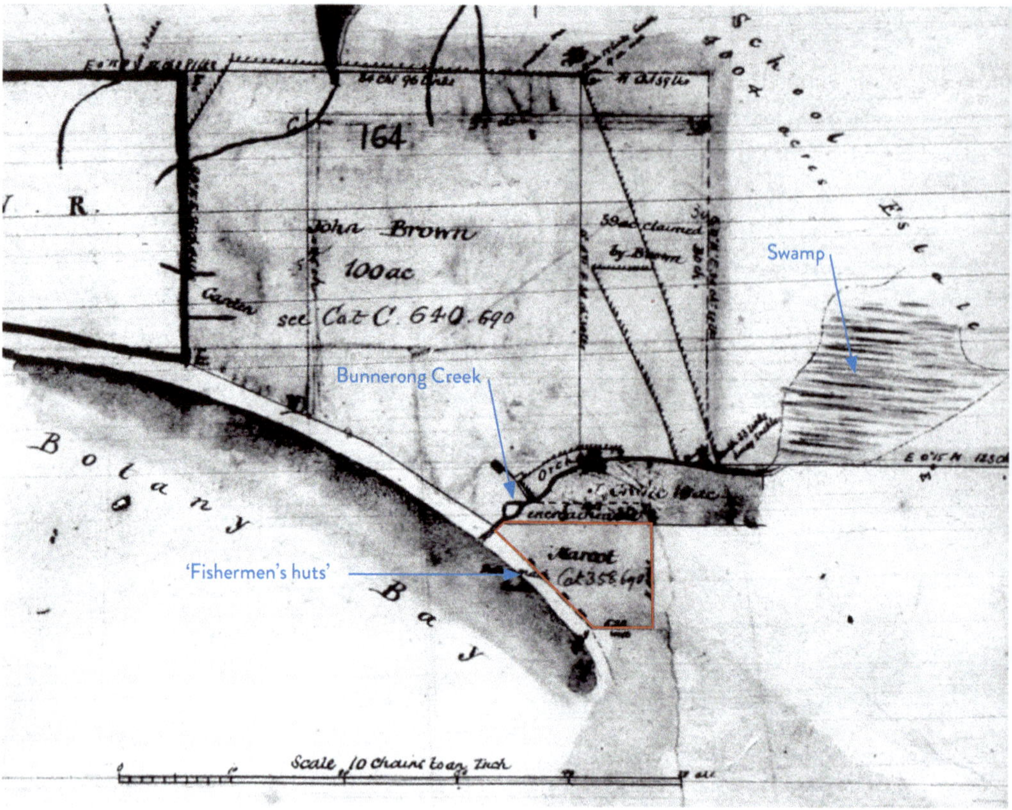

2.5 *Above* Mahroot's land and the 'fishermen's huts' of his tenants dotted on the Botany Bay shore. *State Archives NSW*

2.6   *Left* These Aboriginal people cooking speared fish at Double Bay in the early 1840s were probably part of Thomas Tamara's group. *State Library of NSW*

2.7   *Top* A 'Blackfellows hut' in the Outer Domain in 1843. *National Library of Australia*

2.8   *Above* Aboriginal people fishing in Woolloomooloo Bay alongside the Domain in the 1830s. *State Library of NSW*

a   Domain (1846)
b   Woolloomooloo (1844)
c   Double Bay (1845)
d   Vaucluse (1846)
e   Camp Cove (1845)
f   Mahroot's Land (1840s)
g   Botany Head (1845)
h   Kurnell Headland (1840s)
i   Goggey's Land (1840s)
1   Charles Smith's house/Sydney Markets: including mourning William Annan (1844), Christmas feast (1844), Smith's funeral (1845), visits nearby (1845)
2   Mahroot's evidence at Select Committee enquiry (1845)
3   European hunting party with Aboriginal people to Kurnell (1845)
4   Sydney tribe fishing from Botany Head to the Illawarra and up to Vaucluse (1846)
5   Trip to Sydney town to announce beached whale near Bondi (1845)
6   'Black Charlie' paid at Vaucluse (1844 & 1845)
7   Helping to fight bushfire at Point Piper (1845)
8   In town near Sussex and Druitt Streets (1845)
9   In town near Post Office (1845)
10 In town near Cattle Markets (1845)
a–11 From Domain to boomerang throwing at Hyde Park (1846)
b–1 From Woolloomooloo to Christmas feast at Charles Smith's house (1844)
c–1 Fish and gum from Double Bay sold at Sydney Markets (1840s)
d–1 Fish from Vaucluse sold at Sydney Markets (1846)

2.9   Recorded Aboriginal activities around coastal Sydney in the mid-1840s.
      See Image References on pages 155–6 for all sources

3.1   Sydney town and its initial suburbs in 1843. *State Library of NSW*

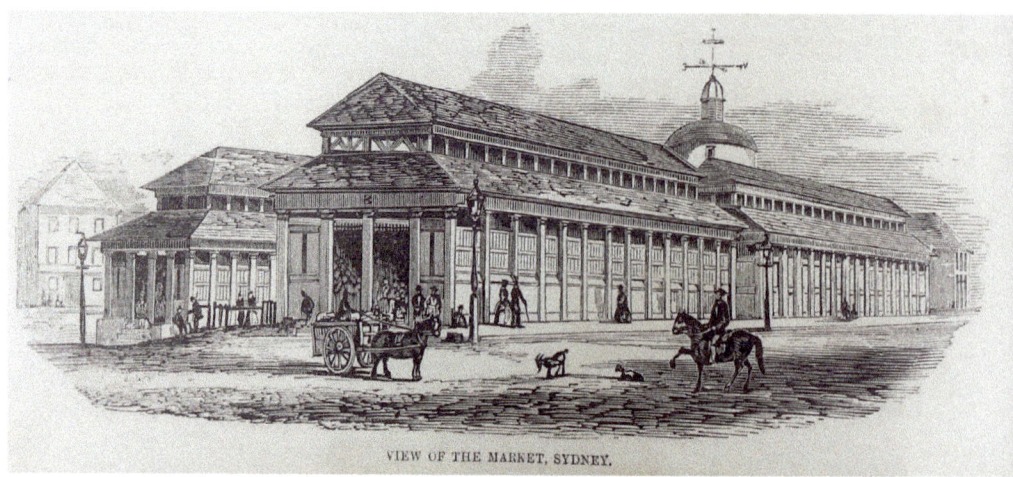

3.2 *Top* The Sydney Markets in the 1850s. The market buildings were located on the southern side of Market Street west of George Street. Building 'A' is the one on the left and this frontage is where Aboriginal people met in the 1840s. The markets were demolished around 1900 to make way for the Queen Victoria Building, which still occupies the site. *National Library of Australia*

3.3 *Above* View north along George Street in the early 1840s from around Bathurst Street. The walled cemetery to the left is the site of the current Sydney Town Hall. The domed building is the Police Court and beyond this are the buildings of the Sydney markets which opened in the early 1830s. *State Library of NSW*

3.4 *Top right* The Cricketers Arms Hotel building. The building is pictured in 1901 in a later iteration as Smart's Hotel. The site of the hotel is now a bank opposite the entrance to Pitt Street Mall. A rum mug used by Cora Gooseberry at the hotel is held in the collections of the State Library of NSW. *City of Sydney Archives*

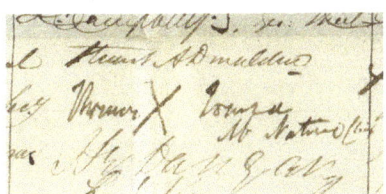

3.5 *Centre* Thomas Tamara's mark on a pledge of allegiance to Queen Victoria in 1837.
State Library of NSW

3.6 *Far right* William Annan in 1843. This image was made the year before Annan died.
State Library of NSW

3.7 *Above* Bob Nichols in 1848, when he was active in local Aboriginal affairs.
State Library of NSW

4.1 The western end of Double Bay (Darling Point) in 1858. This was the likely location of the shelter used by Tamara's group in the 1840s, but by the 1850s the area was densely settled and the slope containing the shelter had been modified. © *The University of Manchester*

4.2 Double Bay in 1880. The view is looking south-east from Darling Point and shows the edge of cleared suburbia. *State Library of NSW*

4.3 William Warrell outside his hut at Rose Bay in the early 1850s. Note the poor construction of the hut, which was built by Warrell's friend George Rawlingson. *State Library of NSW*

4.4 Daniel Cooper's Rose Bay Cottage in 1857. The view is from Point Piper. William Warrell's hut would have been in centre left just behind the foreground trees. *National Gallery of Australia*

a   Richard Hill rowed to Lane Cove by Aboriginal people (up to 1850s)
b   WC Wentworth and Daniel Cooper looking after William Warrell (1850s–1860s)
c   Bobby working for Wentworth family (1860s)
d   Aboriginal people visiting Edward Smith Hill (1860s–1870s)
e   Johnny Baswick visiting EL Clarke, befriends son Bonus (1870s)
f   Aboriginal people supplying seafood to Woollahra House (1870s)
g   'Johnny' (Baswick?) visiting Vaucluse House (1870s)
h   Johnny Baswick visiting WB Dalley (1880)
i   Johnny Baswick dies at EL Clarke's house (1880)

4.5   Cross-cultural interactions in the eastern suburbs 1850s–1870s.
See Image References on page 157 for all sources

3

Cross-cultural relationships (1790s–1840s)

On an autumn day in 1838, Port Hacking man William Annan (c.1790s–1844) was out fishing in Darling Harbour with a group of Europeans that included local butchers George Hill and Charles Smith. They were net-fishing from their boat, and had just hauled in a load of fish when the venomous spine of a catfish stung William on the hand. He was in great pain; Hill and Smith took him to the General Hospital and paid for his stay and the necessary eventual amputation of his right arm.[1] Fortunately he survived, and continued to fish and hunt with Hill, Smith and others. He even later displayed a sense of humour about his brutal experience by convincing a naïve tourist that his arm had been removed according to Aboriginal practice with a 'sharp shell'.[2]

Cross-cultural relationships like this had been forming since Europeans arrived in Sydney half a century before. They were a key part of the Aboriginal response to the growth of colonial Sydney. Their webs of connection within and beyond coastal Sydney gave their groups stability and longevity; they continued to fish, providing them with food and a source of income to obtain other things they needed; and these relationships helped them to maintain access to lands and waters. While cross-cultural relationships were a common feature of life in colonial Sydney, they were neither random nor universal. Aboriginal people formed relationships selectively and strategically, and not all Europeans were inclined to reciprocate. These relationships formed part of the daily dynamics of Aboriginal life, but as we will see, they also came to define the longer-term fate of Aboriginal people in coastal Sydney in the 1840s, and one-armed William Annan was central to that story.

Early relationships

Aboriginal people were aware from the earliest days of the colony that Europeans were not an undifferentiated group. They quickly identified who wielded physical, political and economic power, and who was *friendly* or *unfriendly*. Cross-cultural relationships initially developed out of curiosity and necessity on both sides, and Aboriginal people tried to bind these new connections into their existing social world. This is probably why Bennelong referred to Governor Phillip as *Beanna* (father), and why other Aboriginal people in the early years of the colony chose the names of European residents for themselves.[3] Major Worgan, for example, took on the name of first fleet surgeon George Worgan (the only European of that name), while two Aboriginal 'Major Whites' were most likely inspired by surgeon-general John White.[4] Many early relationships were fleeting, as governors and naval officers left the fledgling colony after a few years, but the idea of maintaining relationships with key Aboriginal people appears to have been passed down to successive governors until well into the 19th century. As we have already seen, they were the basis for Macquarie's grant of land to Bungaree's group in the 1810s, and they foiled an attempt to push Mahroot off his land at Botany in the 1840s. Though these 'chief-to-chief' relationships were important, it was the bonds that formed between Aboriginal people and ordinary Europeans that proved the most enduring and essential.

From the 1790s, as Aboriginal people regrouped their bands in the wake of the smallpox epidemic, they began to interact with a wide range of Europeans in Sydney town and in the rural settlements that sprouted along the major waterways across the Sydney region. Typically these early relationships involved Aboriginal people providing labour or services that Europeans needed, in exchange for money or goods. They were born of economic necessity and both parties' practical desire for security. For Aboriginal people, they also had an element of traditional reciprocal exchange, where an investment would be made on the understanding that the favour would be returned when needed in the future.[5] When violent conflict arose from the European failure to recognise these protocols, and from their relentless appropriation of Aboriginal lands, it was often in the context of these prior peaceful interactions. As historian Grace Karskens points out, antagonists were often 'intimate enemies', who already knew 'their attackers and their victims by name and face'.[6] We can see this dynamic at work during the several years of armed conflict in southwestern Sydney that culminated in the massacre of Aboriginal men, women and children by a posse of soldiers and landowners at Appin in 1816.[7] The fine-grained differentiation of friend and foe meant that Europeans like John Wentworth could feel safe fishing with local Aboriginal men near the Georges River in 1814, despite the nearby fighting.

When the Appin massacre effectively ended armed Aboriginal resistance in Sydney, personal cross-cultural relationships continued to form, and they were not the actions of a defeated people seeking to eke out a dependent existence on the colonial margins. Aboriginal people in coastal Sydney actively engaged with Europeans to shape their futures as much as possible on their own terms. They placed their main settlements some distance from Sydney town, not to shun Europeans, but to allow them to choose when and how they interacted. They entered Sydney town regularly by boat from these settlements, or on foot from closer staging post camps, to buy and sell goods and to meet Aboriginal or European acquaintances. As Judge Barron Field observed in the 1820s, Aboriginal people were 'the carriers of news and fish; the gossips of the town; the loungers on the quay. They know everybody; and understand the nature of everybody's business'.⁸ These regular interactions provided the basis for enduring relationships between European and Aboriginal men and women, and importantly between their children.

For the first generations of Aboriginal and European children born after the colony was established in the 1790s and 1800s, encountering each other was a fact of life. That is not to say that all children played together or became friends, but some developed relationships in those early years as they both tried to figure out what it meant to be *native born*. For Aboriginal people this was a period of great change and challenge, redefining who they were and how they could live; locally born Europeans were trying to make sense of a country that was foreign to their parents, but was the only one they knew. By the 1820s Australian-born Europeans represented about a quarter of the colony's population, and the oldest were adults.⁹ Some of them maintained their relationships with Aboriginal people, and it is primarily those that formed between men that are described in surviving records. Their relationships deepened over a shared passion for hunting and fishing that was both a defining feature of coastal Aboriginal identity and part of being a colonial man in Sydney.¹⁰

By the 1840s colonial sons such as George Robert 'Bob' Nichols, William Charles 'WC' Wentworth, George Hill, Richard Hill, Daniel Egan and James Oatley had acquired influence in Sydney as parliamentarians, newspaper editors, businessmen, magistrates, lawyers and aldermen. They had risen from humble beginnings, often as the children of convicts, and they felt a sense of patronage to the less fortunate that informed their support for a range of benevolent institutions. It also inclined them to assist local Aboriginal people, but their actions were local and personal, and sat outside the broader currents of philanthropy that flowed through the colony at this time. Few if any joined the Sydney branch of the international Aborigines Protection Society when it formed in 1838, and their attitudes in the same year towards the eleven Europeans on trial for the massacre of at least twenty-eight Aboriginal people at Myall Creek differed greatly.¹¹ Both WC Wentworth and Bob Nichols were politically aligned in the pro-Australian independence movement, but while Nichols decried the barbaric acts at Myall Creek through his newspaper *The Australian*, Wentworth's firm view was that Europeans should not be subject to 'judicial murder' for killing Aboriginal people.[12] In terms of their interactions in Sydney, though, these views mattered far less than their personal familiarity with local Aboriginal people. They knew them from hunting and fishing trips, and encountered their settlements on their way to and from Sydney town.

Two important facets of European and Aboriginal life sustained and deepened cross-cultural relationships in colonial Sydney. On the European side, the sense of patronage was nurtured by the linkages between many Australian-born families. It was not a large city, and historian David Denholm has explored the networks of intermarriage, business, friendship and personal patronage that bound many influential families together. He concludes that to understand many of their activities, 'we need to know [...] who was married to whom and who was patron to whom'.[13] These networks helped to maintain charitable activities as the right thing to do across families and through generations. For example, D'Arcy Wentworth, as Police Superintendent from 1811 to the mid-1820s, was known to Aboriginal people – in fact they goaded Europeans into attacking them on the streets of Sydney and then taunted that they would tell 'Massa Wenta' (Wentworth) if they did.[14] The relationship transferred to D'Arcy's sons John Wentworth on the Georges River, and to the highly influential colonial figure WC Wentworth, who established a century-long familial association with the Vaucluse Estate from the 1820s. WC Wentworth was related by marriage to the neighbouring Cooper and Hill families, who also developed relationships with local Aboriginal people, in some cases lasting into the 20th century, as we will see.[15]

Aboriginal people were motivated to maintain relationships because they needed to retain a place for themselves in colonial Sydney, but there were probably also deeper cultural factors at work.

Their adoption of European names in early colonial times indicates a desire to weave selected outsiders into their social world, with its strong ethic of reciprocity. Through Aboriginal eyes, the power that Europeans held in colonial Sydney carried with it a responsibility to meet Aboriginal needs, something that historian Richard Broome has called 'right behaviour'.[16] The expectation of right behaviour is why Aboriginal people saw the annual distribution of blankets as an ongoing entitlement, and they probably regarded their requests to Europeans for assistance in times of need in the same way.[17] The longer and deeper cross-cultural personal relationships became, the closer the European idea of patronage aligned with the Aboriginal notion of right behaviour.

Navigating the town

To get a sense of how cross-cultural relationships influenced the lives of Aboriginal people in coastal Sydney on a daily basis, we can look at how they used the urban space of Sydney town. By the 1840s, Sydney town was home to over thirty thousand Europeans, mostly within the Tank Stream valley, but the town was also expanding south and beginning to sprout suburbs to the east and west (see Figure 3.1).[18] New suburbs like Elizabeth Bay were the preserve of wealthy families who had private means of travel, for Sydney was still a walking town devoid of public transport.[19] Though the population had tripled since the 1810s, the geography moulded under the Macquaries remained. The main retail centre was still around the lively trading spaces of the city markets at George and Market streets (see Figure 3.2), fed by the recent expansion of shipping from Sydney Cove onto the wharves of Darling Harbour immediately to the west. Banking and commercial activity was situated north of the markets, while the government buildings to the north and east housed the colonial administration of the entire eastern Australian mainland.[20]

Convict transportation from England to Australia ended in

1840, and a growing middle class of free settlers was trying to turn Sydney town into a respectable colonial city.[21] There was a wide gulf though between aspiration and reality, which was captured well by artists John Skinner Prout and John Rae in their serialised book *Sydney Illustrated* in the early 1840s.[22] They portray newly gas-lit thoroughfares like George Street along which 'stately structures of polished freestone' were replacing older timber and stone structures (see Figure 3.3). But their tidy depiction of buildings like the Police Court are at odds with their accompanying description of it as the 'Drunkard's Tribunal' and 'a popular resort for the idlers of Sydney, who flock to it in crowds'.[23] Perspective was crucial. As historian Grace Karskens points out, 'Sydney was literally a different town to different people as a result of their expectations, experiences and background'.[24] One person's 'idler' was another's companion, and where visitors perceived bacchanalian chaos across a town awash with drinking holes (there were over two hundred), residents knew the difference between the 'respectable' portion of the Rocks and 'that part where the whalers, sailors and old hands used to congregate'.[25]

To understand how different people used and experienced Sydney town, we can think of each of them having what archaeologist Denis Byrne calls a 'mental map' onto which was imprinted familiar places and areas to avoid.[26] These mental maps operated at the large scale of entire beats around coastal Sydney and beyond, but also at the much more detailed level of city streets and houses. The mental maps of Aboriginal visitors to Sydney town had shifted over the decades, as their use of the town space had changed. The bloody ritual contests that had previously been held on the ceremonial grounds at the south end of Hyde Park had shifted out of town, and Aboriginal people now used the same space to spruik the sale of their expertly carved implements by holding demonstrations of boomerang throwing.[27] Aboriginal people entered the town to sell fish and other goods, to socialise (with both other Aboriginal people and Europeans), to bring news or to collect participants in their guided hunting and fishing trips. Most Aboriginal people had acquiesced to European expectations and wore (some) clothes in the town, though they often cast them off on their return home.[28]

Aboriginal people could freely enter and move around the town, but they had to watch their step. As the population of Sydney town swelled due to immigration, the streets were increasingly filled with Europeans who had no experience of local Aboriginal people and were often indifferent or even hostile to them, as were some of the locally born Sydneysiders. Roaming this pedestrian town were groups of youths who liked to hurl stones and abuse at vulnerable passers-by. Aboriginal people were often in their sights, and some took to carrying clubs with them to ward off attacks. Others were charged at by horse-drawn coaches and abused for getting in the way.[29] These ever-present dangers did not keep Aboriginal people out of town, but their mental maps focussed their movements between friendly places, such as the homes and businesses of a number of sympathetic Europeans.

A prominent example was Charles Smith (1800–1845), a successful convict-turned butcher, racehorse breeder and philanthropist, who had been Port Hacking man William Annan's fishing companion when he was stung by a catfish in 1838.[30] Annan was not Smith's only Aboriginal acquaintance, and he was known for having 'long fed and protected' local Aboriginal people.[31] His house and butcher shop had been located opposite the Sydney Markets (the site of today's Queen Victoria Building) on the corner of George and Market streets since at least the early 1830s, and was known to Aboriginal people as a safe haven in the town. In the early 1840s, coastal Sydney people often met directly across the road from Smith's home and business 'at their old place of rendezvous, the George Street Market Buildings, letter A' (see Figure 3.2).[32] The location features regularly in short paragraphs in local papers, mentioning the presence of Aboriginal people in the town and bemoaning their drinking, but there was more to their visits than this. They came to sell their fish and other wares, as well as to socialise, and knew that this was a place where they had an understanding and generous friend.[33]

Close relationships also developed between coastal Sydney people and ex-convict turned hotelier Edward Borton (1795–1867). Like Charles Smith, Borton was known as a 'friend to the blacks', and developed a particularly strong bond with Sydney woman Cora Gooseberry (1770s–1852), whose husband Bungaree (1770s–1830) had been a well-known figure in the early colony.[34] Cora and her cousin William Warrell (1790s–1863) frequented Borton's Cricketers Arms hotel, located just a hundred metres east of the Sydney Markets at the corner of Market and Pitt streets (now the site of a bank, see Figure 3.1 and Figure 3.4). Borton also allowed Cora to sleep in the kitchen of his residence at the Sydney Arms Hotel a block or so away on Castlereagh Street.[35] When she died there one night in 1852, Borton paid for her burial and headstone in the Devonshire Street Cemetery (see Figure 5.3).[36]

Aboriginal people also maintained a number of other personal relationships across the town, often by working for local households. This ensured that there were friendly doors on which to knock when they were sick or needed shelter. The Prescott family in Clarence Street, for example, had engaged an Aboriginal man known as Shingleman to fetch their water from the town fountains in the 1840s. When he became very ill in 1849, he knocked on their door and was allowed to spend the night in the kitchen.[37] And in the early spring of 1846, Jack Stewart and another Aboriginal man knocked on the door of an acquaintance near Darling Harbour asking for 'a bit of fire' to keep them warm.[38] An employee of the house let them in, gave Stewart tea, and left him by the fire to go to bed. These stories show a degree of trust and familiarity, and highlight how Aboriginal people navigated the town according to cross-cultural relationships. They also show the brutal reality of life for Aboriginal people at this time. We only know these stories because both Shingleman and Stewart died in their host's houses during the night of cold-related ailments and became of interest to local newspapers. But we can assume that there were also many unrecorded visits that did not end in tragedy, and formed part of life in mid-19th-century Sydney.

The patchwork of cross-cultural relationships across Sydney town and beyond was the basis for Judge Barron Field's 1820s observation that Aboriginal people had their finger on the pulse of the town.[39] They were aware of upcoming special events and often came to town to spectate or even participate. When news of the death of King William IV reached Sydney in 1837, around a hundred influential Europeans organised to sign a document pledging their allegiance to Queen Victoria. Among the signatories was Sydney/Illawarra man Thomas Tamara (1800s–c.1860s), who signed his 'X' as 'A Native Chief' (Figure 3.5). Whether he was invited or just turned up is not known, but of greater significance is that he knew of the event and that he was not turned away. When the first Sydney municipal elections were held in late 1842, a large number of Aboriginal people were seen to enter the town.[40] They knew the election was happening, and although they were not voting themselves, they probably knew a number of the candidates personally.[41] Just a couple of years later at least five of them, native-born Sydneysiders James Chapman, Daniel Egan, John Little, Thomas Smidmore and George Hill, signed up to help local Aboriginal people when the government suddenly ceased all involvement in their welfare.

Colonial indifference

By the 1840s, there was a growing feeling among the government and people of the New South Wales colony that missionary and other charitable efforts over previous decades had achieved little.[42] From their perspective, they were right to be pessimistic. The early state-sponsored missions at Lake Macquarie (1824–1841), to the north of Sydney, and Wellington (1832–1842) over the mountains to the north-west, were closing due to dwindling Aboriginal attendance, and could boast few conversions.[43] Humanitarian criticism of the way indigenous people were treated throughout the British Empire had been growing, and as a result in 1839 Governor George

Gipps engaged several Europeans to act as 'Aboriginal Protectors' in the new colony of Port Phillip (Victoria). They were to ensure that Aboriginal people were protected from harm and provided with food, shelter and religious instruction, but over several years, and despite great expense, they had done nothing to stem rampant frontier violence. Sydneysiders did not just read about this in their newspapers; they could see the human cost of the frontier around them. Aboriginal prisoners from distant districts were marched along the streets in shackles after being drawn along the veins of the colonial justice and penal system to its Sydney heart; orphaned Aboriginal children were sent to Sydney for schooling or to work as domestic servants; and everyone had an opinion on the trial of Europeans for the 1838 massacre of Aboriginal people at Myall Creek in northern New South Wales.[44]

As a humanitarian, Governor Gipps was keen to improve the lot of Aboriginal people, but in keeping with the widespread colonial view and the sentiment underpinning the new British Poor Law of 1834, he believed that this was best achieved by providing opportunity rather than charity.[45] Accordingly, from 1838 he began to wind back the annual distribution of government blankets from the universal entitlement it had become, to a merit-based reward. It was in this context that the government conducted a broader review of expenditure on Aboriginal affairs in 1841, as a devastating economic depression swept the expanding colony after the 1830s property speculation bubble burst.[46] Historians have reviewed the effects of the ensuing spending cuts in detail at the colonial scale.[47] Governor Gipps' decision to stop handing out blankets in 1844 heralded the start of what historian Ann Curthoys has aptly described as a period of 'colonial indifference' to Aboriginal welfare across the New South Wales colony that lasted well into the 1870s.[48] But the end of blanket distributions also had very local consequences for Aboriginal people in coastal Sydney, and here we pick up the story of Port Hacking man William Annan once more (see Figure 3.6).

Annan was known as a 'Chief of the Port Hacking Tribe' in

southern Sydney and was brother to Botany Bay 'chief' Bulkabra.[49] He was named (perhaps through his father) after the whaling ship *William and Ann*, and had worked with whalers and sealers.[50] In the late 1820s he worked in Sydney as an armed police tracker with Constable Benjamin Nichols to pursue the infamous bushranger John Hayden. He spied Hayden and one of his gang while out hunting to the south of Botany Bay with a young European companion, and when they refused his order to surrender, Annan knocked Hayden down 'with a swinging blow from the butt of his fowling-piece' (an early form of shotgun). Hayden escaped but Annan later used his intimate knowledge of the forests and mudflats of southern Sydney to track him down with the police, and he was eventually brought to justice.[51] Annan was a valued hunting and fishing companion to Europeans, both before and after he lost his right arm to a catfish bite in 1838. But the amputation made it more difficult to earn a living, and by the early 1840s he was also seeking 'charitable donations of those to whom he was known in former days', and had unsuccessfully requested a boat and tackle from the government.[52] In the winter of 1844 Annan came into Sydney town, probably to collect a blanket, as he and others had done at this time of year many times before.[53] Finding that there were none to be had, he left empty-handed and was found dead of exposure in Hyde Park a short time later.[54]

Annan's decades of building and maintaining cross-cultural relationships had the effect in his death of fostering right behaviour among the Europeans he knew. Some linked his death to the pettiness of the colonial government in denying Aboriginal people 'the boon of a blanket each', and their indignation quickly galvanised into action.[55] Lawyer and native-born Sydneysider Bob Nichols (1809–1857; see Figure 3.7) organised a meeting the following week to form a private committee to raise funds for the 'Sydney tribe', which soon had thirty subscribers.[56] His contemporaries would not have been surprised to find Nichols leading the committee. His former editorship of the liberal, emancipist newspaper *The Australian*, his political alignment with WC Wentworth's Australian Party, his past representation of Aboriginal prisoners in court, and his support for causes such as self-government and an end to convict transportation had already earned him the derisive title 'Radical Bob'.[57]

His actions were probably also personal to some extent. As a young boy growing up on the Parramatta River, he would have heard stories of local Aboriginal people, such as the attack on his parents' farm along the Parramatta River several years before his birth. His police constable uncle Benjamin Nichols had probably told him about tracking bushrangers with William Annan in the 1820s.[58] Perhaps he had even hunted or fished with Annan himself, as other committee members such as George Hill had. Within six months Nichols' committee had donated a fishing boat and supplies to the 'Sydney tribe'. This was almost certainly the group led by Botany Bay/Illawarra man Thomas Tamara and his Botany Bay wife Nanny Nellola, as Tamara was recorded soon after as having 'been presented with a boat, in which he fishes outside the heads and brings his fish to Sydney Market'.[59]

In his own way, Annan's former fishing companion Charles Smith also did right by his friend. Soon after Annan's death, his group gathered, as they had done many times before, outside Smith's home and butcher shop opposite the Sydney Markets. This time though, they were in mourning, 'lamenting his loss', and refraining from speaking his name, in accordance with ongoing custom.[60] Charles Smith did not join Nichols' committee, but it was probably in response to this outpouring of grief on his doorstep that he organised a lavish Christmas feast six months later at his premises for 'the Aboriginal tribes of Woolloomooloo and Shoalhaven'. Feasts had long been used in English culture (and by past governors at Parramatta) as a way of making amends and bringing people together, and it was certainly a lavish affair. As newspapers reported, over forty Aboriginal men and women attended, including 'a chief called Tarban, Boatswain, and a Queen of the tribe. The whole of the males underwent the operation of shaving and washing previous to the dinner, and Mr. Smith kindly presented to each of them a new shirt on the occasion as a Christmas box.' A sumptuous feast ensued under a specially erected awning in his yard, observed by some of the town's well-to-do and supplemented by 'ale, porter and wine'.[61] While Smith's right behaviour of holding the feast was an appropriate response, it had no lasting impact, as he died suddenly just a few weeks later. His Aboriginal friends from Sydney and the Shoalhaven district were in mourning once again, and 'huddled together round the corner of deceased's residence [...] silent and mute as if some awful calamity had overtaken them'.[62]

The colonial government was not inspired by the actions of these Sydneysiders, and was not about to rediscover an interest in Aboriginal welfare. It focussed the little attention it gave to Aboriginal issues throughout the next thirty years on more remote regions.[63] Its 1845 *Select Committee on Aborigines*, for example, was established to deal with the plight of Aboriginal people in the wake of the rapidly expanding frontier.[64] The appearance of Botany Bay man Mahroot (1790s–1850) as its sole Aboriginal witness has been interpreted as evidence of government concern over a declining Aboriginal population in Sydney, but this was not a factor in their decision.[65] The government had intended to call Aboriginal witnesses from across the colony but this did not eventuate.[66] Mahroot probably became the first and only one interviewed because he was known to Select Committee members and lived nearby. In any case, his moving description of decline and hardship among Sydney's Aboriginal people elicited no action from the government.

From this time, though, several members of the 1844 fundraising committee took up where the government left off, and maintained an interest in the welfare of Sydney's Aboriginal people. Bob Nichols' brother Isaac, for example, was among those who were concerned by the apparent disappearance of Thomas Tamara's group from Botany Heads in 1846. Though it turned out that they were far from lost and had merely been fishing their way south to Wollongong along familiar waters, he nonetheless took his boat to Port Hacking to ensure they returned safely to Sydney.[67] In 1847 Bob Nichols, George Hill and others informed the Colonial Secretary that they had formed 'a committee for the purpose of affording some relief to such aborigines as may visit Sydney during the ensuing winter'.[68] Their request for a 'bale of blankets' was granted and for many years the Sydney Aborigines Committee (it had no official title), comprising Nichols, Hill and Daniel Egan, distributed blankets and requested fishing boats, supplies and repairs on behalf of the Aboriginal people of coastal Sydney.[69] As we will see, their activities helped these groups to maintain a foothold in the area.

SINCE THE EARLIEST DAYS OF THE COLONY, ABORIGINAL PEOPLE AND Europeans had largely worked things out for themselves, and from the 1840s there was little if any direct government involvement in the welfare of coastal Sydney people. In 1848, Governor FitzRoy ended his predecessor's ban on the distribution of blankets, but while elsewhere in the colony this was managed by government representatives, in Sydney town he was content to leave the Sydney Aborigines Committee in charge. The longstanding Aboriginal strategy of engaging creatively and selectively with the colony had reaped the reward of fostering right behaviour among sympathetic Sydneysiders. Along with the economic underpinning of fishing, and their sustaining web of connections across the affiliated coastal zone, Aboriginal people had found a way to meet the challenges of the early colony. But more changes were just around the corner in the mid-19th century. As Europeans began to occupy coastal Sydney more densely and pressures increased on Aboriginal people, their new way of life led to an unexpected outcome.

4

Entangled lives (1850s–1870s)

Almost a century after Europeans first pitched their tents in Sydney Cove, a group of Aboriginal people were fishing about five kilometres down the harbour at Rose Bay. They were gathering oysters from the rocks and fishing with traditional spears, though they had swapped the wooden prongs for umbrella wires. A local resident later recalled that 'standing on rocks above the water, and with spear poised to strike, they seldom failed in their unerring aim'.[1] The group were locally connected people who lived nearby, and were continuing to fish familiar waters using long-honed skills. But they were not just fishing for themselves. They took some of their catch up the hill to Woollahra House, and supplied its residents with fresh seafood, both as a commercial transaction and to foster goodwill, ensuring they could continue having access to private lands in the area.

This was the reality of Aboriginal life in coastal Sydney in the latter half of the 19th century. In earlier decades, Europeans had inhabited coastal Sydney fairly sparsely, giving Aboriginal people a degree of choice in where to live. They could set up camp next to rich fishing grounds in areas to which they had existing connections through ancestry or marriage; they formed relationships with Europeans; and they strategically engaged with the colony so they could continue living as much as possible on their own terms. As Europeans increasingly came to occupy coastal Sydney from the 1850s onwards, this decreased the choices available to Aboriginal people.

But while it has long been assumed that the growth of suburban Sydney forced the remaining Aboriginal people out of Sydney, something much more interesting occurred. Instead of leaving, Aboriginal people engaged more deeply with Europeans. As a result, both personally and economically, they became even more enmeshed in colonial Sydney.

Accommodation

After gold was discovered west of the Blue Mountains in 1851, a steady flow of immigrants turned Sydney town into a city. The number of people crammed into the Tank Stream valley grew by a third each decade to more than seventy-five thousand by the 1870s. Across the rest of coastal Sydney the European population grew even more dramatically, from around a thousand to tens of thousands in the same period.[2] Inner residential and industrial suburbs pushed outwards from the city, while the first outer suburbs in places like Newtown, Randwick and Waverley were tethered back to the city by road. Even the more remote areas began to be dotted with pleasure ground hotels carved out of the bush to serve a growing middle-class demand for leisure activities. These hotels, and the outer suburbs, were made viable by a network of regular steam ferries and horse-drawn omnibus services from the 1860s.[3] Although suburban Sydney spread unevenly, leaving some forests, sandhills and swamplands alone, there were many more Europeans living in, and travelling across, coastal Sydney than there had been before the 1850s.

The Aboriginal population, meanwhile, had remained relatively stable across coastal Sydney, comprising between fifty and one hundred people at any one time. Aboriginal mobility and a lack of record-keeping prevent us from being more precise, but at least fifty to sixty Aboriginal people collected blankets across coastal Sydney each year in the 1850s and early 1860s, and other records of the various Aboriginal settlements suggests that a population within this range was fairly constant.[4] Comparatively, though, this made Aboriginal people an ever-shrinking minority across coastal Sydney. They had to contend with the increasing European occupation of land and a greater number of visitors to formerly secluded locations. Just inside the southern entrance to the harbour at Camp Cove, for example, Aboriginal people had been able to live around the lagoon behind the rich fishing grounds of the cove up into the 1840s, on land that had been granted by the government but had no permanent European occupants. By the 1850s there are no further records of an Aboriginal settlement at Camp Cove. From this time, weekend daytrippers from Sydney town regularly invaded the beach, and a growing number of permanent residents began to clear the land around the lagoon and build huts (see Figure 2.3).[5] It no longer offered Aboriginal people the seclusion and security that it once had (though they did not desert this part of the harbour entirely, as we will see in later chapters).

Closer to Sydney town at Double Bay, Thomas Tamara and his group had lived in a large rock shelter in the 1840s, but photos like Figure 4.1 show that by the 1850s this was either destroyed or surrounded by suburban housing, and there are no further records of Tamara at Double Bay or elsewhere. While we do not know what happened to Tamara's family, it would be a mistake to assume that Aboriginal people were disappearing from coastal Sydney. If we zoom a bit further out from Tamara's rock shelter or from Camp Cove lagoon, we can see that the new suburbs were still islands surrounded by expanses of uncleared forest, scrub and swamp (see Figure 2.3 and Figure 4.2). Some of this land was public common, while much of it was still bound up in the large country estates of locally born families. Many of them were sympathetic to the continuing Aboriginal use of the area, forming a small but sufficient network of friendly landowners and settlement space around which Aboriginal people continued to circulate. But the decreasing number of other settlement options made them more reliant on this network of places and their European owners.

A good way of imagining this increasing personal and economic engagement is the concept of 'entanglement'. Historians, anthropologists and archaeologists use this term to evoke the two-sided nature of cultural and material interactions between indigenous people and Europeans.[6] Entanglements can be physical, personal or economic and they can be short moments or last much longer. It is a useful shorthand in coastal Sydney because it gives a sense of the space in which cross-cultural interactions took place, as well as the interactions themselves. The process of increasing entanglement is particularly evident across what is today known as the 'eastern suburbs' – the southern side of the harbour to the east of the city. In the first half of the 19th century Aboriginal people had lived in settlements in virtually every bay of the eastern suburbs, and by the 1840s they had established relationships with many landowners. They were described as a 'tribe of friendly blacks' who fished the harbour, sold wares (probably fish) to the large estates and used their local knowledge to help the police catch bushrangers.[7] Recorded events from this time reveal how much a part of the local scene Aboriginal people were. When a bushfire engulfed Point Piper in 1845, local Aboriginal people helped fight it alongside assigned convicts and local residents. When one of the convicts was bitten by a snake, Aboriginal people were asked to participate in his treatment using their traditional medical knowledge.[8]

As the city expanded in the 1850s, and the Watsons Bay fishing village grew into a permanently populated and regularly visited place, Aboriginal settlements began to cluster in the less-populated areas between Rushcutters Bay and Vaucluse. Sydney/Illawarra man William Warrell (1790s–1863) for example, came to reside at Rose Bay in the late 1840s, where he remained until his death (Figure 5.1).[9] As we saw in earlier chapters, he was a cousin to Cora Gooseberry, and had lived and travelled with her in and around Sydney town in previous years.[10] He was influenced by many things when he chose to live at Rose Bay. He knew of its use as a ceremonial combat ground called Pannerong from his childhood, and would also have been aware of the Aboriginal burials there, including those of his cousin Cora's husband Bungaree, and Bungaree's first wife, Matora. But as well as these links to its Aboriginal past, he had known George Rawlingson, the groundskeeper of Daniel Cooper's Rose Bay Estate, since the 1820s. It was perhaps this relationship that determined the exact site of his settlement, for Rawlingson built him a hut on 'a dry patch of land [...] close to the main road' near Cooper's residence (near today's intersection of Norwich Road and New South Head Road; see Figure 4.3).[11]

Warrell was a Sydney identity and knew some of his other neighbours, including Cooper's brother-in-law WC Wentworth at the nearby Vaucluse Estate. He made use of these connections and his acknowledged status as the so-called 'last of his tribe' to extract money from his neighbours and other travellers along the South Head Road in front of his hut; a kind of toll for passing through his traditional lands. As he became frail with age and increasingly immobile, Cooper and Wentworth gave him regular donations of food and clothing. Wentworth gave Rawlingson 'half-a-crown a week [...] to attend to him, and supplied him with two meals per day'.[12] These wealthy and influential people clearly accommodated Warrell's desire to remain at Rose Bay, despite the eyesore his hut and 'toll collecting' created in their genteel neighbourhood. The dynamics of this coexistence are neatly summarised in a painting of Rose Bay Cottage that Cooper commissioned at the time, in which Warrell's hut was kept discreetly out of frame (see Figure 4.4).

Warrell was not alone in cultivating relationships with his European neighbours, as the interactions summarised in Figure 4.5 show. Thomas Tamara's group had lived on the Wentworth estate at Vaucluse in the 1840s, while other senior men from the area such as Wingle (1790s–1868) and Jack Harris (1810s–1863) knew WC Wentworth well enough to personally greet him on his return from England in 1861.[13] These relationships also deepened when the Wentworth family engaged a local Aboriginal man, Bobby, as their servant in the 1860s. Bobby was said to be a local 'chief' and lived with the family for a number of years.[14] Other members of the intermarried Wentworth, Cooper and Hill families lived in the vicinity and also had relationships with local Aboriginal people. Edward Smith Hill (Daniel Cooper's brother-in-law) lived next to Rose Bay at Point Piper, for example, and was said to have 'understood their language and encouraged their camping about his residence'.[15] As well as having a keen ethnological interest in local Aboriginal culture, he was also on the 1840s fundraising committee for the Sydney tribe with his brother George. Their other brother Richard (WC Wentworth's brother-in-law) had lived on the Vaucluse Estate until the 1850s, and was said to have hired Aboriginal men to row him up the harbour to his Lane Cove orchard.[16]

Earlier in the 19th century these relationships had been about Aboriginal people investing in the future by fostering right behaviour, but as Europeans intensified their occupation of eastern Sydney, the needs of Aboriginal people became more acute and immediate. They did the rounds of this network of patronage and benevolence, binding it together to ensure they had continued access to land. Johnny Baswick (1820s–1880), also known as Bankie, lived in the area in the 1870s with his wife Rachael, their three children and others. He was said to be from 'the coast south of Port Jackson or Botany', and ranged between coastal Sydney and the Shoalhaven district, where his son Freddy had attended school in the early 1870s.[17] When in Sydney they moved between settlements at Bondi Beach and Rose Bay, visiting the Clarke family at their dairy on the ridge above Rose Bay, William Bede Dalley at Vaucluse and Edward Smith Hill at Point Piper.[18] It was Baswick's group that we have already seen spear-fishing at Rose Bay and supplying the residents of Woollahra House with 'fresh fish and oysters'.[19] These activities encouraged right behaviour from their European neighbours by strengthening relationships and building up reciprocal obligations.

The strategy worked. Aboriginal people were able to continue living on private lands at Rose Bay and Vaucluse for decades after the 1850s. At Rose Bay, they lived along New South Head Road in the vicinity of William Warrell's former hut into the 1890s.[20] The wider community did not emulate these wealthy Europeans' patronage of Aboriginal people, but the idea of at least tolerating their settlements appears to have filtered through to the broader Sydney population. At Rushcutters Bay, Aboriginal people had established a settlement by the 1850s, and probably earlier, in the bush about fifty metres back from the tollhouse on New South Head Road (see Figure 4.6), in what is today Rushcutters Bay Park.[21] Local residents knew it well, and it was later recalled by Alfred Gelding and WH East, who grew up in the area in the 1860s and 1870s.[22] Gelding remembered men spearfishing and ceremonies taking place. He also recalled Aboriginal women bailing up the carriages of rich passers-by by standing in front of them, asking for money or gifts for their children, just as William Warrell had extracted a kind of toll from travellers further down the road.

There were altercations at Rushcutters Bay between local European youths and Aboriginal people, as well as a number of assaults and alcohol-related deaths at this settlement.[23] WH East recalled that 'residents found it impossible to retain their female servants, who were [...] compelled to return home in daylight or undertake the dreaded lonely walk with the ever present fear of meeting aboriginals'.[24] Children experienced similar fears.[25] Yet despite these anxieties, and the obvious inconvenience and unsightliness of the settlement to European residents and road users, not a single letter of complaint was written to newspapers or the government; no action was taken to shut the settlement down or to move Aboriginal people on. It is not clear what mechanism the authorities could have used, in any case. As we saw in Chapter 2, the *Vagrancy Act* excluded Aboriginal people, and the authorities do not appear to have contemplated acting outside the law to forcibly move them on. Perhaps the government realised that they had nowhere to move anyone to, and in this era of colonial indifference, did not wish to take responsibility for Aboriginal welfare. Whatever the reasons, residents and wayfarers seem to have accepted that Aboriginal people had to live somewhere. Consequently, the Rushcutters Bay settlement endured through to the end of the century, despite being increasingly surrounded by densely populated suburbs.

Smaller groups and individuals also continued to live at other locations across the eastern suburbs outside the main settlements of Rose Bay and Rushcutters Bay. As the population of Double Bay increased, this may have destroyed Tamara's rock shelter at its western end or prevented people from occupying it, but in the 1860s Aboriginal couple Gurrah and Nancy were living along what is now known as Seven Shillings Beach and Redleaf Pool at the opposite end of the bay. When the Walker family moved into their newly constructed Redleaf House (today the heritage-listed Woollahra Council office building) above the beach in 1863, Gurrah and Nancy continued to live just outside the property fence and, to the Walkers' frustration, saw no reason to move. The facts are hard to distil in this local legend, but the Walkers negotiated some form of payment (seven shillings is suggested) in the late 1860s as recognition of the Aboriginal couple's rights to the area and to compensate them for moving away. Gurrah and Nancy viewed the transaction differently however, moving a few hundred metres up the hill to a sympathetic neighbour, and returning soon after when more accommodating owners took over at Redleaf. Gurrah continued to visit Redleaf after Nancy's death in the early 1870s, probably to fish its familiar waters.[26] Further east above Rose Bay at Vaucluse, Nancy's sister Sophia was said to have lived next to a spring-fed stream.[27] Although details are often scant about many of these Aboriginal people and their settlements, they were a fact of life for Europeans across the eastern suburbs throughout the 19th century. And while Europeans increasingly occupied the eastern suburbs, decreasing the range of spaces available for Aboriginal settlement, their intensifying use of other parts of coastal Sydney opened up new opportunities.

Making a living

Since the earliest days of the colony, Aboriginal people had participated in the European economy to supplement their subsistence fishing and food gathering. Their work ranged from unskilled labouring to jobs which made use of their existing abilities, such as commercial fishing and whaling. By the mid-19th century, Aboriginal people were finding work harder to obtain. Whaling operations that had previously engaged Mahroot and a number of other local Aboriginal men were no longer based in Sydney, an ever-increasing number of Europeans were taking up the market for menial jobs around the town, and other briefly popular occupations such as bare-knuckle boxing in pubs had passed their heyday.[28] The settler population of coastal Sydney was sufficiently large that even the 1850s exodus to the goldfields did not create a noticeable demand for Aboriginal labour as it did in rural areas.[29] Compounding this was the fact that few Aboriginal children attended school, due to pessimism about their abilities rather than segregation. Experts consulted during an 1853 government enquiry 'could offer no suggestions' to solve this problem, ensuring that most Aboriginal people did not receive any formal education for decades to come, which further limited their prospects for employment.[30]

Examining a similar period in colonial Adelaide, historian Michael Parsons has observed that decreasing economic options often led Aboriginal people to 'seize [...] the opportunity to market their cultural knowledge and skills'.[31] In Adelaide this took the form of tourist corroborees, while in coastal Sydney, Aboriginal people marketed their intimate knowledge of the local environment. As we have seen, some had been fishing commercially and acting as fishing and hunting guides for Europeans since the early 19th century. Exchanging their traditional *nowie* for wooden boats changed the context of Aboriginal fishing from an individual to a group activity, but it gave them a degree of autonomy as well as a means of travelling longer distances. While the growing European population decreased economic options in other ways, it increased the market for Aboriginal guides.

By the mid-19th century the growing middle-class desire for weekend leisure activities spawned the construction of pleasure ground hotels in secluded parts of coastal Sydney. The earliest and most prominent of these was the Sir Joseph Banks Hotel at Botany, which survives today, converted into apartments with some of its grounds preserved as the adjacent Sir Joseph Banks Park. It was constructed in the 1840s among the dunes along the foreshore of Botany Bay, and was accessed by omnibus or ferry from Sydney town. By the 1850s hundreds of visitors flocked to the hotel each weekend to enjoy the bars; the dance hall with visiting bands; the 'tastefully laid-out garden', which included a zoo with a range of local and imported animals; and to swim, fish, hunt and sightsee (see Figure 4.7).[32] Aboriginal people took advantage of the economic opportunities provided by these latter activities. Previously they had relied on word of mouth among Sydneysiders to provide them with customers for fishing and hunting trips, but the Sir Joseph Banks Hotel brought hundreds of potential customers to their doorstep on the shores of Botany Bay each weekend.

Botany Bay man Mahroot (1790s–1850) was the first to exploit this situation. Also known as 'Boatswain', Mahroot had an existing fishing business and a plot of land a couple of kilometres south along the bay shore from the Sir Joseph Banks Hotel. By the late 1840s he had set up a shelter in the hotel gardens and was working as a guide and ferryman for visitors, probably using his own fishing boat.[33] One of his customers later recalled that 'to many a fishing excursion, through many a hunting bivouac had old Boatswain guided and watched the white young native', which acknowledged his seasoned and steady-handed expertise in the lands and waters of the bay.[34] When he died in 1850 he was buried in the grounds of the hotel, but the entrepreneurial business he had started did not die with him.[35]

Botany Bay man Johnny Malone (c.1820s–1880s) had grown up around the bay while Mahroot was still plying its waters (see Figure 5.8). He may have been a relative or one of the 'young fellows' that Mahroot sometimes had with him on hunting trips.[36] Either way, his own intimate knowledge of the lands and waters of the bay was recognised by the late 1850s, when Aboriginal sympathiser and ethnologist Edward Smith Hill of Woollahra sought him out to help an Austrian visitor find an Aboriginal burial site.[37] A few years later, Malone's local knowledge came to the attention of the new proprietor of the Sir Joseph Banks Hotel, Vickers Moyse. In the first advertisement for his new venture, one of his main selling points was that 'arrangements for boat excursions and fishing parties are most complete, Johnny Malone and tribe being engaged by me for the same'.[38]

To take advantage of this opportunity, Johnny and his Illawarra wife Lizzie (1830s–1901) built or occupied a hut on the nearby Botany Reserve, in which he stowed spare sail canvas and a looking glass for his vessel. They raised a family there in the 1860s alongside a number of other Aboriginal residents.[39] Whether or not their arrangement with the hotel continued, the residents of the Botany settlement kept working as local guides, and built their reputation to the point that customers actively sought them out. A newspaper article in 1870 informed those wishing to hunt in the vast expanses of bushland to the south of Sydney that 'the assistance of a few blacks […] can always be obtained at Botany'. Typically groups of European and Aboriginal men made these trips, sailing south from Sydney to Kurnell, Port Hacking or what is now Royal National Park for several days to hunt. On one such trip in 1870 participants shot 'fifty-one head of fine wallaby, and captured two others, which they brought alive to Sydney, besides shooting for their table a number of parrots, gill-birds, wonga wonga pigeons, and other birds'.[40]

European leisure seekers also sought out the guided tours of Botany Bay woman Biddy Giles (c.1810–1888) from the 1860s (see Figure 5.9). The details of Biddy's early life are poorly known, and have been subject to conjecture, as historians Heather Goodall and Allison Cadzow have discussed.[41] What we know with some certainty is that she had lived in southern Sydney and the Illawarra, and had at least two daughters to Illawarra man Burragalong (aka Paddy Davis, 1810s–1877). By the late 1850s, though, she was living with Englishman Billy Giles and two (possibly unrelated) Aboriginal boys on a farm at Mill Creek, off the Georges River. Biddy was intimately acquainted with the surrounding countryside and moved onto the 120-acre property when she discovered that owner James Cuthill had departed permanently to Fiji.[42] She and Giles lived in a 'two-roomed slab structure […] kept in a clean and tidy state' and kept a small herd of goats and an orchard of quince trees. They were self-sufficient, but supplemented their income with guided tours.[43]

Individually and together, Biddy and Billy guided hunting and fishing parties across the bushland south of the Georges River throughout the mid- to late 19th century. Later published reminiscences by participants have allowed Goodall and Cadzow to explore the nature of these expeditions. Wielding a large pack of hunting dogs, Biddy and Billy ranged south over the Hacking River and into the Heathcote area in what is now Royal National Park, areas 'in which Biddy clearly felt comfortable and to which she belonged'.[44] Biddy and Billy also knew the Europeans sparsely scattered across this landscape, staying with them on occasion or at other settlements of their own in addition to their base at Mill Creek. Their clients included George Hill, who was part of the Sydney Aborigines Committee, which distributed blankets and helped obtain boats and other provisions, as well as James Oatley, another native-born Sydneysider who had dealings with local Aboriginal people.[45]

The role of Aboriginal guides was sometimes downplayed to that of 'wallbungers' (beaters to spy and startle game), but they were clearly in control of their often flat-footed companions, and their knowledge and prowess impressed those who were prepared to admit it. Just as Mahroot was said to have 'guided and watched the white young native', a participant in one of Biddy Giles' trips marvelled at her incredible fishing skills and her mastery of a large pack of hunting dogs to herd game.[46] She was simply at ease and at home in the bush in a way that impressed those who had spent most of their lives in and around the bustling port of Sydney. She knew exactly where she was going and all about the plants and animals they encountered, often giving the local Dharawal language name as well as the English. Biddy, Johnny and others were intimately familiar with the local landscape before they started running tours, and their trips helped to maintain and nurture these links.[47] Aboriginal people also travelled through their lands to visit family or to bring back specimens of birds and other creatures to supply the booming natural history trade in Sydney.[48]

The cultural dimension of Aboriginal travelling is hard to gauge from the sparse historical record. We do not know the extent to which Aboriginal people maintained or adapted their traditional custodial activities relating to land and to specific places of significance, but they continued to associate with areas of family affiliation, which suggests a degree of continuity, as do some other documented incidents. In 1845 for example, visiting Frenchman Eugène Delessert participated in a hunt in southern Sydney with around a dozen Aboriginal guides. After rowing across to Kurnell on the southern shore of Botany Bay, they set up camp 'in a small isolated and deserted cabin next to which our blacks made a big fire'. As the Europeans retired for the night, Delessert heard the Aboriginal guides start singing and dancing. What they sang is not recorded, but this was clearly not entertainment for their sleeping charges; it was ceremony for its own sake and was most likely related to their ongoing cultural obligations to the area.[49] Biddy Giles was maintaining her relationship to the land when she took visitors to a significant whale engraving site at Jibbon Head near Bundeena on some of her tours in the 1860s and 1870s, but she also used the opportunity to develop cross-cultural understanding. She took the time to explain the engravings, and to share her knowledge of language and culture more generally.[50]

Some of the European participants on these tours were very interested in what their guides did and said, as it indulged their ethnological interests. One of them was Edward Smith Hill, who was part of the Sydney Aborigines Committee in the 1840s, and whose brother George remained a key member in the following decades. Hill participated regularly in fishing and hunting activities with Aboriginal people from Sydney through to the Illawarra. He had developed many personal relationships through these activities and consequently, Aboriginal people often visited him at his home at Point Piper in the 1860s and 1870s.[51] Hill could be as pompous and paternalistic as his contemporaries when speaking to a European audience about Aboriginal people, as some of his letters to the *Sydney Morning Herald* reveal.[52] Nonetheless, he knew that obtaining local Aboriginal traditional knowledge enhanced his reputation and social standing, allowing him to give lectures, provide expert advice for books and exhibitions, and act as a cultural go-between for visitors curious about Aboriginal people.[53]

It was in this capacity that he chaperoned visiting Austrian Karl Scherzer in 1858, visiting a number of Aboriginal people in Sydney and the Illawarra, including Johnny Malone at his Sans Souci settlement. During this visit, Scherzer noted Hill's 'natural generosity' at mealtimes, for he 'shared everything he had brought with him with the Aborigines, who for their part were extremely forthcoming with him'.[54] This simple gesture had a much deeper meaning. Hill wanted knowledge, and Aboriginal people wanted continuous access to land and more general support. Aboriginal people were aware that they had something of value to offer, and viewed these knowledge transactions along the lines of reciprocal exchange, where gifts were made in order to foster right behaviour from the recipient, such as assistance when needed in the future. The Aboriginal people who visited Hill's Point Piper home were most likely his informants and hunting guides, seeking to deepen their relationship or to cash in a favour.

Building reciprocity and encouraging right behaviour also appears to have been the basis for some local Aboriginal people working as domestic servants. Though historians have studied Aboriginal domestic service for some time, they have mostly focussed on situations of forced labour through child abductions on the frontier, or later government child 'apprenticing' schemes.[55] Most of the eighteen Aboriginal servants so far documented in coastal Sydney between the 1840s and 1870s probably fall into one of these categories. They were young boys and girls between ten and eighteen years of age, mostly (or perhaps all) from outside Sydney and the affiliated coastal zone, who had probably moved to Sydney together with a European family. The remainder, by contrast, were locally connected adults, and it seems likely that they provided labour in a broader context of fostering mutual obligation, because they all worked for local settler families who were sympathetic to Aboriginal people.

At Kurnell in the mid-19th century, elderly local woman Sally Mettymong worked for the Laycock family, including as nanny to the young Elias Connell Laycock. Elias recalled Sally walking along the beach with him when he was a young boy in the 1840s, pointing out where Cook's crewman Forby Sutherland had been buried in 1770 when she was a young girl (the monument to Sutherland in Kamay Botany Bay National Park is based on Elias's memory of this).[56] By the time Elias was born, the cross-cultural relationships at Kurnell were several generations old. His great-grandfather John Connell had advocated on behalf of local people to the government in the 1820s, and Aboriginal people had lived around the family house and fished the waters below for decades.[57] At Woolloomooloo in the late 1860s, Thomas Potallick worked for James Oatley, a member of the 1844 Aboriginal fundraising committee and hunting companion of Biddy and Billy Giles. Oatley had probably known Thomas's father, a prominent Shoalhaven man of the same name, who had lived nearby in the Domain and died there in the 1850s.[58] Further east at Vaucluse in the same period, local 'chief' Bobby worked for the Wentworths, who regarded him highly. He travelled to England with the family, and was described by daughter Laura as 'naturally so clever and sensible'.[59]

It is no coincidence that Aboriginal people continued to live in the same areas in which these servants worked. Their apparently servile positions had a broader strategic context, maintaining the network of influential Sydneysiders who could assist them with access to land and in other ways. It was a deliberate strategy which helped elicit right behaviour among this group, even if they could not foresee the exact results. At the very time when the government withdrew its interest and involvement in local Aboriginal affairs, the cross-cultural relationships of William Annan and others had led directly to the formation of the Sydney Aborigines Committee, which filled the gap. Several decades later, the relationship between Emma Timbery (nee Waldron/Lowndes, c.1842–1916; see Figure 7.3) and Richard Hill had a similar effect.[60] As we will see in the following chapters, their relationship proved pivotal to the welfare of Aboriginal people in coastal Sydney as the government began to intervene in their lives once again.

Drawing closer

As Aboriginal people increasingly intertwined their lives with the people, urban space and economy of Sydney, this was both a deliberate strategy and an organic consequence of the city's growth, and it developed out of their existing cross-cultural relationships. Whatever choice Aboriginal people had was informed by a deep desire to stay connected to coastal Sydney, and an equally strong impulse to retain as much control over their lives as possible. Their lives remained hard, and too many continued to die before their time, but a generation of future leaders including Ellen Anderson, Emma Timbery, Kate Foot and William Rowley all grew up in this time of entanglement – it was what they knew. There was strength in community, and they were also aware of the alternatives.

There was no effective safety net for those who fell on hard times in the mid-19th century, black or white. Those without a family or community to support them often found their way into the city's growing slums, where life rarely ended well. Such was the case for young Newcastle Aboriginal woman Mary Ann Burns (1830s–1857). Mary Ann was born within the affiliated coastal zone but was 'brought up at a Catholic school', suggesting that she lived apart from the broader Aboriginal community.[61] By the mid-1850s she had moved to Sydney and was living in the Durand's Alley slum near Haymarket, one of the city's most notorious crime streets. She was a hard-drinking prostitute who stole from customers, got into fights, and spent several spells in prison.[62] After a couple of years of this life, and when she was still just a young woman, she suddenly fell ill and died.[63]

If Mary Ann had sought poor relief, the outcome may well have been the same. Private charities like the Benevolent Society ran the Benevolent Asylum at the south end of George Street (under what is today Central Railway Station), where people could temporarily obtain food and a bed. Access was difficult due to consistently high demand, but it was literally a last resort. The asylum had a high death toll due to disease and overcrowding (on average several people per week), and inmates regularly leapt the walls and absconded as soon as they could.[64] Local Aboriginal people like Thomas Tamara and William Warrell attended the asylum in the 1840s after European acquaintances recommended it, but Warrell refused to return even when he was old and infirm and living on the street at Rose Bay.[65] Coastal Aboriginal people in Sydney realised that they had a much better chance of making a life for themselves by living in their own settlements, however hard that life might be.

Aboriginal people valued their independence, but were prepared to seek help from neighbours and colonial authorities to achieve this end. They were also aware of their rights. They did not yet feel the widespread distrust of authority and government that developed because of later government policies of segregation and assimilation. That is not to say that all Aboriginal people felt able or confident to use the colonial system to their advantage. It was often leaders of groups who interacted with authorities, but they did so expecting that these authorities would take appropriate action. We have already seen how men like Mahroot directly petitioned the government, and this approach extended to all levels of authority. Johnny Malone, for example, reported the theft of goods from his hut at Botany in 1868 to local police, and they dealt with it just as they did other similar crimes involving non-Aboriginal people.⁶⁶ Senior Gundungurra man Billy Russell, leader of a group of Aboriginal people in south-western Sydney, contacted Camden police in 1862 to report a local doctor who had disinterred his recently buried cousin to examine his body. Russell's claim was not ignored, but was sent to the Attorney General, who recommended that the police enforce the law and arrest the guilty party.⁶⁷

A case like Russell's paints a ghoulish picture of the realities of life for Aboriginal people at this time, but it also highlights the need for Aboriginal people to know the system and be able to access it, both to get what they needed and to hold onto it. Following in the footsteps of many leaders before him, Georges River man Jackey Goggey did both of these things on behalf of his group in the mid-19th century. Since the 1830s, Goggey and his family had lived on a piece of land along Harris Creek near Liverpool, where they grew crops and fished the river. Their neighbour John Rowley ran a shipbuilding business and water mill. When Goggey's family needed a fishing boat in 1850 to remain self-sufficient on their land, he enlisted Rowley and the Sydney Aborigines Committee to successfully petition the governor for one.⁶⁸ Seven years later though, as historians Heather Goodall and Allison Cadzow relate, Rowley forced the Goggeys off their land.⁶⁹

Rowley's motives are not clear, but records of several insolvencies since the 1840s suggest that he was a poor businessman, and the move may have been his latest attempt to expand his enterprises.⁷⁰ Knowing that land policy at this time awarded title to whoever could prove the strongest claim to the land, Goggey protested about his eviction to the government via the Liverpool magistrate on the grounds that Rowley had no 'just claim' to the land. The surveyor-general did not ignore Goggey's letter, but contemplated making the courts request Rowley to show a 'better title than the 20 years possession which Goggey alleges, and can possibly prove'.⁷¹ Whether the authorities would have taken further action is not known. By the following year Rowley was bankrupt once again, and it appears that the Goggeys were able to return to their land.[72]

While these informed and strategic responses of Aboriginal people to the expansion of Sydney were important, it does not follow that they could foresee or control the longer-term consequences of their decisions. As Sydney expanded in the mid-19th century and available land decreased, Aboriginal settlement was concentrated in fewer locations. From the 1850s Rose Bay and Rushcutters Bay became the two main centres of Aboriginal occupation in the eastern suburbs, while at Botany Bay it was Johnny Malone's settlement at Botany and another at Sans Souci. While they still served as stopover points on broader coastal beats, it is likely that these settlements were not left abandoned for as long as in previous decades, and were perhaps permanently occupied by older, less mobile people. People used fewer settlements more intensively because their options were decreasing and they were more entangled with the European population, but this became a self-reinforcing process based on the nature of Aboriginal attachment. Historical and anthropological studies around Australia have shown that as Aboriginal settlements were more intensively used, associations of birth, death and other events that were once dispersed across the landscape began to accumulate in one place, giving them even more 'pull' and increasing their permanence.[73] This is one reason why many of the settlements that were occupied in the 1850s were still in use nearly half a century later.

The increasingly permanent association of individuals with particular places from the mid-19th century is probably the reason why Europeans named several places at this time after their Aboriginal occupants.[74] For example, the eastern half of the beach at Double Bay was named Seven Shillings Beach after Aboriginal couple Gurrah and Nancy, who we met earlier in this chapter. The name commemorates the Walker family's naïve attempt in the 1860s to dislodge Gurrah and Nancy's deep connections to the area with a few coins.[75] Nancy's sister Sophia lived next to a spring-fed stream at Rose Bay, which still bears the name Sophia's Spring, and another nearby cove was known locally in the 19th century as 'Black Gin Beach' after its Aboriginal occupant.[76] Yet despite this local recognition that Aboriginal people were present, Europeans were not aware of their personal stories, their connections, and the beats that tied them to coastal Sydney. Over the preceding decades, the gap between the European idea of Aboriginal authenticity and the actual existence of the Aboriginal people living alongside them in Sydney had steadily widened to a point where perception and reality could no longer be reconciled.

5

Strangers in their own land (1850s–1870s)

On 24 May 1850, more than sixty Aboriginal people entered Sydney town to receive their annual gift of a government blanket from the Sydney Aborigines Committee. It was a high-profile event. The committee comprised Sydney mayor George Hill, alderman Daniel Egan, and parliamentarian Bob Nichols, who personally supervised the distribution. They diligently recorded the name and 'tribe' of each recipient, which included coastal Sydney people of the Sydney, Botany, Georges River and Port Hacking 'tribes', as well as others with affiliations elsewhere across the coastal zone a hundred and forty or so kilometres to the north and south.[1] After receiving their blanket, the assembled Aboriginal men, women and children gave three cheers for the queen, the governor and the mayor, and departed. In leaving town, it is as though many of the Aboriginal people of coastal Sydney walked out of history, for few of them are identified as individuals in later records. Instead, over the following decades Europeans documented the deaths of the so-called 'last of their tribes', and increasingly cast other Aboriginal people living across coastal Sydney as outsiders.

How can we reconcile this with the fact that locally connected people were not only still living across coastal Sydney at this time, but were becoming more entangled with the city and its economy? How was it that Aboriginal people could be conceptually alienated from their own lands even though they were still there? There was no calculated or coordinated attempt to deny Aboriginal connections, but rather a steadily widening gap between the European perception of Aboriginal life and the reality. To understand this process, we need to look at developments in European thinking about Aboriginality. We also need to consider whether Aboriginal people *were* in fact changing their sense of local identity. Ultimately though, what affected Aboriginal people most in coastal Sydney was the way the influential network of sympathetic Europeans reconciled personal experience with popular myth. They had the opportunity to reject stereotypes and see continuities among their Aboriginal associates, and their actions, more than those of the general public, influenced the fate of Aboriginal people across coastal Sydney.

Tribal celebrities

Since the earliest days of the colony, Europeans compared the living Aboriginal people they knew to an imaginary, authentic version, based on a mixture of initial observations and pre-existing assumptions about the 'primitive' state of Indigenous people.[2] According to Europeans, the authentic Aborigine lived a traditional life within a bounded 'tribal' territory; an identifiable area of origin to which they belonged. The more complex, far-reaching and dynamic connections bound up in Aboriginal beats across the affiliated coastal zone were not recognised. Aboriginal people could never conform to this artificial benchmark, and as their lives changed in colonial Sydney, they were seen to fall further and further short of this ideal. Their refusal to adopt a fully European way of life confirmed that their unchanging 'primitive' existence was a cultural dead end, but if they adopted European goods and practices they were viewed as less authentic. The bands that regrouped in the wake of the smallpox epidemic were named the 'Sydney tribe', 'Botany tribe' and so on to recognise some kind of ongoing link to land, but these links were seen to be weakening in step with their declining authenticity.

Without any reliable way of quantifying this imagined process of decline, the changing fortunes of a few well-known Aboriginal personalities became the narrowly focussed lens through which Europeans viewed the impact of colonial settlement. These early 'tribal celebrities' included Bennelong (c.1764–1813), Bungaree (1770s–1830) and Cora Gooseberry (1770s–1852), all of whom were acknowledged leaders of their regrouped bands. Because they were born before Europeans arrived, their knowledge of language and cultural practices was considered 'authentic', but the changes in their lives became parables about the inevitable demise of Aboriginal culture in the face of European civilisation. On Bennelong's death, for example, he was remembered as a 'thorough savage' with a 'propensity to drunkenness' and resistance to civilisation, while Bungaree's 'naturally strong constitution gave way under a predilection for hard drinking'.[3] These stories of sad but unavoidable decline became the standard way of referring to the fate of Aboriginal people more generally in the early 19th century, and have become deeply embedded in the broader public consciousness. To this day, there is a preference in media reporting and popular books for simplistic parables of tragic decline over the more nuanced pictures of Bennelong and Bungaree that have emerged from the work of historians in recent years.[4]

With the next generation of tribal celebrities, the story of decline reached its end point. William Warrell (1790s–1863), and to a lesser extent Mahroot (1790s–1850) and Wingle (1790s–1868), were seen to retain some authenticity through their cultural knowledge and their links to land and language, even though they were born after the colony was established. When they died, though, they were said to be the 'last of their tribes'. This was meant to signify the imagined end of the last vestiges of authentic Aboriginal life in coastal Sydney rather than the literal death of all people of Aboriginal ancestry.[5] Their deaths were markers of colonial progress, paralleled by similar reporting of the deaths of pioneer settlers. The difference was that European pioneers were seen as having founded the future, whereas Aboriginal people represented the flawed and dwindling past.[6]

This was perfectly illustrated by the most famous of the last tribal celebrities, William Warrell (see Figure 5.1). Though he has proven far less enduring in the popular imagination than Bennelong and Bungaree, he was just as widely known in Sydney in the mid-19th century. By 1840, when he began to frequent the town, his partially crippled frame soon earned him both mockery and the enduring nickname 'Ricketty Dick'.[7] As we have already seen, he often visited Sydney town with his cousin Cora Gooseberry over the next decade, before moving to a hut along New South Head Road at Rose Bay. With age Warrell's condition worsened and he became less mobile, and the apparent symbolism of his declining health was too tempting for observers to ignore. As visiting Austrian Karl Scherzer wrote in 1858, Warrell was 'a wretched crippled native, the sole survivor of his tribe, once the lord of all this country, who now stretches out his horny hand to receive charity'.[8]

This decline was captured in contrasting statuettes by famed local silversmith Julius Hogarth in the 1850s (see Figure 5.2). One was created for an international audience and depicted an idealised Warrell as a noble figure in classical pose, while the other showed him as a cripple huddled in his hut, a more recognisable scene to the Sydney resident for whom it was made.[9] As with previous celebrities Bennelong and Bungaree, newspapers of the time portrayed Warrell's fate as his own choice. Having lived alongside Europeans, he had been given the opportunity to be 'engrafted on a nobler stock only to wither and decay'.[10] On his death in 1863, reports highlighted his paralysis, drinking habits, and propensity to shun his leaky hut to sleep in the open air.[11] This was despite the same reports noting that Warrell had not built the poorly constructed shelter; his European friend and neighbour George Rawlingson had. The picture of a withered cripple matched too closely the fatalistic stereotype of a race doomed by its own inability to change to be complicated by such facts.

As the last tribal celebrities from the 1850s passed away, an increasing European desire to commemorate them reflected this sense of finality. Europeans paid no attention to the burials of

Bennelong and Bungaree despite their notoriety; we do not even know exactly where Bungaree is buried. But when Cora Gooseberry died in 1852, her friend Edward Borton paid for her burial in the Sydney Burial Ground complete with a headstone commemorating her as a 'Queen of the Sydney tribe' (see Figure 5.3). A similar memorial was planned for the Aboriginal burial ground maintained by local Europeans within the grounds of the Sir Joseph Banks Hotel at Botany, which contained the graves of Wingle, Mahroot and perhaps Mahroot's wife.[12] These memorials reflected genuine personal affection, but as historian Tom Griffiths has written, they were also intended as 'milestones of progress' which celebrated 'white philanthropy' while mourning the 'inevitable decline of another race'.[13] Silversmith Julius Hogarth continued to commemorate William Warrell after his death, using his likeness as the template of the 'ex rex' (former king) for souvenir medallions at the 1873 Sydney Intercolonial Exhibition. Visitors could stamp their own medallion to commemorate, simultaneously, their trip and the supposed end of a local Aboriginal presence, despite the fact that Aboriginal men, women and children were also perusing the exhibits. The design proved so popular that Warrell became the generic face representing the idea of a former Aboriginal leader (or 'king' in the terminology of the day), and was used for similar commemorative purposes in Queensland and Victoria, amended with a local name as Figure 5.4 shows.[14]

The 'last of their tribe' parable relied on ignorance and ambiguity. It is hard for us today to see how anyone could have been viewed as the 'last' of a particular tribe when Europeans did not even agree on what constituted these groups, and who belonged to them. The 'Sydney tribe', for example, was said to number both four and eleven in 1844, around twenty in 1845 and twenty-four in 1846, and its supposed last member, William Warrell, was also said to be 'from' Botany Bay, the Illawarra and Broken Bay at different times.[15] Nor did 'last' mean 'only'. When Jack Harris died in 1863 his tribe was said to be 'nearly extinct', though his wife and others continued to live at the Rushcutters Bay Aboriginal settlement.[16] Similarly, mid-19th-century resident Godfrey Charles Mundy saw no contradiction in calling the recently deceased Mahroot 'the last of the Botany tribe' barely a sentence after describing another Aboriginal man spearfishing at La Perouse, near Mahroot's land.[17] In the myopic logic of the time, the direct descendants and contemporaries of tribal celebrities were not considered to retain any knowledge or authenticity, especially if they also had European ancestry.

Petrified Aborigines

By the 1860s, Europeans largely believed that there was no longer a living Aboriginal culture in coastal Sydney. Whether every last person of Aboriginal descent had died or moved on was less important than the certainty that any survivors had no authentic local connections and were no longer *real* Aborigines. Authentic Aboriginal experiences in Sydney, they assumed, could only come from somewhere else or from the imagined past. Visiting Russian naval officer Pavel Mukhanov, for example, was far more satisfied during his visit to Sydney in 1863 with the 'native' exhibits of the Australian museum than the 'crippled brownish figure' of William Warrell that he encountered at Rose Bay. The assembled artefacts allowed him to picture an imagined past where 'men and women [...] dance wildly before the dimly flickering fire', an image more real to him than his encounter with a living Aboriginal person.[18]

This preference for an idealised and exotic past over present reality was typified by the so-called 'petrified Aborigine' that had been exhibited in Sydney the previous year. It was the body of an Aboriginal man seemingly turned to stone that had been stolen from a South Australian cave by showman Thomas Craig (to add to his travelling sideshow of two giant stuffed crocodiles). In fact, the body had simply dried out in the arid cave, and closer inspection revealed a bullet protruding from one arm, suggesting that the man was a victim of recent frontier violence; but no one was interested in such details.[19] They wanted an exotic spectacle and were willing to suspend any disbelief. This was a time when Aboriginal remains were displayed in the windows of natural history traders and in museums, serving to reinforce the view that Aboriginal people were either distant or dead, and in death became natural specimens.[20]

Aboriginal people had been entertaining Sydneysiders for decades as boxers and show-riders, and as part of choreographed corroborees, but these activities were thought to harness their natural abilities and were not considered evidence that they had acquired European cultural sophistication.[21] In the 1860s, though, as theories about supposed racial differences became more prevalent, a new kind of Aboriginal spectacle emerged in the form of touring teams of Victorian Aboriginal cricketers. They captured widespread settler curiosity about whether Aboriginal people were intellectually capable of learning, let alone excelling at, such a complex sport.[22] The teams toured Sydney several times, and many thousands of people attended the first match in February 1867 at the Albert Ground in Redfern. The players' manners and their grasp of the game suitably impressed observers, as did their performances between innings in a series of athletics races against Europeans, and demonstrations of boomerang and spear throwing. The *Empire* reported that among the audience:

> [...] were a few aboriginal men and women, and one or two half-castes, their companions, who watched, with unwearying interest, the feats of their brethren from the south, on a spot where, in all likelihood, similar performances, but without the humanising influence that now regulates them, were witnessed eighty years ago.[23]

The message was clear. *Real* Aboriginal culture in Sydney belonged to the past or had to be sourced from elsewhere, and was also most appropriately consumed as entertainment in a form moderated by, and palatable to, Europeans.

By the 1870s European perceptions of Aboriginality were completely divorced from reality. Consequently, when Sydney was selected to host the prestigious International Exhibition in 1879, it was highly unlikely that anything of local or contemporary Aboriginal culture would be represented in the imposing Garden Palace exhibition hall (see Figure 5.5). Although one member of the public urged the organisers to 'induce' some Aboriginal people to erect traditional shelters next to the enormous Garden Palace, this living stereotype was rejected in favour of a static, comparative display of Aboriginal and Pacific Islander artefacts; a petrified version of Aboriginal culture, frozen in time.[24] The display, in the exhibition's Ethnological Court, was packed to the roof with thousands of indigenous artefacts from around the world (see Figure 5.6). The handful from Sydney would have been indistinguishable to visitors, but that was the point. The display was all about contrasting the technological development of a generic Australian Aboriginal culture with other 'native' cultures of the region.[25] There was literally no place in this cluttered comparison for local history or people. In the space of less than a century, Europeans had ideologically alienated Aboriginal people from the Sydney landscape, and denied them any role in interpreting their own past.

This is my country

Aboriginal people were among the many thousands of visitors to peruse the dense forest of artefacts in the Garden Palace; they would have seen Aboriginal skulls and other grisly trophies on display there and in shopfronts as they walked the city, and in several previous intercolonial exhibitions they would have watched visitors stamping likenesses of their countryman William Warrell on souvenir medallions (see Figure 5.4).[26] What they made of all this we will never know, but it would have been evident to them that their way of life was not the picture of Aboriginality held by the European population. Their lives *were* changing, but not in the way, or with the speed or finality Europeans imagined. Language and ceremony were declining (but far from forgotten) and European clothing was now the norm, but most Aboriginal people in coastal Sydney were still affiliated with the area, lived in separate settlements to Europeans, continued to fish by traditional and other means, and maintained their coastal beats. Their connections to coastal Sydney may not have been recognised by the general population, but that does not mean they were not asserting them.

Aboriginal people were still occasionally making explicit statements of affiliation. Sydney man Jack Harris (1810s–1863), for example, engaged regularly with Europeans in town, and was known for his emphatic retort 'this is *my* country' when anyone annoyed him.[27] More often though, they conveyed a sense of connection and belonging by actions rather than words. Long after the deaths in 1863 of the so-called 'lasts of their tribe' Jack Harris at Rushcutters Bay and William Warrell at Rose Bay, Aboriginal people with local connections continued to live in both places, while as we have seen at Double Bay, Aboriginal couple Gurrah and Nancy stubbornly maintained their presence in the 1860s and 1870s despite some local opposition. Further south along the Georges River, a review of the area's history in 1870 noted that part-Aboriginal people in the area, though 'changed in character and habits by European contact, still retained a strong preference for the district in which they were born'.[28] But how much can we discern about the continuity of connections from looking at these settlements, when we know that the increasing Aboriginal entanglement with Sydney was also creating new links to particular places?

To answer this we need to zoom out from the fragmentary record of particular settlements and look at whether broader patterns of coastal Aboriginal beats were changing with the times. We have already seen how Aboriginal movement in the first half of the 19th century continued to be bounded by the affiliated coastal zone about 140 kilometres either side of coastal Sydney. In this period, a number of Sydney-based settler families who had relationships with Aboriginal people (such as the Wentworths and Macarthurs), established rural landholdings within and beyond the affiliated coastal zone. These properties opened up new means of travel for Aboriginal people working or living around them, and meant they could travel more frequently. From the 1830s, for example, Aboriginal people often came to Sydney from Alexander Berry's estate in the Shoalhaven district (at the southern end of the affiliated coastal zone), bringing produce and stock or running errands, as did others from areas such as Eden further to the south. While these new opportunities and means of transport (such as European sailing boats) probably intensified some intergroup relationships over time, there is little evidence to suggest that Aboriginal connections expanded beyond the affiliated coastal zone in this period. The Shoalhaven people intermixed with local people, living in settlements like the Domain and participating in ceremonies, while those from outside the affiliated coastal zone kept more to themselves.[29]

From the 1850s, a rapidly increasing European population and the advent of steamship services up and down the New South Wales coast from Sydney created an unprecedented opportunity for Aboriginal people to travel (see Figure 5.7). Aboriginal people were often provided with free (or perhaps working) passage on steamers, meaning they could travel longer distances more independently than in previous decades, when such travel was often tied to the timing or needs of European landowners.[30] From the 1860s, more frequent (often weekly) services also meant that Aboriginal people could use this new independence to travel to and from distant locations without planning far ahead, or risking being stranded for long periods at the other end. If passenger lists were kept at all, the names of these free travellers were not recorded, so it is difficult to know which services they used most frequently. But we can use other records to examine how coastal steamers affected Aboriginal movement within and beyond the affiliated coastal zone.

Surviving correspondence between the colonial secretary's office and local magistrates, parliamentary records and newspaper reports all give a relatively good guide to the number of blankets distributed annually at a number of centres across the affiliated coastal zone between 1849 and 1861 (shown in Figure 1.5).[31] Four to five hundred blankets were distributed each year across these centres, but the records show no indications of inward migration to Sydney. As we have already seen, in 1850 small groups of Aboriginal people came from a number of areas across the coastal zone to Sydney to collect a blanket, but the majority of people from each area did not; they chose to receive their blanket in their local district. Similarly, by the late 1850s some Aboriginal people from Port Stephens were visiting Sydney annually for several weeks at a time, probably via steamer. In 1857 they were recorded receiving blankets in Sydney, but they did not stay, and far more blankets were distributed locally at Port Stephens.[32] This suggests that the people coming into Sydney were those connected to the area, and that movement into Sydney was still overwhelmingly drawn from within the affiliated coastal zone.

After the early 1860s, the blanket distribution records are missing, so we cannot trace continuing Aboriginal beats in this manner. However, the 1868 royal visit of Queen Victoria's son Prince Alfred gives us another way to investigate the effect of steamer travel on Aboriginal movement and settlement. The prince arrived in Australia in late 1867 and briefly visited Sydney before touring the Hunter Region and Queensland. Aboriginal people were well aware of the queen's overarching authority, and knowing that the prince was due to spend several more weeks in Sydney in March 1868, many came from across New South Wales intent on meeting him there. By early February, Aboriginal sympathiser George Thornton reported to the government that:

> there are at present in and around Sydney, a great many Native Blacks – who have come from various parts of the Colony to see 'The Queen's Son' – they have a great desire to see, and also to be seen by, him [...] [and] [...] are also very desirous of being permitted to show His Royal Highness one of their 'corrobborees'.[33]

These people had made their own way to Sydney; they had not been invited. Thornton relayed their request to perform for the prince the following month to the colonial secretary, and a day was duly set for an Aboriginal performance and feast, with funds obtained to feed and clothe them in the weeks leading up to the event. As word spread of the approaching visit, more Aboriginal people arrived in Sydney by steamer from the mid- and far north coast as well as two hundred from the south coast, and others from western New South Wales and the southern highlands. They appear to have been generally well treated in Sydney. Advertisements for the event enlisted the public to help the visiting Aboriginal people find their way to the steamers specially commissioned to ferry them across the harbour to the feast location at Clontarf.[34]

This was the largest gathering of Aboriginal people in Sydney since early colonial times, comprising about three hundred men, women and children. But their time with the prince was to be denied. As they made their final preparations for the performance over the hill from the prince, he was shot and injured by an Irish nationalist and was rushed from the scene. The attempted assassination caused such a sensation that newspaper reports hardly mentioned the Aboriginal gathering, and the ensuing colonial shame ensured that no detailed account of the aborted event was ever published.[35] The performers were not given another opportunity to stage their event, but descriptions of rehearsals suggest that it was to have been an impressive display. A young Livingston Mann watched Aboriginal people living near his home on the north side of the harbour 'practising for this great event, making their boomerangs from the local trees and using them, as they danced round with their bodies painted in many designs'.[36]

We can only speculate on how the event affected Aboriginal people in a broader colonial context. It was the first time Aboriginal people from such a wide area had gathered together since the arrival of Europeans, and possibly the first time some groups had met. It is almost certain that Aboriginal people shared their experiences of spreading European settlement; perhaps they formed new bonds, and reinvigorated ceremonies. What did *not* happen, however, was any discernible Aboriginal migration to Sydney. Aboriginal people were understandably angered by the attack on the prince, but when it was clear that there would not be another opportunity to meet and perform for him, they returned to their own districts 'in a very sorrowful mood'. A small group performed for the recovering prince at Double Bay several weeks later, but these were most likely local people living in the adjacent settlements.[37]

While steamers probably changed the frequency and timing of Aboriginal movements from the 1850s, they did not enlarge Aboriginal beats beyond the affiliated coastal zone. This suggests that Aboriginal people retained a sense of their areas of affiliation despite the changes around them, and this is confirmed when we zoom back in to look at the movements of well-documented individuals like Botany Bay man Johnny Malone (c.1820s–1880s), as summarised in Figure 5.8. Johnny was born decades after European arrival to an Aboriginal mother from Botany Bay and a European father, and later married Lizzie (1830s–1901), an Illawarra woman. He continued to live in areas to which he was affiliated, fishing the waters of Botany Bay, establishing a settlement at Botany, and conducting guided fishing and hunting tours to the south of Sydney. In the 1870s he provided samples of his 'Sydney tribe' language to anthropologists. Johnny included words for fish and game as well as Aboriginal translations of English phrases, demonstrating that his language was alive and being adapted to new circumstances.[38] A similar pattern can be seen in the life of another guide we have already met, Botany Bay woman Biddy Giles (c.1810–1888). Although many aspects of Biddy's life are not clear, all of her family relationships and her movements continued to be contained within the affiliated coastal zone throughout her long life (see Figure 5.9).

Both Biddy Giles and Johnny Malone were motivated and active people; they were familiar with colonial society, had their own boats and ran their own businesses roaming the countryside around Sydney. If anyone could have travelled far beyond the affiliated coastal zone it was them; and perhaps they did at times. But if so, it was brief, and they chose to spend most of their lives in the country of their parents and relatives. This pull to return can also be seen in the case of Jimmy Lowndes (1830s–1900), one of the few people connected to coastal Sydney who lived beyond the affiliated coastal zone in the mid-19th century. Lowndes was born at Camden, near the western edge of the affiliated coastal zone. For some time in the mid-19th century he worked west of the mountains around the Castlereagh River area north of Dubbo, before returning to Sydney and settling along the Georges River with his family by the 1870s.[39] Half a century later, Aboriginal families from the Castlereagh area were living on the Georges River, and historians Heather Goodall and Allison Cadzow have speculated as to whether Jimmy's travels created the links that took them there. As we will see, though, this movement had a very different cause stemming from events in the 1890s, so while Jimmy's movements were important in his own life, they do not appear to have had a lasting impact in Aboriginal Sydney. In the second half of the 19th century, the affiliated coastal zone was still the main influence on Aboriginal movement, and most Aboriginal people living in coastal Sydney continued to be linked to the area despite the popular belief to the contrary.

Missing the links

While misinformed popular views of authentic Aboriginality affected the lives of Aboriginal people, what mattered more was whether their small but influential group of locally born European acquaintances recognised their ongoing connections to coastal Sydney. Aboriginal people had cultivated relationships with these people since the early 19th century by visiting them, working for them, supplying them with food, passing on traditional knowledge, hunting and fishing with them, and sometimes living on their properties. These

Sydneysiders potentially had a far greater insight into the nature of Aboriginal life than the general population; an opportunity to see continuities and connections as well as changes, and to reject popular myths. We have no direct record of how most of them felt about local Aboriginal people, but we can learn something of this from the actions of members of the Sydney Aborigines Committee.

As we have seen, the committee was formed in 1844 to address the welfare needs of Aboriginal people around coastal Sydney. It remained active until at least the early 1860s and its key members were Bob Nichols (1809–1857), George Hill (1802–1883), Daniel Egan (1803–1870) and George Thornton (1819–1901), who are shown in Figure 5.10. Though all of these men shared a common background of local birth, convict roots and a long association with Sydney, this did not result in uniform attitudes towards local Aboriginal people. Europeans involved in Aboriginal affairs across Australia in the 19th century have long been assumed to be 'benevolent' simply for having an interest in Aboriginal issues, but as historians are now discovering, each had their own reasons for the particular approaches to Aboriginal welfare they favoured.[40] In the case of the Sydney Aborigines Committee, the divergent views of Bob Nichols and George Thornton had lasting effects on local Aboriginal people.

Bob Nichols had founded the committee in 1844 and remained its key figure until his death in 1857. As a colonial radical and supporter of causes such as emancipation, he was probably naturally sympathetic to the downtrodden, but there are few specific clues to the origins of his attitudes to Aboriginal people. His general sympathies can be seen from statements he made as a lawyer and parliamentarian. In his 1834 defence of Hunter Valley Aboriginal man and accused murderer Wong-ko-bi-kan (Jackey) for example, he argued for acquittal on the grounds that Aboriginal people were 'the primary tenants of the soil' and that it was illegal for Europeans 'to disturb them in possession of these natural rights'.[41] Even allowing for the hyperbole of a defence lawyer, this was a line of thinking that was far from typical at the time. A more revealing episode was his argument against the prohibition of alcohol sales to Aboriginal people as a member of the Legislative Council in 1849. Apart from believing that prohibition was ineffective, Nichols argued that it was discriminatory because 'many of the blacks were industrious, and comparatively civilized [and] consequently […] had a right to equal liberty with the whites'.[42] As he made his speech, it is likely that he had in mind his associates from the Sydney tribe, plying the harbour fishing grounds in the boat he had acquired for them several years before.

Nichols viewed Aboriginal people as entitled to equal rights as well as to special charitable consideration, and there is no evidence that he had the kind of ethnological interests that inspired some of his contemporaries. As leader of the Sydney Aborigines Committee, Nichols saw its main role as 'affording some relief to such aborigines as may visit Sydney in the ensuing winter' through distributing blankets.[43] The phrasing is significant, for it reveals that Nichols' sympathies were with Aboriginal people in need, irrespective of where they were *from*. His apparent indifference to their point of origin is curious. He had formed the fundraising committee in 1844 specifically to assist the 'Sydney tribe', and several years later had sought money to repair the boat that these funds had purchased.[44] By the mid-1850s Aboriginal people expected to receive a blanket if they were in Sydney at the appropriate time, but Nichols did not seem concerned that this may have been acting as a magnet to draw people in from areas outside Sydney. He continued to seek fifty to sixty blankets each year from the government, and sometimes extras as needed, and these were always provided without query.[45]

Nichols' attitude clearly troubled George Thornton. As his later actions showed, Thornton believed that charity should be extended to Aboriginal people in their home districts, and to others only in exceptional circumstances. The origins of his view are hard to trace, though earlier blanket distributions in the 1830s had a similar (rarely realised) aim of only assisting local people in their place of origin.[46] Thornton was not an evangelist, and came to his charitable activities with considerable knowledge of Aboriginal people from his early years. He had probably met local Aboriginal people during hunting and fishing excursions to the Coogee area in the 1830s, and in the 1840s he 'camp[ed] out among the blacks about Wollongong, Kiama and Jervis Bay' and hunted with others on a trip with the Hill brothers to Port Stephens.[47] He had therefore had considerable opportunity to understand the long-distance connections and beats that were a feature of Aboriginal lives, but he was also influenced by broader ideas about 'authentic' Aboriginal people and culture, and retained a belief that Aboriginal people had a single, definable 'home district'.

Thornton joined Bob Nichols, George Hill and Daniel Egan on the Sydney Aborigines Committee in 1854, and did not initially try to restrict blankets from being distributed to all comers. In 1855, he was receptive to local Aboriginal requests to distribute blankets earlier in the year than mid-winter, and successfully petitioned the colonial secretary to allow this.[48] Perhaps he was held back by the dominating presence of Nichols, for when Nichols died in September 1857, Thornton immediately moved to stamp his own authority on the committee's activities. The committee usually corresponded with the colonial secretary at the start of each year to organise the next blanket distribution. Thornton, however, took the unprecedented step of contacting the colonial secretary within weeks of Nichols' death, supplying an annotated list of the 1857 blanket recipients, and stating his disapproval that most of the fifty blankets issued had been given to visiting Aboriginal people from Port Stephens.[49] They were huddled in the Domain in severe wet weather and Thornton had only reluctantly given them blankets as 'a case of urgent necessity [...] saving as I am sure it did some of them from perishing'. But he also sent their names to the local magistrates in Raymond Terrace and Maitland asking that they prevent them from coming back the following year. Thornton further stated that he had retained fifteen leftover blankets and considered these more than sufficient to meet the needs of the few remaining local people and any cases of absolute emergency for the following year.

Thornton thought he had taken control of the annual blanket distribution, but he had not told Hill and Egan. Consequently, in April the following year they wrote to the colonial secretary and requested the usual fifty blankets 'for the use of the Aboriginals'.[50] When the colonial secretary decided to issue them with thirty-five and asked Thornton to hand over his remaining fifteen, an indignant Thornton forcefully restated his position from the previous year in writing. He argued that additional blankets were not required because:

> the number of Blacks now belonging to the Sydney district are reduced to two – viz 'Wingle' and 'Bill Worrell', as I am positive in this assertion, I can disprove any statement to the contrary, although some of the Botany Blacks sometimes visit Sydney, yet it has been ascertained that Blankets for them are issued at Liverpool.[51]

Thornton's words show that he was influenced by the idea of authenticity, whereby local Aboriginal culture was represented by a shrinking group of tribal celebrities with deep links to the local area. He knew of others such as Jack Harris and Johnny Malone, who appeared on his list of blanket recipients the previous year, but as they had mixed ancestry, he did not consider them *real* Aborigines and worthy of charity. He also disregarded a number of others who were living along the southern side of the harbour at the time, perhaps seeing them as visitors from other places. His intention to restrict the distribution of blankets shows he was already aware that charity could be used to entice Aboriginal people to stay in their home districts. This demonstrated his ignorance (or perhaps studious ignoring) of the continued reality of Aboriginal movement and connection within the affiliated coastal zone.

Thornton's attempt to retain control of the blanket distribution in Sydney included a rather sycophantic plea not to 'deprive me of that which under present circumstances I consider a privilege', which clearly strained the colonial secretary's credulity. He made enquiries and discovered that blankets had *not* been requested at Liverpool for the Botany tribe that year as Thornton had asserted.[52] Hill and Egan were duly issued with thirty-five blankets and Thornton was advised to distribute his supply together with theirs. Thornton appears to have bowed out of the committee after this time, and for several years thirty-five blankets were issued to Hill and Egan in Sydney and twenty to the Liverpool magistrate, allowing them to continue distributing blankets to any Aboriginal person in need, regardless of their assumed place of origin.[53]

Though Thornton's plans to use donations and inducements to reduce Aboriginal migration to Sydney were thwarted on that occasion, from the late 1860s he became the most active public figure in local Aboriginal affairs. It is not clear whether the Sydney Aborigines Committee disbanded after the early 1860s, as records are incomplete or missing. Daniel Egan, however, does not appear to have continued his public Aboriginal welfare, pursuing commercial activities in the later 1860s, and acting as Postmaster General from 1868 until his death in 1870. George Hill also appears to have retreated from public charity, though he retained a private interest in advocating for Aboriginal people. In 1870, he petitioned for the early release of Hunter Valley Aboriginal man Billy from Darlinghurst Gaol. Hill stated his longstanding interest in Aboriginal people and that he had been 'looked upon by them as their general advisor and protector'.[54] Thornton, meanwhile, was actively assisting the Aboriginal people around Jervis Bay to obtain fishing boats and supplies.[55] While his generosity cannot be denied, it was motivated by a calculated rationale of trying to keep Aboriginal people in their home districts, and out of Sydney.

Thornton's views gained a disproportionate influence over the lives of Aboriginal people, largely because he outlived fellow committee members Nichols (d.1857), Egan (d.1870) and Hill (d.1883), as well as most of the other prominent Europeans who sustained the Aboriginal network of cross-cultural relationships, including

Edward Smith Hill (d. 1880), WC Wentworth (d. 1872) and James Oatley (d. 1878). Though some of their children retained an interest in Aboriginal affairs, they were neither as active nor as influential as their parents. By the early 1880s, the very time when the government and church groups were awakening from decades of indifference towards Aboriginal people, Thornton was in a particularly influential position. His views about the identity of Aboriginal people in coastal Sydney were to have far-reaching consequences. It was the question at the heart of the New South Wales government's re-entry into Aboriginal affairs, an action which unleashed a wave of bureaucratic intervention that radiated out across the state from Sydney like a second frontier.

6

Intervention (1870s–1880s)

In May of 1880, Reverend John Gribble was in Sydney to seek public and government support for his newly opened Aboriginal mission in western New South Wales. He was trying to shake the government out of three decades of indifference by highlighting the needs of Aboriginal people in country areas, but had not expected to see the same situation in Sydney. Walking through the city, he 'came in contact with no less than twenty-six aborigines', and was surprised and saddened to learn that 'they have a camp so near to the city as Double Bay, and there they are quite unprovided for, both as regards food and protection from the force of the elements'.[1] The calls to action of Gribble, George Thornton and others brought the Aboriginal people of coastal Sydney back into public focus. They had never left, of course, but Europeans in Sydney no longer recognised their local connections. As a consequence, when the government began to notice Aboriginal people in Sydney again in the early 1880s, they were seen as migrants who did not belong; a moral and social problem that needed to be solved. The government was persuaded to intervene, and in so doing became responsible for Aboriginal welfare in Sydney and across New South Wales.

This development has often been viewed by historians as a decisive moment in Sydney's Aboriginal history. Whether they believed that the Aboriginal residents of coastal Sydney were locals or migrants, they considered this the point when Aboriginal people were banished from the city and sent to a settlement beyond suburbia at La Perouse. Adding what we now know about the ongoing patterns of Aboriginal settlement and connections in coastal Sydney, and the vested interests of George Thornton, we can see that neither the origins nor the initial effects of government intervention were this clear cut. Instead, a more nuanced and personal picture emerges.

Myths of migration

In the 1950s and 1960s, anthropologists and historians started to piece together the events surrounding the origins of the La Perouse Aboriginal settlement and its link to the advent of government intervention in Aboriginal welfare three-quarters of a century before. No history of these events had been written at this time, so they relied on three main sources of information: mid-19th-century observations about the deaths of the so-called 'lasts of their tribe'; the writings of George Thornton, whose deeply held view was that all Aboriginal people in Sydney were migrants; and descriptions from the late 1870s and early 1880s of a number of Aboriginal settlements across coastal Sydney. Putting this information together, it seemed apparent that Aboriginal people had more or less disappeared from coastal Sydney by the middle of the 19th century, and that by the late 1870s Aboriginal groups from outside of Sydney had moved in to this abandoned area.[2]

For the past thirty years most historians have accepted this version of events, though Aboriginal communities have asserted continuous connection and some historians have acknowledged this.[3] Clearly the idea that local Aboriginal people disappeared does not fit the evidence that they continued to use coastal Sydney, and of their broader connections and beats within the affiliated coastal zone. We have already seen that Sydneysiders at the time did not understand these extensive networks of Aboriginal connection, so it is not surprising that Aboriginal people were thought to be *from* somewhere else. But this still leaves open the question of whether there was an influx of Aboriginal people into coastal Sydney in the late 1870s, either from inside or outside the affiliated coastal zone, as some historians have suggested.

The historical record is sparse and fragmented, but a close reading of the available information does not support the idea of migration into Sydney. The supposed Aboriginal migrants are said to have come from the south coast, both within and further south of the affiliated coastal zone, but the records of blanket distributions from the surviving years of 1861 and 1880 contain no evidence of this. Even though these records only indicate population numbers imprecisely, the combined distributions for all south coast centres remained remarkably similar at 475 and 430 respectively, and there was also no *increase* in the numbers of blankets distributed in coastal Sydney in the same period.[4] If any Aboriginal people did migrate permanently to Sydney at this time, it was certainly only a small number, and they are undetectable within broader, ongoing patterns of movement in and out of Sydney within the affiliated coastal zone.

What do we make then of the settlements that Aboriginal people supposedly established around coastal Sydney in the late 1870s at Rushcutters Bay, Rose Bay, Circular Quay, North Sydney, Manly, Botany and La Perouse?[5] References to these come largely from the observations of visiting missionaries who were documenting what they saw and had no prior knowledge of coastal Sydney people. They did not know, and did not comment on, when the settlements were established or where their residents were *from*. It was later historians who interpreted these settlements as new Aboriginal colonies, influenced by George Thornton's recorded view that all Aboriginal people in Sydney at this time were from other places. As Figure 6.1 summarises, and as we have seen in past chapters, almost all of these 'new' settlements had already been in use for many years. The Rose Bay and Rushcutters Bay settlements had been occupied since at least the 1850s, and were home to a fluctuating population of up to several dozen people. On the opposite side of the harbour, Aboriginal people had been camping on the North Shore since the 1860s. They used several different locations in the wooded areas between Lavender Bay and Neutral Bay during visits to collect blankets in Sydney, for the visit of Prince Alfred in 1868, and probably at other times.[6] As a local resident later recalled, they would 'forage for miles around and pretty well clean out all the opossums and other matter fit for digestion'.[7] Further east at Manly, the harbourside beach had housed an Aboriginal settlement since at least the mid-19th century, and although records are patchy, it appears to have remained in use through to the 1870s.[8]

South of the harbour, Johnny Malone's family and others had been using the Botany settlement since the early 1860s as the base for their commercial guiding activities. Aboriginal people had also used the nearby La Perouse area regularly throughout the 19th century, but it became a more permanent settlement in the late 1870s when several families set up camp behind the beach at Frenchman's Bay (see Figure 6.2). They were reported to have 'several boats, by which means – catching fish and letting their boats to visitors – they were able to earn some money'.[9] But these were not outsiders. Early La Perouse residents included southern Sydney woman Emma Timbery (c.1842–1916; see Figure 7.3), her Illawarra husband George 'Trimmer' Timbery (c.1839–1920), Botany Bay man William Rowley (1856–1941) and Botany Bay man Johnny Malone's children to his Illawarra wife Lizzie (1830s–1901).[10] Like the other settlements around coastal Sydney in the 1870s, La Perouse was established by people with local knowledge and connections who were continuing to use an area with a long history of Aboriginal occupation and excellent fishing.

The only truly new settlement to be established in the late 1870s was at the government boatshed, located where the Opera House forecourt now stands on the eastern side of Circular Quay at Bennelong Point (see Figure 6.3), but even this was linked into the broader Aboriginal landscape of coastal Sydney. The boatshed was used as a repair and storage shed for government boats from the 1860s, but by the late 1870s it had fallen out of regular use, and Aboriginal people moved in.[11] It functioned as a staging post for visits to the city, and as a gathering place for Aboriginal people entering Sydney by steamer from across the affiliated coastal zone. It may have taken over this function from the settlement in the extensive eucalypt forest of the outer Domain, from which Aboriginal people had visited the city to sell wares and obtain supplies until at least the late 1850s. By the 1870s the forest was dying of natural decay, and in early 1879 a large portion of this area was taken over as exhibition space for the upcoming Sydney International Exhibition.[12] If Aboriginal people were still using the outer Domain settlement by then, they would have had good reason to seek another location. The government boatshed was ideal. It was just as close to the city as the Domain, and although naval and police personnel and commercial traders were using the area during the day, it was not on a public thoroughfare and was significantly less busy than the head of the quay to the south, as a comparison of Figure 6.4 and Figure 6.5 shows.

The boatshed housed a fluctuating population of between ten and thirty residents, who stayed for up to several weeks at a time, camping together in one corner of the shed around an open fire. It was a domestic and social space, but also a place of work. While their children played in the water, women at the boatshed made shell-encrusted decorative baskets to sell in the city, a practice adopted from a form of Victorian English craft that was popular at the time.[13] Residents were drawn from coastal Sydney, including 'Botany fisherman' Charlie Lambert and Ellen Davis, the daughter of Botany Bay woman Biddy Giles and Illawarra man Burragalong (aka Paddy Davis).[14] Others were said to have come from places within the affiliated coastal zone such as the Illawarra, Kiama, Shoalhaven, Port Stephens and the 'Hunter' (probably Newcastle/Maitland). The boatshed was also linked to the other Aboriginal settlements around the harbour and Botany Bay, particularly Rushcutters Bay. For example, boatshed resident Frank Foster died at Rushcutters Bay in 1880, and Kate Foot and her husband Joe Bundle had their son Joseph at Rushcutters Bay in 1880 before moving to the boatshed.[15] People arriving at all of these coastal Sydney settlements were travelling around the established beats of decades past, following well-worn pathways to centres of Aboriginal occupation, where the hearths of Aboriginal people to whom they had affiliations awaited.

Concocting a moral panic

In the two years prior to 1881 there were no calls to evict Aboriginal people from the government boatshed at Circular Quay. Indeed, the government had encouraged them to remain there by providing weekly rations to residents.[16] The rising interest in Aboriginal welfare among some politicians was based on the growing issue of what to do with Aboriginal populations in rural areas. There was no groundswell of public concern about a new or increasing Aboriginal presence on Sydney's streets or suburbs. In fact, with the exception of one or two letters to the editor there was complete silence on the matter. This was in stark contrast to the very public opposition at the same time to Chinese migration, based on racialised fears of takeover and disease.[17] There is no evidence in police records or newspapers of an increase in Aboriginal criminality or public nuisance at Circular Quay, or around the city more generally. If newspapers mentioned Aboriginal people in Sydney at all, it was usually to lampoon them as figures of pity or ridicule, as Figure 6.6 shows.

By the middle of 1881 though, the government had been convinced of the need to take action. In the space of a few weeks between mid-July and early August, Aboriginal people moved out of the boatshed, while others left Sydney entirely for an Aboriginal mission on the Murray River. The sudden exodus of Aboriginal people from the city has the appearance of a coordinated and enforced plan, reflected in the use of terms such as 'broke up', 'closed down' and 'forced out' when historians discuss these events.[18] But on closer inspection, it emerges as the result of the intersecting personal crusades of

Aboriginal sympathiser George Thornton and missionary Daniel Matthews (see Figure 6.7).

From the 1860s, George Thornton had been actively trying to keep Aboriginal people from coming to Sydney by lobbying the government to provide them with fishing boats, rations and other assistance in their own 'district'. He believed that there was no need to dispense charity in Sydney as there were no authentic coastal Sydney people left, and he did not believe those of mixed ancestry deserved assistance.[19] Beginning in early 1881, he wrote a series of letters to the premier and colonial secretary Sir Henry Parkes, alleging the 'abominable state of things [that] now exists with these people in Sydney and Botany, and especially at the boat-sheds', and urging an enquiry that he anticipated would end what he later called the 'misplaced charity' of providing rations to Aboriginal people in Sydney.[20] His timing is curious. As a parliamentarian and unofficial advisor to the premier Sir Henry Parkes on Aboriginal matters, he had been aware of the boatshed settlement for several years, and as president of the Sydney Rowing Club he passed it every month to attend meetings in the clubhouse just a hundred metres further along the shore (see Figure 6.3). He seems to have been prompted to act when he recognised some of the Port Stephens and Shoalhaven people at the boatsheds for whom he had recently organised the purchase of a boat and supplies. Despite his best efforts, they had still been 'attracted to Sydney, and encouraged to remain here, by having shelter and rations given to them'.[21] Thornton could see that his approach of localised charity was being actively subverted at the very time when government intervention in Aboriginal affairs was becoming inevitable and imminent. He realised that he would have to take the initiative to ensure that the government pursued his model of restricted, localised welfare distribution over the generalised approach that missionaries and some parliamentarians were promoting.

To elicit action from the government, Thornton had to convince them that there was a problem. His first letter to Parkes in January 1881 alleged vice and depravity at the boatsheds, and prompted enquiries among the police, Marine Board and Water Police Magistrate. To disagree with Thornton's assertions would have been to suggest that Aboriginal slums in the city were acceptable, but they were in the awkward position of having to highlight the nuisance Aboriginal people presented while admitting that they had done nothing about it for the previous two years. Water Police Constable Little detailed prostitution, drinking and fighting at the boatshed, and the trouble Aboriginal people created at the quay wharves, pushing in and out of steamers and causing brawls that attracted large crowds and 'frequently stop[ped] the public thoroughfare'.[22] Parkes agreed that action should be taken, and offered Thornton the role of distributing rations and supplies to Aboriginal people across the state.[23] Thornton accepted, but for reasons that are not clear, nothing happened. Police and newspaper reports do not record any of the arrests and public complaints alleged in Constable Little's report, and the bustling quay was a well-known place of petty crime, drinking and riotous behaviour among Europeans, so perhaps Parkes regarded the claims as exaggerations. Or maybe he acknowledged the limited powers of the government to move Aboriginal people on. As we saw in Chapter 2, the *Vagrancy Act* exempted Aboriginal people, and even if it was invoked, it would have involved arresting several dozen men, women and children, which probably seemed out of proportion to the problem, especially in the absence of any public outcry.

Thornton did not give up, and wrote again to Parkes in May 1881 urging action.[24] Once again nothing was done, but events began to swing back in his favour in the following weeks with the arrival of missionary Daniel Matthews (1837–1902; see Figure 6.7). Matthews had established the Maloga Mission on the Murray River near Echuca with his wife Janet in 1874, and by 1880 had formed the Aborigines Protection Association (APA), consisting of religious and lay supporters of the Maloga Mission and John Gribble's Warangesda Mission about 200 kilometres to the north. Matthews was in Sydney to raise funds, and to convince the government of the need for more general action on Aboriginal welfare through the APA.

While in town, Matthews took up the cause of Aboriginal people in Sydney, giving them practical assistance with rations and medical aid, and urging APA members and the government to intervene on their behalf.[25] Matthews saw Thornton as a potential ally and tried to enlist his help, but after an initial meeting, Thornton avoided him and the APA, having little time for their religiously motivated do-gooding. For his part, Matthews found Thornton's belief that localised charity was the best means to care for Aboriginal people to be a 'great fallacy.'[26] Though the two men appeared to be working at cross-purposes, any focus on the conditions of local Aboriginal people was to their mutual advantage, and Matthews shared Thornton's desire to remove Aboriginal people from the boatshed, publicly stating his intention to take 'a number of them to our mission station at Maloga'.[27]

The catalyst for government action came with the tragic death of Kate Foot and Joe Bundle's infant son Joseph Bundle at the boatshed on the afternoon of Thursday 7 July 1881. Joseph had been playing with friends near the water while Kate sat nearby making shell baskets, when he fell in. Kate saw him floating in the water, and rushed over and grabbed him. With her husband Joe and others she desperately tried to revive him, rolling him in a blanket to warm him next to the boatshed fire, but it was too late.[28] The very next day the Inspector-General of Police Edmund Fosbery sent Sub-Inspector John Donohoe to investigate claims that European men were living with Aboriginal people at the boatshed, in contravention of the *Vagrancy Act*. Fosbery had been aware of these claims for at least six months, so it seems more likely that the well-publicised tragedy of young Joseph's death persuaded him of the need to intervene. European vagrants were not mentioned in Donohoe's report, suggesting that it was indeed a ruse for intervention. Instead, he detailed the undesirable activities of the twenty or so Aboriginal residents and called for their 'removal from the shed'.[29] He asked George Thornton about the best means of doing so, and Thornton recommended that he seek Parkes' permission to effect the 'immediate removal of these aboriginals to their own districts'.³⁰ Parkes agreed, and Donohoe was immediately ordered to clear the boatshed by offering residents free steamer passage back to their places of origin.

The end result of Thornton's six-month campaign to evict residents of the boatshed looked more like bribery and inducement, indicating the limits of government power. Donohoe went to the boatshed on 14 July and made the offer, telling residents that they would no longer be permitted to live in the boatshed. They refused to leave Sydney, but agreed to cross the harbour to other existing settlements at the North Shore and Manly.³¹ It is not clear what Donohoe could have done if they had not left, but once they were gone, the authorities began issuing rations at the La Perouse Aboriginal settlement instead, and ordered the local police to ensure that Aboriginal people did not re-establish a settlement within the boatshed.³² As removing Aboriginal people from the boatshed was not part of a broader government strategy of banishment, it did not make similar moves at other coastal Sydney Aboriginal settlements, but soon afterwards, some Aboriginal people did leave Sydney on steamers bound for the Hunter River, Kiama and Wollongong (all within the affiliated coastal zone). Perhaps they realised that they would not be allowed back to the boatsheds and that they would no longer be issued with rations in the city, or perhaps these events merely coincided with, or accelerated, the timing of their intended departure from this stop on their coastal beat.

The more significant and lasting demographic shift at this time occurred through the actions of Daniel Matthews. He saw no hope of converting Aboriginal people in the vice-ridden environs of Sydney, and in the weeks after the boatshed settlement closed he recruited Aboriginal people at the North Shore, Manly, Botany and La Perouse settlements to accompany him back to Maloga Mission. Most Aboriginal people were aware of the concepts of Christian religion, having been baptised or married by the Catholic or Protestant church, or preached to at Botany, and Matthews' exhortations about Christian salvation may have convinced some.³³ He probably also exploited the uncertainty created when the boatshed settlement closed and ration distributions were changed to persuade Aboriginal people to come with him. Fellow APA member Richard Hill (see Figure 6.8), who was well connected with the local Aboriginal community, assisted him in these endeavours. Hill and his son had been active in distributing rations to Aboriginal people at Botany at their own expense, and he also employed the Aboriginal couple Emma and George Timbery at his city abode on Bent Street (see Figure 6.9).[34] The Timberys were living at La Perouse, and George appears to have assisted Matthews with introductions to the local community there and at the boatshed.[35] It seems unlikely though that the Timberys actively promoted Matthews' aim of removing Aboriginal people to Maloga among their community, as they refused to let their own young girls go with him.[36]

Matthews had more success at Manly, where he 'broke up' (in his words) the settlement several weeks after people had moved there from the boatshed, taking eight men, women and children back to Richard Hill's house.[37] He also appears to have persuaded a number of people from the Botany settlement to go with him, effectively shutting it down, as the remainder moved to nearby La Perouse.[38] In the end, Matthews was able to persuade twenty-five Aboriginal people to go with him, mainly families and their children, as well as several single men and women. On the eve of their departure on 2 August, they were all taken to Richard Hill's house in the city, where a 'fire, plenty of food and blankets' awaited in his yard. Two people had second thoughts and left during the night, but the remaining twenty-three accompanied Matthews the next day by train to the Maloga Mission.[39] At least a quarter of the Aboriginal people living in coastal Sydney had gone, and some would never return.

Intervention (1870s–1880s)

Protectors and patrons

The government's decision to shift the distribution of welfare to La Perouse was easily made, but there was no policy to guide the ensuing activities, such as *who* should receive aid. Wanting to ensure that his approach of localised and restricted charity was adopted as policy, George Thornton wrote to Parkes again at the end of 1881, encouraging the premier to make him Protector of Aborigines, and suggesting how such an office might work. Parkes was about to leave the country and hastily appointed Thornton as 'Protector of the Aborigines' in New South Wales. Thornton was to have the:

> authority to dispense and expend moneys set apart for the sustenance and comfort of the Aboriginal race, to distribute articles of food and clothing among persons belonging to the said race and to give advice and instructions to other persons who may be variously concerned in the case and treatment of the said race.[40]

As historian Ann Curthoys has pointed out, it was a disorganised start to the state's re-entry into Aboriginal welfare, and with Thornton's autocratic style, problems soon arose.[41]

Thornton suddenly found himself solely responsible for administering Aboriginal welfare around New South Wales, with the fine details left largely up to him. He immediately began to define and centralise his powers, asking the colonial secretary's office to notify government departments of his appointment, to stop them dispensing the kind of 'irregular issue of provisions' he so despised.[42] He then undertook the first census of Aboriginal people in New South Wales, strategically listing those of mixed ancestry separately to allow him to quantify how many of these 'unworthy' people were potentially receiving government aid.[43] The census showed that Aboriginal people had survived in greater numbers than had previously been assumed, highlighting the inadequate resources at his disposal. This in turn raised the issue of who qualified for government assistance, which was largely debated in the context of the La Perouse Aboriginal settlement.

Given Thornton's aim of removing Aboriginal people from Sydney to their 'home districts', his tolerance of the La Perouse settlement with its mainly part-Aboriginal and (in his opinion) migrant population, seems contradictory. As historian Maria Nugent discusses though, in Thornton's view the settlement was far enough from the city not to 'pose a threat or cause a nuisance', and he also regarded the industrious fishing and craft activities at the settlement as worthy of support.[44] His view was underpinned by knowing he lacked the power to move Aboriginal people away except by inducement. This had succeeded at the government boatshed, but it was another matter entirely to try to move Aboriginal people away from a fishing village which they had established and which had the support of some influential Europeans. Thornton instead made government aid at La Perouse conditional. As he later stated in a letter to the *Evening News*, 'I think they should be helped, but also be made, so far as practicable, self-reliant. They are all young and able men, mostly half-castes.'[45] He reduced rations from a weekly universal right to a needs-based request system, and focussed his attention instead on providing 'boats and gear, fishing-tackle, some clothing [...] [and] materials for building five houses or huts'.[46]

With his official position and the endorsement of the premier, Thornton probably felt that he was at liberty to devise and implement policies as he saw fit. But he had underestimated the established culture of patronage and right behaviour that had developed during the decades of colonial indifference. Aboriginal people had become increasingly entangled with Sydney through their relationships with key locally born European men and their families, and although many of these Europeans had died by the early 1880s, those remaining, such as Richard Hill, took their obligations seriously. Hill had been supplying La Perouse residents with meat and rations for some time before Thornton became Protector.[47] There would have been no apparent and compelling reason for Hill and others to abandon such behaviour simply because of Thornton's appointment. For their part, most of the Aboriginal people living at La Perouse had spent their entire lives under this system of privately negotiated charity, where they had some influence over the process and result, and would have been reluctant to abandon it.

Thornton made the additional mistake of opposing the expanded role of the APA, and missionary aid in general, making him a marked man in the eyes of some APA members. In December 1882, APA member and parliamentarian John McElhone, who favoured Richard Hill as Protector over Thornton, wrote to Treasury accusing Thornton of having starved La Perouse residents at Christmas by withholding rations.[48] He then launched stinging attacks in parliament and through the newspapers in early 1883, aided in the latter by other supporters including local Presbyterian minister Thomas Curtis.[49] It was a strategic character demolition at the very time when a new government was replacing Thornton's main supporter, Premier Henry Parkes. Thornton desperately tried to save his reputation in a series of bitter letter exchanges, but the incoming premier was an APA supporter, and soon decided that a board should replace the lone Protector. The Aborigines Protection Board was duly established in June 1883, and though Thornton was appointed as the Board's first Chair, his position was untenable and he resigned shortly afterwards, ending forty years of involvement in Aboriginal welfare.[50] He was replaced as Chair by Richard Hill. With Hill in charge, it may have seemed to Aboriginal people at La Perouse and elsewhere around coastal Sydney that a new version of the Sydney Aborigines Committee had been formed, and that their strategy of personal negotiation could continue. In the short term, this was not far from the truth.

Continuing coastal beats

Several years after the boatshed settlement closed and the Aborigines Protection Board formed, Sydneysiders could have been forgiven for wondering what had actually changed. In the mid-1880s, Aboriginal people still frequented the city, lived in many of the same settlements, and continued to move in and out of coastal Sydney, primarily from within the affiliated coastal zone. While several of the twenty-three men, women and children who had accompanied Daniel Matthews to the Maloga Mission in 1881 tragically died soon after arriving, some others found their way home over the next two years. These included Bill and Kate Foot and Harry Davis by the end of 1882, while a number of others were probably among the thirteen people who left the mission in April 1883.[51] By the mid-1880s, there were again between fifty and one hundred Aboriginal people living in coastal Sydney.

One of George Thornton's key aims in closing the boatshed settlement in 1881 and shifting the distribution of welfare to La Perouse had been to prevent Aboriginal people from visiting the city, but he was thwarted by urban growth. The population of Sydney nearly tripled during the 1870s and 1880s to more than 350 000 people, and most immigrants chose to live in the new inner (working-class) and outer (middle-class) suburbs rather than the city itself.[52] To facilitate this growth, the city constructed an extensive rail and tram network in the 1880s, as Figure 6.1 shows. A tramline covering three-quarters of the distance to La Perouse opened in 1882, and Aboriginal people were often allowed to travel free.[53] Within a year of the boatshed settlement closing, Aboriginal people were once again entering the city by tram or on foot from their settlements across coastal Sydney.[54] The Protection Board had no power to stop them. It was essentially a 'small administrative body' in this period that reacted to requests put to it, and had little ability to impose particular policies. The Board periodically sought to restrict free travel on the tram network, but having no legal powers, it could only entreat that conductors enforced their request, which some at least refused to do.⁵⁵

Aboriginal people shifted the way they used the city in response to its changing commercial geography. They focussed their visits on areas such as Haymarket and Paddy's Market in the city's south, where many Sydney residents went to shop and socialise, particularly on Saturday nights. They sold 'native weapons', shellwork, bush honey and wild flowers, and obtained other goods they needed.⁵⁶ European observers recorded only the drinking and petty crime, as well as the harassment and assaults Aboriginal people suffered in the city, but Aboriginal oral histories stretching back to this period provide another perspective.⁵⁷ Harriet Neville, who moved to Sydney with her family from Port Stephens in the early 1880s, later recalled childhood excursions from La Perouse to the city with her grandfather in the late 19th century as a 'pleasure', and stressed the kindness of Sydney people. She related that 'we used to walk barefoot in those days, and when people saw us passing they would give us a shilling or bread and butter. Butchers and bakers would sing out to us and give us bread and meat.' Another La Perouse resident, Charley Wells, had similar memories of Christmas visits into the city at this time from the Rushcutters Bay settlement.⁵⁸

To compensate for its lack of explicit powers, the Protection Board hoped to use welfare distribution to entice Aboriginal people to La Perouse. This settlement was initially similar to the others around coastal Sydney, but as historian Maria Nugent notes in her history of Botany Bay, the focus of Board activity there from the early 1880s changed this dynamic. Rations and other supplies could most easily be obtained there, but this also meant that from then on La Perouse residents 'were forever within the government's orbit'.⁵⁹ Aboriginal people took advantage of government aid to turn their fishing settlement into a permanent village, consisting of five windowless, clay-floored corrugated-iron huts as shown in Figure 6.10, each sleeping a family on stretcher beds, with another hut for single men. New residents or temporary visitors whom the Board did not wish to encourage at La Perouse had to make do with whatever building materials they could buy or find, and lived in shelters made of portions of canvas tents, or iron sheeting covered with stretched blankets.[60]

Several families had sailing boats, around six metres long with a 'sprit sail and jib', which they used to fish the bay and range along the ocean coast.[61] They sold their catch to local middlemen to take to the markets, just as Mahroot had done half a century before, and the Board supported them through supplying and repairing fishing boats and purchasing oars, sails and fishing tackle for them.[62] Aboriginal people also rented out their fishing boats to make money, sold shell-work and other goods in the city, and worked as domestic aids and on nearby construction projects.[63] Their earnings were supplemented by the Board's weekly issue of flour, sugar, tea and sometimes meat to selected residents such as 'full bloods', the elderly and women caring for their children.[64] In combination, this provided an economic stability unmatched at other settlements around coastal Sydney, but it did not override the ongoing beats of Aboriginal people.

Across Botany Bay at Sans Souci, for example, Aboriginal people had been living since the 1850s in the vicinity of what became the Ellesmere estate (see Figure 6.11; Ellesmere House still stands today on the corner of Vista and Endeavour streets). By the early 1880s, the settlement housed locally affiliated people including the Botany Bay Malones, and the Georges River–oriented Lowndes and Fussell families. Theresa Fussell and her non-Aboriginal husband William (who worked as an oyster-dredger on the large Holt Estate across the Georges River), lived with their four young children in a hut with a fireplace, while others may have lived in tents.[65] Despite extended families like the Malones living at both Sans Souci and La Perouse, the Board did not seek to combine the two settlements. Instead, they supported the Sans Souci settlement by providing rations there throughout the 1880s.[66] As historians Heather Goodall and Allison Cadzow have discussed, a number of European residents also accepted the settlement. In 1884 Anna Lowndes, Theresa Fussell and Johnny Malone's daughter Agnes were asked by local European residents to sign a petition to establish a local school, which some of their children subsequently attended.[67]

Aboriginal people also continued to live in settlements that were not officially recognised by the Board, such as within the public reserve at Rushcutters Bay.[68] A description from 1895 reveals that residents lived on the eastern side of the reserve near Darling Point, in shelters made of slabs of wood leaning against a fence and covered with iron, sheets and other materials, around a central campfire.[69] Residents moved between the settlement and La Perouse, and engaged in a similar economy of fishing, shellfish gathering and selling boomerangs and shellwork in the city. As La Perouse resident Charley Wells later recalled, Rushcutters Bay had a few permanent residents; Aboriginal people from other areas regularly visited them at times such as Christmas and Easter and 'brought birds and honey with them, and exchanged them for fish'.[70]

These Aboriginal beats were continuing not just around coastal Sydney in the 1880s, but across the affiliated coastal zone. Richard Hill acknowledged that the Board could do little to curtail this movement.[71] As La Perouse resident Harriet Neville later expressed it, her family had relocated from Port Stephens in the early 1880s because 'we like to move about, and to be with friends. We knew people at La Perouse, and there was a livelihood there. There were fish and shellfish, and they used to dive for lobsters'.[72] A census of the La Perouse settlement in 1887 showed that the sixty-four residents consisted entirely of local families like the Malones and others from places within the affiliated coastal zone, such as the Illawarra, Kiama, Newcastle, Port Stephens and Camden.[73] But the 1880s were to be the final decade in which the affiliated coastal zone dominated Aboriginal beats. When the Aborigines Protection Board was established, it did not bring sudden or sweeping changes, but over time the effects of closer government and religious intervention accumulated to a tipping point, beyond which new influences merged with old ways to produce a new pattern of Aboriginal movement and settlement.

7

New links and old ways (1890s–1930s)

In November 1900, a reporter from the *Evening News* caught the tram to Botany and walked the last few kilometres across the sandy scrub to the La Perouse Aboriginal settlement. He spoke with some of the fifty or so people living there in galvanised-iron huts, including the oldest resident, Lizzie Golden (formerly Malone; see Figure 7.1). Lizzie spoke of how she had spent most of her life in the area, and how her people used to range 'all up atween here and the head of the George's River' on their coastal beats.[1] But this way of life, which had been such a stable feature of coastal Sydney Aboriginal life throughout the 19th century, was changing. Many of the stopover points on coastal Sydney beats were being abandoned. People such as Lizzie's own son Charles Golden (c.1877–1919), who was a preacher for the newly established mission movement, and had married a western Sydney Aboriginal woman, were forging new links beyond the affiliated coastal zone. Sydney was also increasingly becoming home to Aboriginal people who had no previous link to the area. The scale of change was much faster and greater than at any time over the previous century, but there was no clean break with the past; nor were all of the changes forced. As before, the responses of Aboriginal people were informed by existing connections and practices, creating something new from what had come before.

Sustained enticement

Since the early 1880s, La Perouse had been the main place in coastal Sydney where Aboriginal people could gain the assistance of the Aborigines Protection Board. Over the following decade this had slowly but steadily enticed Aboriginal people to live there from across coastal Sydney. Most Aboriginal settlements in the 19th century contained no more than ten or twenty people, but La Perouse rarely housed *fewer* than thirty or forty residents, and sometimes substantially more.[2] Within a population of just fifty to one hundred across coastal Sydney, this left less and less people to populate other settlements, and by the century's end most had closed. La Perouse grew at the expense of other coastal Sydney settlements in a time of increasing government and religious intervention, so it can appear to be the result of a deliberate policy of relocation. Historian Maria Nugent describes La Perouse in this period as a place 'where Aboriginal people from other metropolitan camps had relocated in the 1880s and 1890s when forced out of the city', though she also notes that Aboriginal people reject this idea of relocation in their own narratives about the settlement's origins.[3] In a sense both views capture the complex dynamics at play, as Aboriginal people had limited alternatives but were nonetheless rarely forced to move. To see these processes at work, we need to zoom in and look at what happened to particular settlements in the decades after the Board was established.

In the 1880s and 1890s, Aboriginal settlements outside of La Perouse were increasingly vulnerable because of their small size. The Sans Souci settlement, for example, was virtually abandoned in 1886 after Theresa Fussell drowned while fishing with her European husband William at Kurnell. William could not work and look after their four children. He asked the landlord of the Sans Souci Hotel to look after two of them, and placed five-year-old Henry and three-year-old Lily in the Benevolent Society Asylum, intending that they would be fostered out while he contributed to their maintenance.[4] The newly created foster care ('boarding out') system was not specific to Aboriginal children, but it aimed to sever contact with birth families and establish the new guardians as the 'real parents' in the eyes of the children.[5] If William's longer-term aim was to take back his children, the system worked against him, and his employer Frederick Holt further decreased his chances by informing the authorities that the children had been corrupted by their parents' drinking and should be placed with a 'respectable married couple'.[6] Henry and Lily were soon fostered out to separate families, and it is unlikely that they came to live with each other, or with any Aboriginal people again. William died just a few months later.[7] With only a few people remaining at the Sans Souci settlement, the Board discontinued its assistance after 1890, which probably discouraged others from living there. An older Aboriginal man, Albert, continued to live at Sans Souci throughout the 1890s, occasionally joined by one or two others, but after his death the settlement fell out of use.[8]

Authorities and the public were also increasingly scrutinising Aboriginal settlements in the 1890s. As large old estates were subdivided and the suburban Sydney population increased rapidly, a growing public awareness of the Aborigines Protection Board and the La Perouse settlement fostered a view that there was a designated place for Aboriginal people in Sydney and an official process for getting them there. Aboriginal settlements that had been used for many decades without any public outcry were now the subject of complaints to the Board, who were already monitoring them through police inspections and an annual census. Although the Board did not gain legal powers over Aboriginal people until the early 20th century, it developed a consistent approach to Aboriginal settlements in its first decades through the unfailing attendance of chairman Richard Hill (1883–1895) and Inspector-General of Police Edmond Fosbery (1883–1904) at its weekly meetings.[9]

The Board tolerated settlements if they were small and did not create a public nuisance. The Board did not intervene, for example, when the annual census recorded a group of five adults living at Watsons Bay in 1892.[10] Their view changed the following year, though, when the population increased to over fifteen people, whom local police said 'were likely to become a source of annoyance' to Europeans in the area. Residents of the settlement were said to be going into Sydney to obtain liquor and had 'no means of earning their living at Watson's Bay', though other records show that they busked using 'spear and boomerang throwing exhibitions in front of the Greenwich Pier Hotel' at Watsons Bay on weekends and holidays. The Board requested that Police 'warn the aborigines away, and [...] furnish requisitions for their passages to the places from whence they came'.[11]

This increasing harassment in other areas made the security and stability of La Perouse more attractive, but the Board and police could not stop Aboriginal people from returning to other settlements on public land if they desired. In 1895, the Board acted on resident complaints about several dozen Aboriginal people from La Perouse, Vaucluse, the Shoalhaven district and the mid-north coast, who had assembled at the public reserve at Rushcutters Bay. Recognising their limited powers, the police were apparently 'loth to move in the matter', and only acted when Aboriginal people shifted beyond public land to colonise the nearby ruins of a former chapel on the privately owned Mona Estate.[12] The police ordered them to move, but they simply moved 'a few yards away' back to the public reserve, and when asked to leave the area, 'could not be got to view the matter in the same light'. The police told the Board that they had persuaded the residents to 'return to their own districts', but the *Evening News* reported that they had simply moved east to Rose Bay and 'were sure to return at night'.[13] Annual Board census records show that Aboriginal people continued to use Rushcutters Bay until 1899, but it seems that all had left by the turn of the century.

The closure of the Rushcutters Bay settlement was later recalled by Trescoe Rowe, whose parents owned the Mona Estate at the time. Born in 1891, his childhood memory was that the Aboriginal residents had been 'removed' to La Perouse, accompanied by his governess Harriet Baker (1860–1951), but there was more to it than that.[14]

Baker was an active member of an evangelical movement called the Christian Endeavour Union, which comprised a number of societies associated with particular churches. Jean Watson and Reverend William Allen of the Petersham Congregational Church had a keen interest in evangelising to Aboriginal people. With the encouragement of the Aborigines Protection Association, they started working at La Perouse in 1893, with Lizzie Malone's son Charles Golden (c.1877–1919; see Figure 7.1) as secretary.[15] By 1895 they had built a church (see Figure 7.2) and established the La Perouse Aborigines Mission Committee, which met at Harriet Baker's home in Paddington.[16] Knowing this, it seems most likely that the few remaining Aboriginal residents at Rushcutters Bay were not forced to leave by the authorities, but were persuaded by Baker and her Aboriginal associates to make the permanent move to La Perouse.

The presence of missionaries at La Perouse, who were prepared to advocate on behalf of Aboriginal people, added to the enticing effect of government assistance. The longstanding personal relationships of residents such as Emma Timbery (c.1842–1916) with Protection Board chairman Richard Hill made that assistance easier to obtain. When requests came to the Board from La Perouse for fishing boats, repairs, equipment or rations, Hill volunteered to take charge of them.[17] Aboriginal people in the Sydney area had this opportunity because Board members lived and met in Sydney. Those living at Blacktown had a similar relationship with 1890s Board member Sydney Burdekin, on whose Richmond Road property they were camped.

Emma Timbery had also developed relationships with other sympathetic Sydneysiders and was able to obtain their support from her base at La Perouse. She had known long-time Double Bay resident Eliza Robinson since they were both young women in the mid-19th century, and Eliza continued to visit Emma when she lived at La Perouse. Her son Leo sometimes accompanied her, and probably took the photo of Emma in Figure 7.3.[18] At Christmas, Eliza personally delivered Emma 'a donation of mighty plum puddings and cakes, and a supply of groceries', and in 1903 she organised the building of a fishing boat for Emma and others at La Perouse. The boat was handed over at a ceremony in Manly attended by 'a number of ladies and gentlemen interested in the welfare' of Aboriginal people, many of whom had assisted Eliza in paying for its construction.[19]

With the support of Hill, missionaries and other private individuals like Eliza Robinson, La Perouse residents were able to assemble and maintain a fleet of six fishing boats, and expand or rebuild their original huts into larger, timber-framed dwellings with fireplaces and chimneys, many of which remained in use for decades (see Figure 7.4).[20] Hill was probably also instrumental in gazetting the settlement as an Aboriginal Reserve in early 1895, which gave some apparent security of tenure.[21] When Hill died a few months after this, men from La Perouse travelled into the city from La Perouse to see if the news of his death was true, but the cross-cultural bonds between the Hill family and coastal Sydney people did not end there. Hill's son George, and his own son George Jnr, continued to provide practical assistance to Aboriginal people in the area in the early 20th century, taking supplies to the settlement and hosting Aboriginal people at their large Coogee estate known as Cliffbrook (NewSouth Publishing is located on part of the former grounds).[22] Two of Richard Hill's other sons, James and William, replaced him on the Board between 1895 and 1910, though they do not appear to have personally intervened in matters pertaining to La Perouse as their father had.

As with other settlements in the past, the longer La Perouse existed, the stronger the sense of Aboriginal attachment became, deepened by their accumulating experiences, and the births and deaths of loved ones. As Emma Timbery stated in response to an attempt to shut down the settlement in 1900, 'there's no more suitable place than this [...] and as we do no harm to anyone they ought to let us stop here [...] 'ere we've been all our lives, and 'ere we want to die'.[23] This sense of belonging partly reflected the lack of comparable alternatives, but Aboriginal people were not prisoners at La Perouse in this period, despite some surveillance and restrictions.

They had broader connections across the affiliated coastal zone, and maintained them by continuing their coastal beats, much to the Board's frustration. When around ninety Aboriginal people gathered at La Perouse in 1894, the Board contacted the Illawarra and Newcastle Steamship Companies (but not other steamer lines or railways that operated outside the affiliated coastal zone) to obtain their help in 'checking the constant travelling of aborigines between the coast districts and Sydney'.[24]

The practical effects of increasing Board surveillance, suburban growth and the consolidation of La Perouse as the main coastal Sydney settlement can be seen through the life of Botany Bay man William Rowley (1856–1941), as shown in Figure 7.5. Born on the southern shore of Botany Bay, he was connected to southern Sydney through his Aboriginal mother, and to areas further south through his wife, Mary Ann, and perhaps his own family as well, as he was said to be related to Biddy Giles' daughter Ellen Anderson.[25] In the 1870s he lived at Kurnell with his mother, and in the early 1880s was one of the key early residents at La Perouse, but by the 1890s he returned to Kurnell on the opposite shore of the bay to establish his own place with his wife (they were officially married later), his brothers Harry and James and other family members. He tended the nearby oyster leases of the Holt family and fished around the bay and along the coast. When he was evicted over a misunderstanding in 1899, he moved to an Aboriginal settlement in his wife's area of affiliation at Port Kembla in the Illawarra and spent the next two decades living there and at La Perouse.[26] From the 1920s to the 1930s, William and Mary Ann lived off the Georges River along Salt Pan Creek, on a block of land at Ogilvy Street, Peakhurst. They resided there next to William's relative Ellen Anderson, before moving to the Roseby Park Aboriginal station on the Shoalhaven River in the final years of his life. Though he lived under the Board's scrutiny at La Perouse on occasion, his overall movement patterns suggest that he tried as much as possible to live independent of government oversight. Throughout his life William Rowley was able to follow the well-worn pathways of the coastal beat that connected his areas of affiliation. For many of his contemporaries, though, past patterns of connection were becoming entangled with new lines of movement created by missionary activity.

New connections

The missionary movement influenced Aboriginal movement along two main trajectories, which are illustrated in Figure 7.6. The Aboriginal people who travelled from Sydney to Daniel Matthews' Maloga Mission on the Murray River in 1881 formed the first, while the second radiated outward from La Perouse in the late 1890s as the La Perouse Aborigines Mission expanded. As we have seen, some of the coastal Sydney people who went to Maloga in 1881 returned soon after. Whether they formed any lasting bonds with other Maloga residents is not clear. Of greater significance were the connections formed by those who stayed, and in particular Ellen Davis (1850s–1931), the daughter of Botany Bay woman Biddy Giles and Illawarra man Burragalong (aka Paddy Davis; 1810s–1877). Soon after arriving, Ellen married Hugh Anderson (c.1856–1928) from the nearby Goulburn Valley in Victoria, and they stayed together for the rest of their lives.[27] Their travels and activities over that time, as summarised in Figure 7.7, demonstrate the lasting effect their union at Maloga Mission created, enlarging their sphere of connections. They moved within areas to which they had affiliations, but this now extended far beyond the coastal zone of Ellen's youth.

The Andersons spent most of the 1880s at Maloga Mission and the nearby Cumeragunja settlement that grew out of it. During this time, Hugh gained valuable experience in public speaking as part of evangelical tours, as well as exposure to Aboriginal political activity at both places.[28] In the late 1880s, the Andersons moved back to the coast near Ellen's birth area, and worked to improve the conditions of Aboriginal people there. By 1889, they had negotiated to live on the corner of a farm at Kangaroo Valley, where they established a settlement and school with fellow Maloga resident and teacher Frank Foster (c.1870–1941), whose own coastal ancestry tied him to the area. They found that the Board was reluctant to support their attempt to live outside of the Aboriginal reserve system with rations and school supplies, and by the following winter Hugh and Ellen and three of their children 'had to leave the place [...] because of the scarcity of provisions'.[29] They walked forty kilometres through rugged country to Moss Vale railway station and returned to Hugh's local area at Cumeragunja. In the 1890s they moved between their inland and coastal areas of affiliation, and while the Board refused to issue them with rail passes on at least one occasion, they managed to attend Ellen's brother-in-law 'King' Mickey Johnson's 'crowning' during the Wollongong centenary celebrations in 1896, and to visit the Burragorang Valley Aboriginal settlement. By the early 1900s they had moved to Sydney, where they lived for the rest of their lives next to Ellen's relative William Rowley along Salt Pan Creek at Peakhurst.

Maloga and Cumeragunja were crucibles of Aboriginal connection, joining people together by marriage and shared experience, and giving residents connections to distant places like coastal Sydney. When Ellen Anderson set up camp at Salt Pan Creek, she brought with her a greatly enlarged sphere of connections. Political activism flourished at Salt Pan Creek in the 1920s and 1930s, and was fostered by the wide social networks that the Andersons had accumulated through their travels and affiliations. It also drew on what historians Heather Goodall and Allison Cadzow have described as a 'Christian ethic of care and an active stance of egalitarian protest' that can be traced back to Maloga and Cumeragunja residents such as Hugh Anderson and evangelist Paddy Swift (1848–c.1920s) from northern Victoria.[30] In the 1890s Paddy focussed his evangelism on coastal Sydney and the south coast due to the connections he had forged at the missions with the Andersons and Frank Foster. By the mid-1890s he was preaching with the newly formed La Perouse Aborigines Mission and was nominated to be its first resident missionary. But his passion for justice proved too much even for those sympathetic to Aboriginal people. At an evangelistic meeting in Sydney in the winter of 1896, Paddy rose up and berated attendees, saying:

> you have come into our land [...] and what have you given us in return? Nothing. Now is the time, then, when we should come round, and take up the rent money; and I think it is only fair, for you white people will all admit that you have taken a good lot out of this colony [...] I know that Christ has prepared a home up there for me as well as for you; and he doesn't build two houses where one will do. He isn't going to build a mansion for you and a bark hut for me.[31]

Shortly after this rousing speech, Paddy was disendorsed in favour of the safer choice of non-Aboriginal Christian Endeavourer Retta Dixon.[32]

In 1899 Dixon oversaw the expansion of the La Perouse Aborigines Mission across and beyond Sydney. To avoid confusion, its name was changed to the New South Wales Aborigines Mission, but its La Perouse origins were key to its southern extension.[33] Retta Dixon understood the evangelical value of being accompanied by converted Aboriginal people who could provide crucial introductions and who embodied what they were trying to achieve. For this reason, when Dixon travelled south from La Perouse in 1899, she was accompanied by La Perouse resident John Bundy. They visited Aboriginal settlements such as Lake Illawarra, where Dixon acknowledged that influential local couple Rosie Johnson (daughter of Biddy Giles and sister to Ellen Anderson) and her husband Mickey, converted 'through the instrumentality' of Bundy. A month later, Mickey Johnson was organising the construction of a mission church at Lake Illawarra when Retta Dixon passed by again on her way further south, this time with Emma Timbery.[34] They walked 100 kilometres across her and her husband's areas of affiliation in the Illawarra and Shoalhaven districts, visiting a number of Aboriginal settlements, where they were 'well received', no doubt because of Emma's existing connections.

While the spread of the mission to the south took advantage of existing Aboriginal connections, its expansion into other areas created new links. Inland Sydney was outside of the affiliated coastal zone and, as previous chapters have shown, there was very little Aboriginal movement between this region and coastal Sydney throughout the 19th century. But as missionary activity began to link the two areas, connections were soon created; Charles Golden married into the Blacktown Road Lock family in 1899, Kate Foot's daughter Adelaide Foster married Sackville resident Wes Barber in 1906, and Ellen and Hugh Anderson's daughter Clara had gone to live in Sackville by 1907.[35] Further east–west connections also came about in this period as the newly founded Gully Mission at Katoomba in the Blue Mountains began to house both western Sydney Aboriginal families and coastally affiliated people from the Burragorang Valley.[36] The expansion of the La Perouse mission north to Bellbrook in the Macleay Valley also created new links between previously unconnected Aboriginal families. Emma Jane Foster, another of Kate Foot's daughters, moved there in the early 1900s and married a local man, before returning to Sydney.[37]

These new connections between coastal and inland Sydney Aboriginal people, forged around the turn of the century, created enduring familial links that over many generations have obscured their historical origins. Together with the relationships established at Maloga and Cumeragunja, these new links permanently diluted the influence of the affiliated coastal zone by creating alternate lines of connection and marriage that cut through, and beyond it. For most of the 19th century, it was more likely than not that an Aboriginal person living in a coastal Sydney settlement was linked to the area through the complex web of connections within the affiliated coastal zone. By the century's end that could no longer be assumed. Aboriginal people were entering Sydney in increasing numbers due to these newly created links, as were many others with no previous connections to the area.

4.6 *Above* Rushcutters Bay in the 1870s. The view is east along New South Head Road. The horse and cart are at the tollgates and the Aboriginal settlement was somewhere behind the stone cottage at centre left. *State Library of NSW*

4.7 *Below* The Sir Joseph Banks Hotel in the 1850s. *State Library of NSW*

5.1 *Right* William Warrell in 1844, when he was a familiar sight around Sydney town. *State Library of NSW*

5.2 *Below* Contrasting statues of William Warrell by Hogarth in the 1850s. An 1855 statue of the noble Warrell (left) and an 1850s inkstand showing Warrell huddled in his shelter (right). *Museum of Applied Arts and Sciences; Sydney Living Museums*

5.3 *Top* Cora Gooseberry's headstone at Sydney Burial Ground in 1900. The inscription shows that a 'Mrs Stewart' was responsible for the gravestone along with Edward Borton, but nothing further is known about her. The grave was removed shortly afterward to Pioneer Memorial Park at Botany to make way for Central Railway Station. *Royal Australian Historical Society*

5.4 *Above* William Warrell's profile on souvenir exhibition medallions in the 1870s. Left is the original Sydney template; middle and right show Warrell renamed as Billi *ex rex* Victoria and Sandy *ex rex* Queensland. *Paul Irish*

5.6 *Above* The Ethnological Court at the 1879 Sydney International Exhibition. The clutter of artefacts was incredible, and was clearly designed as a visual spectacle rather than an informative educational display. *State Library of NSW*

5.7 *Above* The *Fire King*, a typical steamer of the 1860s. The *Fire King* transported Aboriginal people from the Manning River to Sydney to perform for Prince Alfred in 1868. Another steamer of this period can be seen in Figure 5.5. *The Great Southern Card Publishers, Australia*

5.5 The Garden Palace behind Bennelong Point around 1880. View is south from north Sydney. The Garden Palace was located on the western edge of the Domain and towered over Sydney. It burnt to the ground in 1882, several years after the International Exhibition. *State Library of NSW*

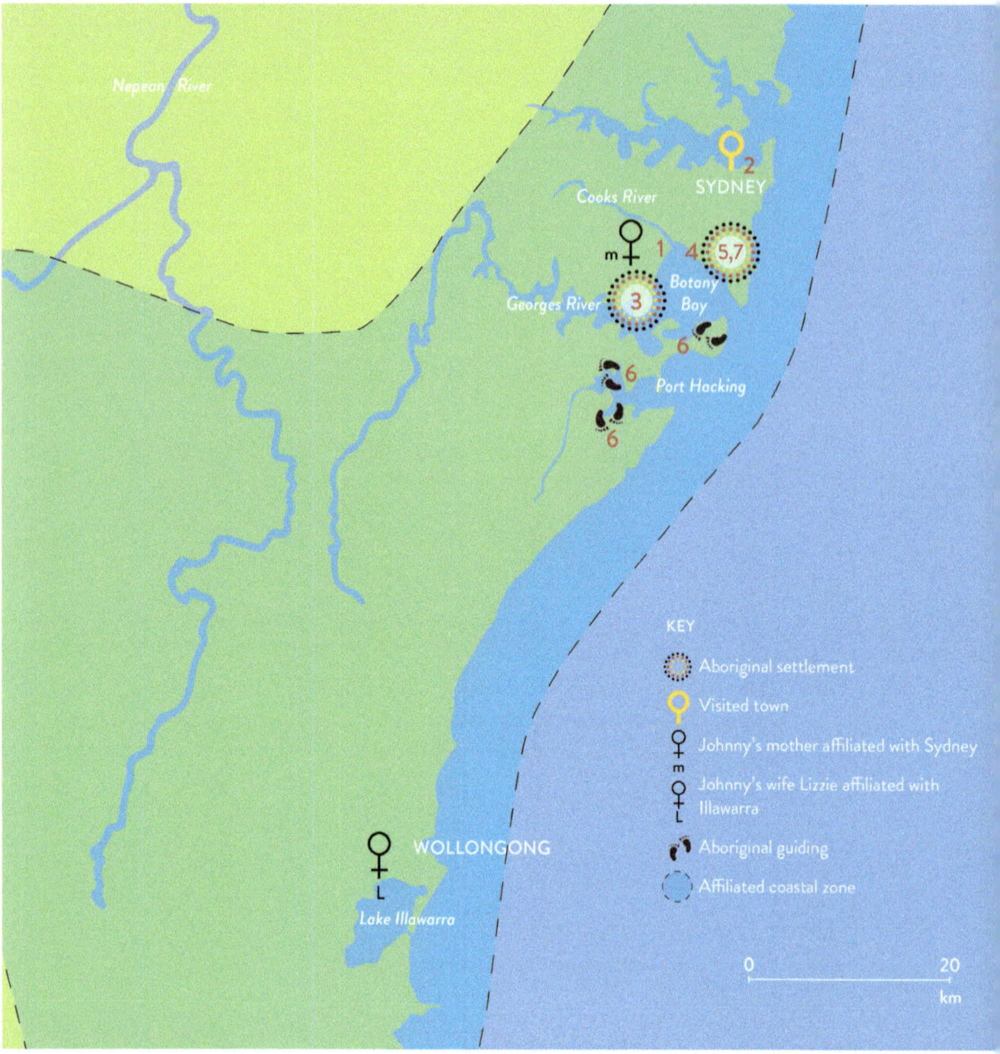

JOHNNY MALONE

1. **c.1820s:** Johnny born around Botany Bay
2. **1857:** Johnny and wife Lizzie receiving a blanket in Sydney
3. **1858:** Johnny visited at Sans Souci by his friend Edward Smith Hill and Austrian explorer Karl Scherzer
4. **1862:** Johnny's group running fishing and sightseeing tours out of the Sir Joseph Banks Hotel using Johnny's boat
5. **c.1867:** Johnny and Lizzie living in a hut at Botany when daughter Elizabeth born. Johnny working as a fisherman and guide
6. **1870s:** Johnny and other men working out of the Botany settlement as guides on fishing and hunting tours at Kurnell and south of the Hacking River
7. **c.1877:** Johnny and Lizzie separated by this time. Lizzie had son Charles to European fisherman Ned Golden

   1880s: Johnny likely to have died by this time. Wife Lizzie and children living at La Perouse

5.8 The recorded movements and connections of Johnny Malone (c.1820s–1880s). *Johnny Malone image – NSW National Parks and Wildlife Service Collection, Kurnell.* See Image References on pages 158–9 for all sources

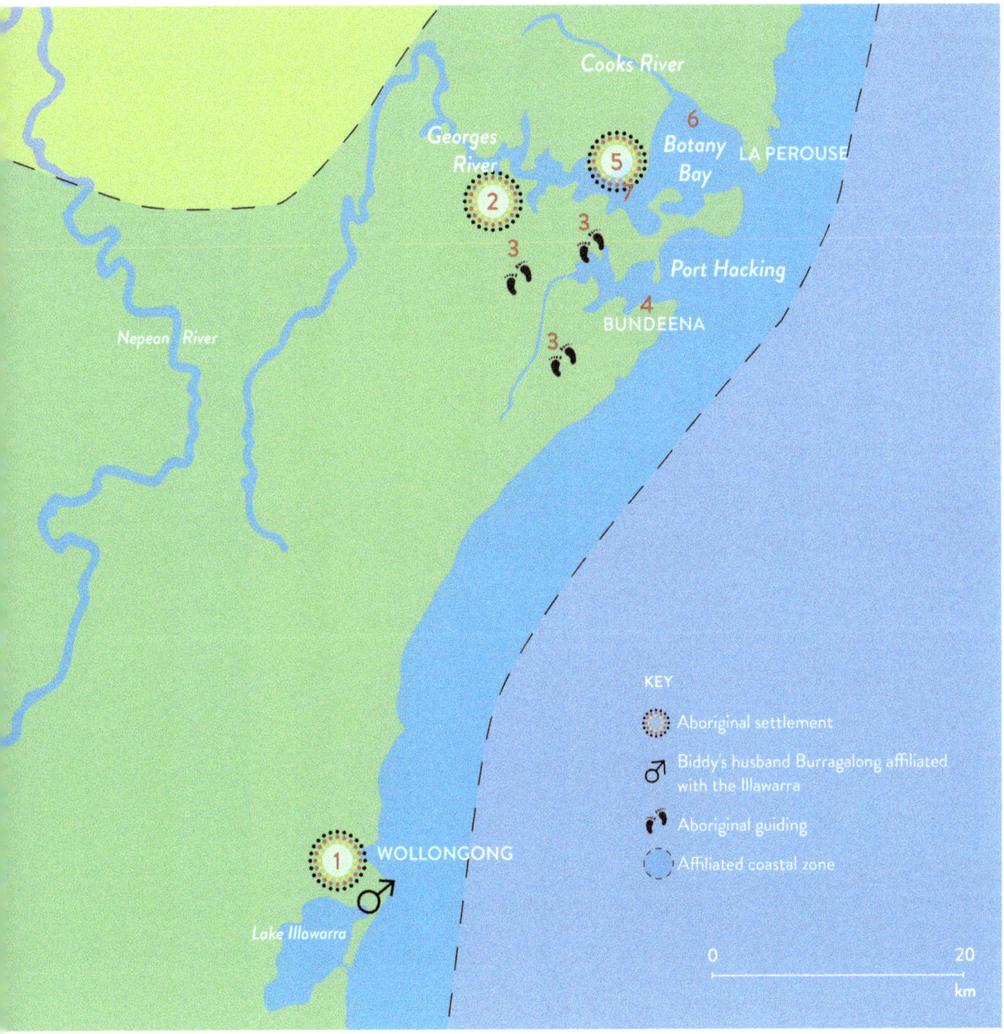

BIDDY GILES

Born c.1810

Aspects of Biddy's early life and relationships are unclear but all known possibilities are within the affiliated coastal zone.

1. **1850s**: living near Wollongong with Burragalong (Paddy Davis), where daughters Rosie and Ellen born
2. **c.1858**: living with Englishman Billy Giles on farm at Mill Creek off the Georges River
3. **1860s**: Biddy and Billy Giles running guided hunting and fishing tours around the Georges and Hacking Rivers
4. **1860s & 1870s**: Biddy sometimes employed at the Simpson Hotel at Bundeena to take visitors on tours of the river and nearby rock engravings
5. **1880s**: living at an Aboriginal settlement at Sans Souci with several other Aboriginal families
6. **1888**: among a number of people rescued from a capsized sailing boat in Botany Bay
7. **1888**: Biddy dies near Tom Ugly's Point

5.9   The recorded movements and connections of Biddy Giles (c.1810 – 1888). *Biddy Giles image – State Library of NSW. See Image References on pages 159–60 for all sources*

Bob Nichols (1809–1857) in 1856

George Hill (1802–1883)

Daniel Egan (1803–1870) in the late 1860s

George Thornton (1819–1901) around 1850

5.10 *Above* Key members of the Sydney Aborigines Committee in the 1850s and 1860s. *From left – Royal Australian Historical Society; City of Sydney Archives; National Archives of Australia; City of Sydney Archives*

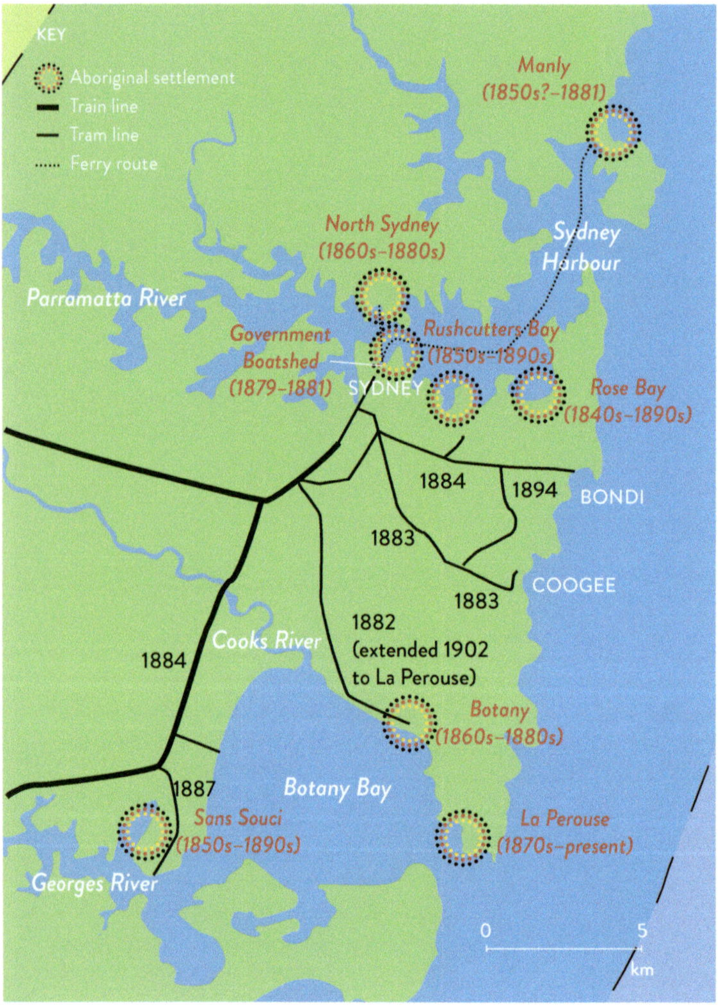

6.1 *Above* The main coastal Sydney Aboriginal settlements in the late 1870s and public transport lines opened over the following decade. Dates of opening are shown next to the line.

.2 La Perouse in 1878. The view is from the La Perouse headland north along Frenchman's Bay. The Aboriginal settlement was established at this time or shortly afterwards, perhaps slightly further north along the beach. *National Library of Australia*

.3 The Government Boatshed at Bennelong Point in the mid-1870s. The boatshed is shown in detail in the image to the right. To the immediate left (north) of the boatshed is one of the two enclosed Water Police sheds and its associated wharf. The image below shows the cluster of nearby buildings. The Sydney Rowing Club building is the furthest left (north), immediately in front of the outer walls and tower of Fort Macquarie. *State Library of NSW*

6.4 *Top* Bennelong Point in the early 1870s. View north along the eastern side of Circular Quay. The boatshed roof is indicated with the arrow, and the two-storey building at the rear is the Sydney Rowing Club. The wharf in the foreground is for the regular Milsons Point ferry to the North Shore. Note the cluttered nature of the buildings in this area, the muddy shore and lack of roadway. *State Library of NSW*

6.5 *Above* Passenger wharves at Circular Quay in the 1880s. View south to the wharves at the northern end of Phillip Street. This area was far busier than the Government Boatshed about 400 metres to the north. People apparently complained to the police about the presence of Aboriginal people from the boatshed settlement in this busy pedestrian area. *State Library of NSW*

6.6 The popular imagining of Aboriginal people in the city in 1880. We do not know how people of the time would have interpreted this image, but it is clear that the 'present' Aboriginal people were hardly an urban menace. *State Library of NSW*

6.7 Daniel Matthews (1837–1902) and George Thornton (1819–1901). Matthews is pictured in 1885, a few years after his visits to Sydney. Thornton is pictured in the 1890s, about a decade after his time as Protector of Aborigines. *State Library of South Australia; State Library of NSW*

6.8 *Above* Richard Hill in 1881. *State Library of NSW*

6.9 *Above* Richard Hill's house in Bent Street. Emma and George Timbery worked at the house, and it was also where Aboriginal people gathered in August 1881 before heading to Maloga Mission with Daniel Matthews. The photo was taken in the early 1900s when Hill's daughter still lived there. *State Library of NSW*

6.10 *Above* One of the original iron sheeting huts at La Perouse. By 1883 when this image was made, this hut appears to have also been used as a stable. Note the fishing boat in the foreground. *State Library of NSW*

Opposite page

7.1 *Mid left* Lizzie Golden (Malone) with her son Charles at La Perouse in 1900. *State Library of NSW*

7.2 *Mid right* The newly constructed mission church at La Perouse c.1894. Missionary Jean Watson is standing to the right of the window, in front of the rear door, among La Perouse residents. *Randwick & District Historical Society*

7.3 *Below left* Emma Timbery at La Perouse in the early 1900s. *Woollahra Council*

7.4 *Below right* The 1890s-era huts at La Perouse. The photo was taken in the early 1900s. *Woollahra Council*

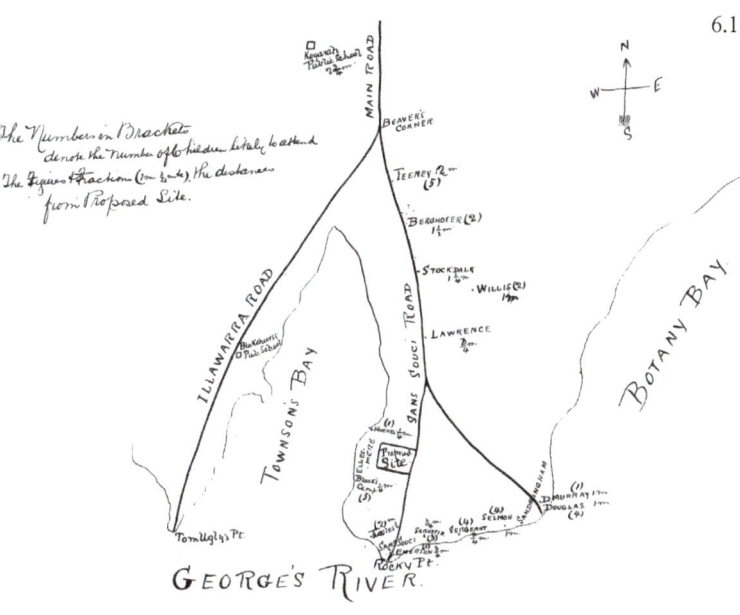

6.11 *Left* The Sans Souci settlement in 1884. The settlement was marked as a 'black's camp', with the number of children as part of a petition made by local residents for a school, which was soon built nearby. *State Archives NSW*

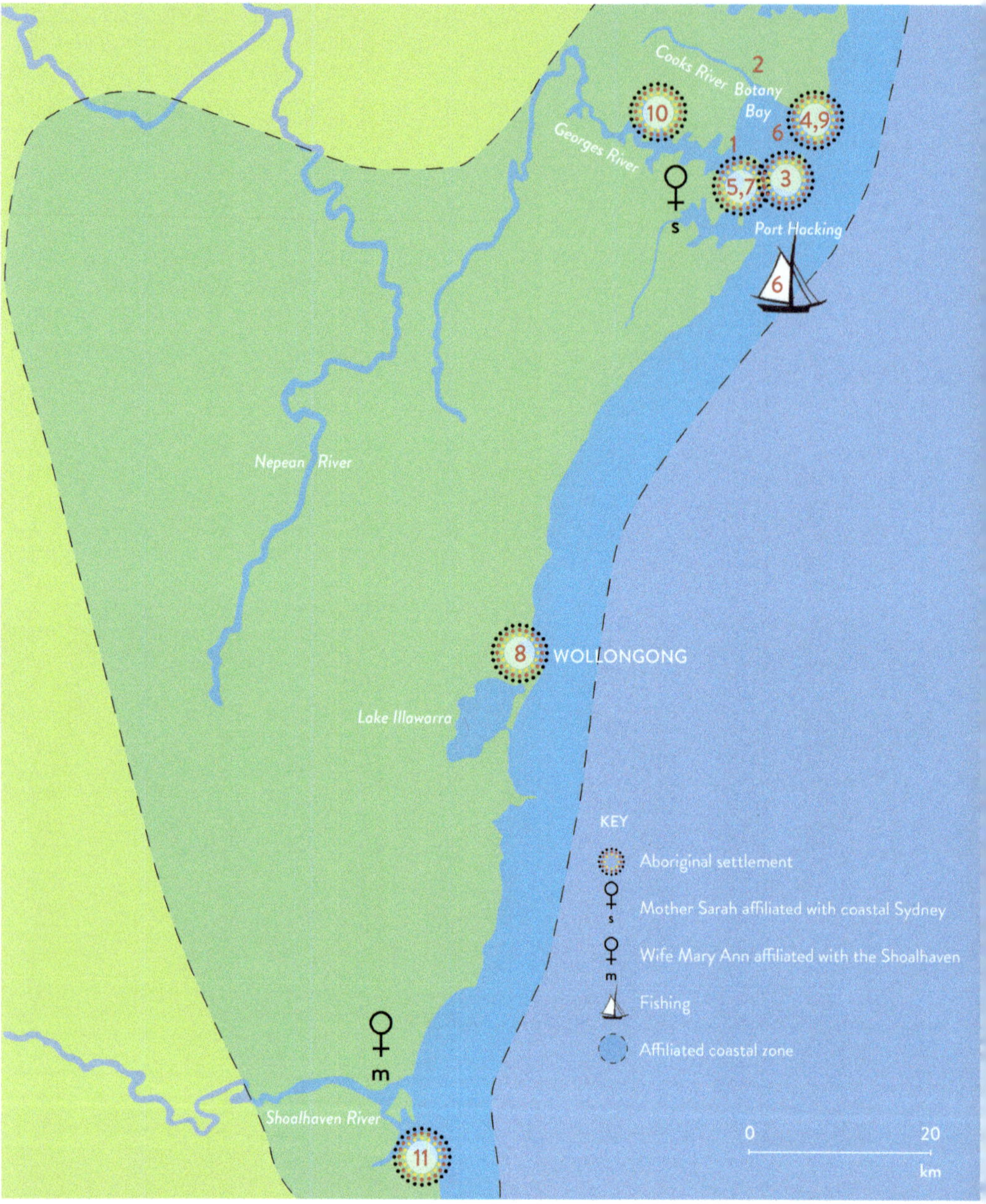

WILLIAM ROWLEY

William and Mary Ann Rowley

1. 1856: born at Pelican Point
2. 1857: baptised at St Peters
3. 1870s: at Kurnell with mother
4. 1883, 1885: living at La Perouse
5. 1891–1899: living at Weeney Bay, tending oysters
6. 1880s–1910s: fishing around Botany Bay and Port Hacking and selling catch at La Perouse
7. 1899: evicted by employer (Holt) from Weeney Bay
8. 1901: living at Port Kembla
9. 1905–1910s: living at La Perouse, marrying Mary Ann Steele in 1905
10. 1920s–1930s: living next to Andersons at Salt Pan Creek, buying land in 1927
11. 1937: moved to Roseby Park with Mary Ann, who died there the following year
    1941: died at Roseby Park Aboriginal station

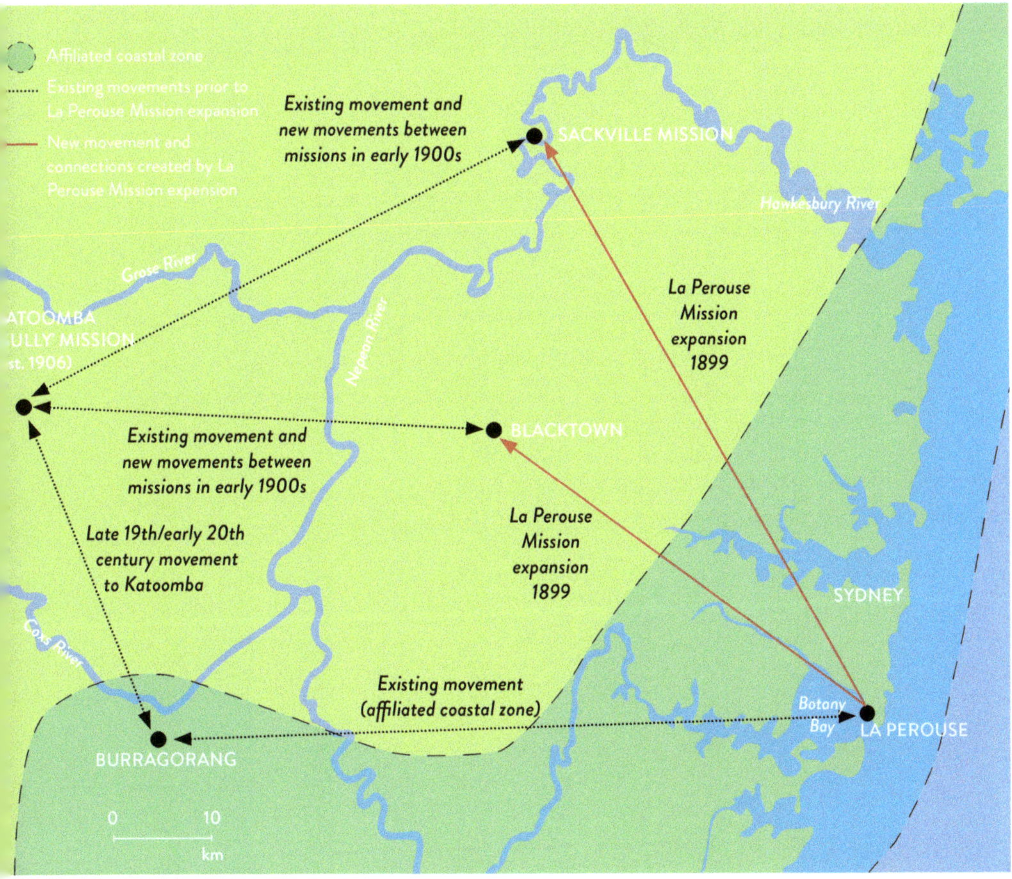

6 New links created by missionary activity in the late 19th century. The bottom map shows the connections created by the Aborigines Protection Association missions in western NSW and the La Perouse Mission. The top map shows how these moves connected coastal people and those from inland Sydney in the 1890s and early 1900s.

5 *Left* The recorded movements and connections of William Rowley (1856–1941). *William Rowley image – Randwick Social History Project.* See Image References on pages 161–2 for all sources

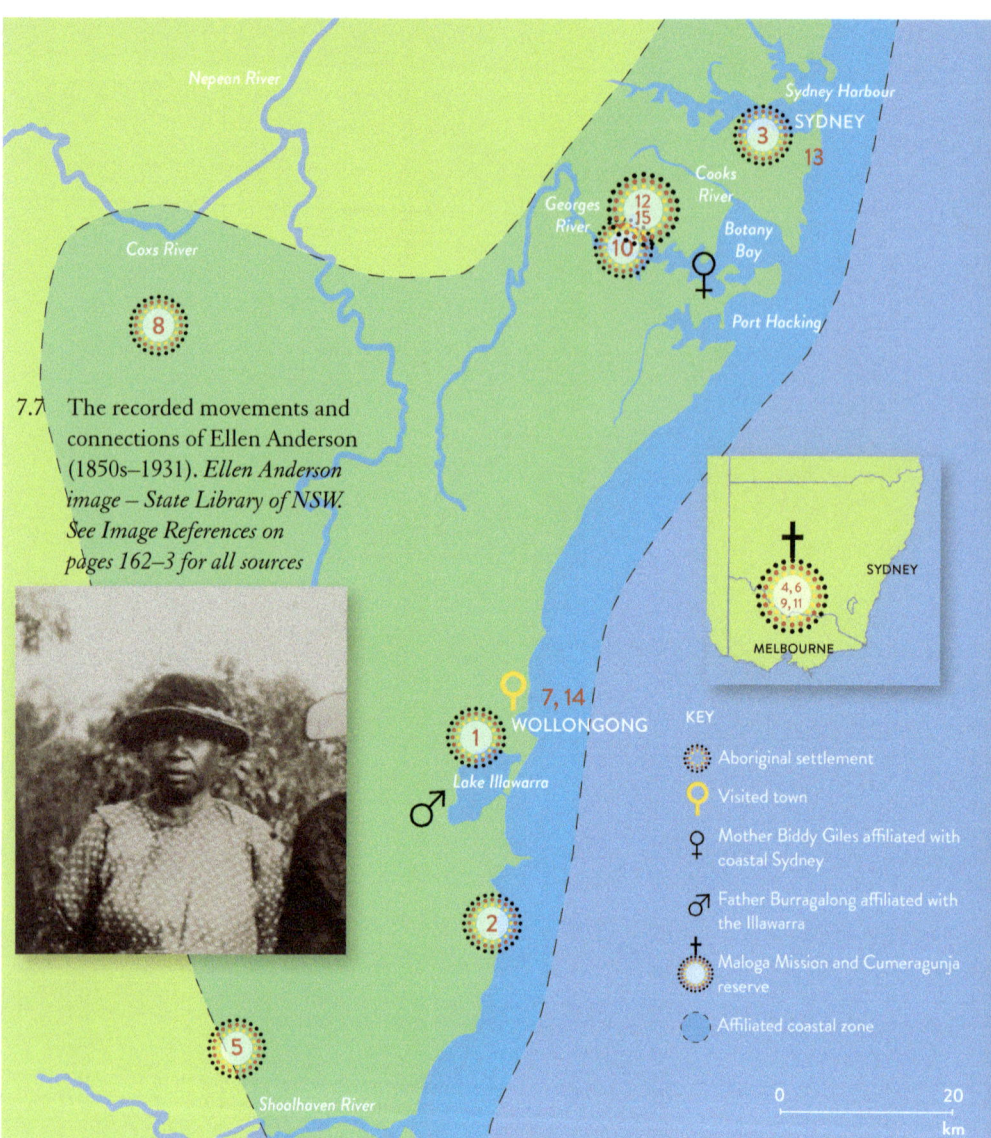

7.7 The recorded movements and connections of Ellen Anderson (1850s–1931). *Ellen Anderson image – State Library of NSW. See Image References on pages 162–3 for all sources*

KEY
- Aboriginal settlement
- Visited town
- ♀ Mother Biddy Giles affiliated with coastal Sydney
- ♂ Father Burragalong affiliated with the Illawarra
- ✝ Maloga Mission and Cumeragunja reserve
- Affiliated coastal zone

ELLEN ANDERSON

1. **1850s**: born at Unanderra near Lake Illawarra to Biddy Giles and Burragalong (Paddy Davis)
2. **c.1879**: birth of son Joseph at Kiama
3. **1881**: living at the Circular Quay boatshed settlement
4. **1881–1889**: living at Maloga Mission and raising family there with Hugh Anderson
5. **1889–1890**: Ellen, Hugh and others establish an Aboriginal settlement and school at Kangaroo Valley
6. **1890–1895**: living on the Cumeragunja Aboriginal reserve and the nearby Maloga Mission
7. **1896**: Ellen and Hugh travel to Wollongong to see sister Rosie and her husband, Mickey Johnson
8. **1890s**: The Andersons lived for a time on a farm in the Burragorang Valley
9. **1897–1900s**: Andersons return to Maloga and Cumeragunja
10. **1910s**: Ellen and Hugh set up camp on private land along Salt Pan Creek
11. **1917**: Visiting Cumeragunja for the birth of daughter Clara's son John
12. **1925**: Purchases block of land along Salt Pan Creek and lives next to Rowleys and with a number of other Aboriginal people
13. **1920s**: Visiting CW Peck at Bondi and allowing him to write down some of her traditional stories
14. **1928**: Visiting relatives at Wollongong
15. **1931**: Ellen dies at Salt Pan Creek and is buried nearby at Peakhurst. Hugh had died in 1928

New arrivals

Aboriginal people had been entering Sydney from beyond the affiliated coastal zone throughout the 19th century, as prisoners from the frontier and elsewhere, as the orphaned victims of frontier conflict, as servants or companions of European visitors and migrants, as pregnant women seeking assistance, as employees of far-flung estates, as entertainers, and for a range of other reasons. Until now I have referred to them only briefly, as most came for a reason and left again, or else entered prisons, hospitals, benevolent asylums, or domestic service. At any rate, few came to live with local Aboriginal people in their settlements. But from the 1880s the records of government, police and charities all chart a rising number of Aboriginal people arriving in Sydney without prior connections, many of whom appear to have stayed. They can broadly be divided into three groups: those who came for economic or social reasons, women and children who arrived in need of charity or medical assistance, and women who were forced to come to Sydney as domestic servants.

Some of those from the first group came to live in Aboriginal settlements around coastal Sydney, and came into contact with local people. Rail lines had expanded across the state in the 1870s and 1880s and the Aborigines Protection Board acknowledged that an unofficial policy of free rail travel was bringing Aboriginal people to Sydney from far-flung regions. In 1886 for example, around thirty men, women and children were living in tents and other shelters in largely uncleared bushland on the North Shore, across the harbour from the city. They included locally affiliated people from La Perouse and the south coast, as well as others from Wellington, Yass and Gundagai, hundreds of kilometres to the west.[38] They travelled regularly across the harbour to Sydney on the ferry and came to police attention because of the noise emanating from their settlement at night. These people came to Sydney because they could, rather than out of existing obligation or connection. Perhaps they chose the North Shore over other settlements because some of them may have stayed there before in the lead-up to the visit of Prince Alfred in 1868, or perhaps it just offered easy access to the city.

Another group of up to sixty Aboriginal people from Sydney and elsewhere set up camp within Moore Park to the east of Redfern in the early 1890s, near the current intersection of Anzac Parade and Cleveland Street.[39] Like the Domain and government boatshed settlements in previous decades, it was a staging post for visits into the city, and also allowed access to the nearby Carrington Ground, where some Aboriginal residents competed in track racing at this time. Track racing (then known as pedestrianism) was at its peak of popularity in the 1880s and early 1890s, and the Carrington Ground and Sir Joseph Banks Hotel (where Aboriginal people had formerly worked as guides) were the premier Sydney venues on the national circuit, drawing crowds of thousands to major events.[40] Aboriginal runners were among the best, and sometimes a dozen or more came from around the country to compete, staying in Aboriginal settlements, perhaps with an entourage of friends and family.[41] Some stayed in Sydney for a time, most notably national champion Charlie Samuels (1864–1912), who lived at La Perouse and the Moore Park settlement in the early 1890s.[42] When the Board tried to shut down both the Moore Park and North Shore settlements, it employed its usual method of bribing residents with free rail and steamer passage to 'their respective homes in the country'. It also increasingly restricted its approval of free rail tickets into Sydney from the 1890s, but Aboriginal people continued to come.[43]

Although Aboriginal runners and other visitors feature more prominently in historical documents, it was the less recorded women who arrived out of desperate need that ultimately had the most lasting demographic impact in coastal Sydney. We know of some of their stories from the records of the Benevolent Asylum, which had operated as a refuge in the south of the city since the 1810s, and by the 1860s was primarily a maternity hospital for married or single women in need.[44] Some women working as domestics in Sydney and elsewhere in the state became pregnant to men who subsequently absconded, and had to rely on the Benevolent Asylum in Sydney when they gave birth. Until the 1880s, there were one or two Aboriginal women giving birth at the asylum each year, but for reasons that are unclear, these numbers more than quadrupled from the 1880s. They were often sponsored by their employers, either out of genuine concern or to remove a 'problem', but not all would take their workers back afterwards, particularly with infants in tow. A typical example was Minnie, a teenager from the Mudgee area who was admitted to the asylum in 1897 in these circumstances. Unable to return home after having her baby, she was discharged into service in Sydney. She gave birth again the following year but lost the baby and had to return to service immediately. In 1900 she, with another infant, had to rely on the charity of the asylum when she was 'no longer required' by her employer.[45] The fate of her three-year-old was not recorded, but Minnie appears to have been effectively stranded in Sydney.

Many more Aboriginal women came to live in Sydney in the early 20th century, as the government intruded into their lives on an unprecedented scale. The 1909 *Aborigines Protection Act* gave the Aborigines Protection Board its first legal powers to directly control Aboriginal movement; these powers increased greatly with amendments in 1915, giving the Board legal guardianship (*in loco parentis*) over all Aboriginal children in the state. Aboriginal children were removed from their families in increasing numbers by people whom the Board grotesquely referred to as 'home-finders'.[46] They were sent to Aboriginal children's homes, where girls were trained for domestic service and boys for menial labouring jobs. After 1915, girls from the Cootamundra Girls Home were mainly sent to suburban Sydney as indentured servants to white families. Some were as young as twelve or thirteen and could be kept in service until they were twenty-one years of age. Their wages were paid into trust accounts, held by the Board, which many never received (an injustice that is only now beginning to be addressed). By the 1920s there were hundreds of Aboriginal girls and young women in domestic service across Sydney.[47] Those interviewed much later in life stressed how they were unable to go out or socialise, and were often completely cut off from their families and other Aboriginal people.[48] When they turned twenty-one and could no longer be prevented from leaving, many returned to their families, but some married and started families in Sydney, while others found themselves eking out an existence on the streets.[49]

By the 1920s the number of Aboriginal women, men and families living in coastal Sydney without prior connections outnumbered the hundred or so locally affiliated people. Their reasons for migrating to Sydney included those already discussed, but others were seeking respite from increasing government intervention. Whatever their motivations, Sydney offered the major drawcard of greater economic opportunity. The son of one family who moved to Redfern in the 1920s later stated that Aboriginal people came to Sydney 'because they want to enjoy life a bit, not just exist. They get a better income here, better food, better houses […] and learn a better way of life.'[50] As they lived outside of Board scrutiny and were therefore not always identified as Aboriginal people in official records, we know little of their lives. Researchers are beginning to piece the fragments together through family histories and innovative historical studies of previously ignored sources like prison photographs. These show that Aboriginal migrants were living in inner-city suburbs like Redfern, Balmain, Waterloo, Darlinghurst and Woolloomooloo. Though some had skilled occupations, most worked as labourers on the docks and in factories or as domestic servants, while others turned to crime to make ends meet. As historian Haidee Ireland has explored, their 'urban identities' were multifaceted, defined by their working-class conditions and poverty as well as by their Aboriginality. The affiliation of some of these people with the workers movement strongly influenced the development of Aboriginal political activism at this time, but domestically, the extensive kinship networks that now extended across the state drew more and more people to Sydney, forming the nucleus of Aboriginal communities in the inner suburbs.[51]

Urban Aboriginal Sydney

It took around 150 years from the devastation of the 1789 smallpox epidemic before the number of Aboriginal people living in coastal Sydney was again comparable to that before European arrival. The difference was that most of them were not ancestrally connected to the area, and they now lived among a settler population of well over one million.[52] In addition to the steady flow of indentured servants, economic migrants and others over several decades, an increasing number of Aboriginal people migrated into Sydney from the late 1920s due to the hardships of the Depression and the increasing closure of Aboriginal reserves by the Protection Board. Suburbs that had housed separate Aboriginal settlements of locally affiliated people half a century before now contained Aboriginal individuals and families in houses and flats.[53] Despite their varied origins and reasons for entering Sydney, by the 1930s a distinct community had formed around several streets within the suburb of Redfern. When Shirley 'Mum Shirl' Smith, later renowned as an Aboriginal social worker and activist, moved there from rural Cowra in the 1930s, she described it as a place where 'we all knew each other, and we had little to do with white people, except that we shopped at their shops, and always had to go to them for jobs and work, but mostly we seemed to be with each other'.[54] The pull of Redfern as a place to find work, family and a sense of belonging saw the Aboriginal community of Redfern and surrounding suburbs continue to grow from that time on.

The La Perouse mission exerted a similar pull, but this was more through extended family connections that traced back to the affiliated coastal zone. The children and grandchildren of Kate Foot, George and Emma Timbery, John and Lizzie Malone and others had married within and beyond the affiliated coastal zone, but still retained a strong bond with La Perouse. As anthropologists in the 1950s found, most families at La Perouse were connected to one another through their forebears, and those connections were still primarily oriented along the coastal zone to the south of Sydney.[55] While movement across this area continued, life at La Perouse was strictly controlled by the mission manager. Resident Iris (Boronia) Williams later recalled that 'the manager's role was to keep us in our place and tell us what we could do and what we couldn't do. We were just treated like children. There was a fence around us, built right around the reserve.'[56]

Beyond the La Perouse Mission fence, Aboriginal and non-Aboriginal people suffering hardship during the Depression established several shanty towns from the late 1920s onwards. Some Aboriginal people came into the mission itself, having been evicted when their reserve, in the Burragorang Valley on the edge of the affiliated coastal zone to the south-west of Sydney, closed.[57] Others chose not to subject themselves to the control of the Board and mission manager at La Perouse, but moved instead to an autonomous Aboriginal settlement established off the Georges River at Salt Pan Creek by locally connected families. In the 1910s Ellen and Hugh Anderson returned with their family to Sydney from Cumeragunja on the Murray River and began living on part of a 165-acre estate along the eastern bank of Salt Pan Creek at Peakhurst, off the Georges River, where they were later joined by the Rowley family and others. In uncertain times, and as the estate's owners began to sell it off into smaller lots, the Andersons and Rowleys secured their future by purchasing two adjacent blocks of land in the mid-1920s.[58]

The settlement strongly resembled those of the 19th century; several families lived near the water, fishing and collecting other wild foods for consumption and sale and working in local industry, while the children attended the local school. It was a beacon of Aboriginal independence, but as had occurred in the previous century, residents engaged directly with their European neighbours, forming close friendships with some local families such as the Webbs and Hannons.[59] When Ellen was forced to sell her block in 1930, perhaps because she could not support the family in the depths of the Depression and after Hugh's death several years before, her son Joe's friend John Hannon purchased it. Hannon allowed the Aboriginal settlement to remain, despite a campaign by some other Europeans to move them away.[60]

Despite their varied origins, in the 1930s the three main centres of Aboriginal settlement in coastal Sydney at La Perouse, Salt Pan Creek and Redfern were linked by the political struggle for Aboriginal civil rights. Activist Fred Maynard's short-lived Australian Aboriginal Progressive Association had lit the fuse in the 1920s; it had formed with the support of sympathetic non-Aboriginal individuals and political groups in reaction to the Board's increasingly harsh regime. People affiliated with the Association passed through the Salt Pan Creek settlement, where political discussions around the campfire were a part of daily life.[61] Many residents and visitors had a shared history of speaking out that traced back to Maloga and Cumeragunja, but for local people it was heightened by their ancestral affiliations to coastal Sydney. Ellen Anderson's sons loudly proclaimed their rights to reside and travel across their areas of affiliation, and Joe in particular actively campaigned for Aboriginal representation in federal parliament.[62]

In 1937 the Aborigines Progressive Association was formed by Bill Ferguson in western New South Wales and quickly gained support in Sydney among Aboriginal people at La Perouse, Salt Pan Creek and the inner city. The Association's inspired and best-known action was to stage an Aboriginal 'Day of Mourning' conference and protest in the heart of the city on 26 January 1938, openly opposing celebrations for the 150th anniversary of the arrival of Europeans in Sydney. Aboriginal people with coastal Sydney ancestry were among the hundred or so who attended the Day of Mourning, and some became actively involved in the Association. Its executive committee included Kate Foot's son Tom Foster (1889–1941) and her nephew Wesley Simms (c.1900–1942) as well as Emma and George Timbery's son Joseph (1876–1952).[63]

Locally affiliated people shared the same grievances as other Aboriginal people, but also had a unique personal connection to the origins of government and religious intervention that the Association was campaigning to end. Their parents and grandparents had lived in the era of relatively independent living in coastal Sydney, enabled by their entanglement with sympathetic Europeans and the city's economy. They themselves had grown up at the end of this period, and had experienced its possibilities again at the Salt Pan Creek settlement in the 1920s and 1930s. When Tom Foster spoke out at the Day of Mourning conference against the 'callous treatment' of the Board and 'the white missionary', he did so in the knowledge that his mother, Kate, had been living at the Circular Quay boatshed half a century before when his older brother Joseph's death by drowning had precipitated the start of Aboriginal 'protection' in New South Wales; he had personally witnessed the expansion of the New South Wales Aborigines Mission movement from its birthplace at La Perouse at the turn of the century; and he had seen the dislocations both of these interventions had caused.[64]

Despite the best efforts of Tom and others, the Day of Mourning and the subsequent actions of the Aborigines Progressive Association had little immediate effect. The Salt Pan Creek settlement was closed down the following year, after a sustained campaign from neighbouring residents.[65] The segregationist Protection Board was disbanded soon after and replaced by the assimilationist Aborigines Welfare Board, but the high level of government control over Aboriginal lives continued. In the longer term, though, the Aborigines Progressive Association created a slow-burning momentum that culminated several decades later in the breakthrough civil rights gains of the 1960s and 1970s. This in turn led to Aboriginal people gaining ownership of land at Redfern (the area known as 'The Block') and at La Perouse.

TOGETHER, LA PEROUSE AND REDFERN HAVE BECOME THE URBAN Aboriginal face of coastal Sydney. They have discrete origins, but are linked by intermarriage and half a century of Aboriginal activism.

They are also now linked to virtually every Aboriginal community across the country, and new arrivals are constantly being drawn along these threads of connection. We should celebrate this diversity, this survival, and we should be eager to hear the compelling stories they have brought with them, as well as the new chapters that they have added in Sydney. At the same time, we should be careful not to let these stories drown out the voices of those whose links to coastal Sydney extend back hundreds of generations; whose ancestors met the first Europeans, and who found a way to create an ongoing place for themselves in the oldest and largest city in the country. Theirs is a remarkable story of survival through cultural strength and cross-cultural entanglement that sits in stark contrast to commonly held views of colonial and Aboriginal Australia, and to the experiences of most Australians today. I hope that the history sketched out in this book encourages more interest in Sydney's Aboriginal history, but I also hope it gives pause for thought about what can be achieved when neighbours engage with each other and work things out.

EPILOGUE

In plain view

The history in this book remained hidden for a long time because of a widespread assumption that locally affiliated Aboriginal people had either ceased to live in coastal Sydney by the mid-19th century, or had ceased to be authentically Aboriginal. We now know that Aboriginal people with local connections have been present throughout the entire European history of coastal Sydney. They were never absent. This is historical fact, not political or symbolic assertion. The tired idea that Aboriginal people disappeared can clearly be put to rest. The basic sequence of white replacing black, historically and physically, is a simplification that needs to be challenged if we want to understand what colonial cities like Sydney truly represent. Between the appropriation of Aboriginal land by Europeans in the late 18th century and the government-administered segregation of Aboriginal people in the early 20th century lies a period of cross-cultural interconnection that deserves greater recognition.

As the reality of Sydney's entangled 19th century becomes better defined, we can start thinking about the other misinterpretations that have arisen because Aboriginal people were assumed to be absent. Key among these is the way that we interpret the physical evidence of Sydney's past. As with its history, Sydney's heritage has long been understood as having two layers – a pre-colonial Aboriginal layer of engravings, middens, stone artefacts and rock shelters, and a colonial layer of European buildings, roads and other structures. If we inject the cross-cultural interactions of the 19th century into this neat division, things get more complex, but also more in line with reality.

A number of buildings around Sydney are known as 'historic houses' for their European associations, but the name is even more apt when we realise that they are sites of cross-cultural entanglement. They have what archaeologist Philip Jones has called 'a double patina [...] of ochre and rust'.[1] In addition, there are many other places where built reminders of the Aboriginal past may not survive, but which can still be recognised for their historical associations. On virtually every trip you take around coastal Sydney, you will pass places that Aboriginal people continued to use during the 19th century. As you drive past the neatly mown Rushcutters Bay Park, imagine the ceremonies and campfires that travellers saw in the 19th century; swimming at Bondi Beach, think of Johnny Baswick and Rachael fishing there in the 1870s, or at Double Bay's Redleaf Pool and Seven Shillings Beach picture Gurrah and Nancy sitting on the same beach a century and a half ago.

Before we go any further with this idea, I want to make clear that I do not wish to replace the erroneous idea of Aboriginal absence with the equally misleading generalisation that Aboriginal people were everywhere, all of the time. Most Sydneysiders did not actively assist Aboriginal people and some were openly hostile. Consequently, Aboriginal people had a tough existence in coastal Sydney and could only cultivate friendships with those who were willing to reciprocate. The places associated with the history outlined in this book do not form one single landscape; rather they can more accurately be divided into a number of layers, each representing the particular patchwork of friendly niches available to Aboriginal people at different points throughout the 19th century. It follows that not all places of European history and heritage have evidence of Aboriginal associations. But if we tune our eyes to distinguish between those that do and don't, we can begin to recognise something of how Aboriginal people lived around coastal Sydney, and how this changed over time. Knowing about the history of different places helps to connect the past and the present. It is what urban historian and architect Dolores Hayden calls 'the power of place'; the ability of historical locations to foster public memory of the ochres, rusts and other patinas of their pasts.[2] By taking a look at just a few of the places that have featured in this book, we can see this power of place.

Vaucluse House, in the city's eastern suburbs, is a 'living museum' that preserves the main house and some of the grounds of the original Vaucluse Estate, primarily associated with the Wentworth family for most of the 19th century. It appears to be European space, but as we have seen, Aboriginal people lived on parts of the estate at times, they visited the house to sell goods, and local man Bobby trod the halls as servant to the Wentworths in the 1860s. Visiting Aboriginal people camped in the back paddock throughout the 19th century, and the house is overlooked by several rock engravings that indicate a much longer history of use.[3] More of the original estate is preserved in nearby Nielsen Park, which includes sandstone overhangs filled with the remains of more than a thousand years of Aboriginal meals of fish and shellfish.[4] Nielsen Park also contains Greycliffe House, the former residence of Aboriginal sympathiser Richard Hill, which was frequented by local Aboriginal people in the mid-19th century. Once these overlapping associations are made clear, it becomes impossible to maintain the fiction of a neat succession from 'Aboriginal' to 'European' history.

Nor did the entanglements at Vaucluse cease when the estate was subdivided in the early 20th century. After Richard Hill's death in 1895, his son George carried on the family's tradition of assisting local Aboriginal people by distributing supplies to the La Perouse mission and hosting Aboriginal people at his Coogee residence.[5] His own son George continued to visit La Perouse well into the 20th century.[6] Other cross-cultural relationships lasted even longer. In the 1960s Billy Wentworth, the great-great-grandson of William Charles Wentworth, still lived at Vaucluse (though not at Vaucluse House). His keen interest in Aboriginal people saw him become Minister in Charge of Aboriginal Affairs in the Gorton government from 1968 to 1971. During that time he opened his Vaucluse residence to La Perouse man and Aboriginal rights advocate Tom

Williams OBE and his wife, Iris, for fundraising functions.[7] By that stage, the cross-cultural relationship involving the Wentworths had lasted for more than a century and a half and had encompassed six generations. Some of the descendants of Billy Wentworth and of Tom and Iris Williams still live in coastal Sydney today and are aware of this history.

Further south at Botany Bay, the Sir Joseph Banks Hotel and pleasure grounds survive as converted apartments and a public park, now cut off from the bay by extensive reclamation works. The hotel complex is commemorated as European historical space, but it is a deeply entangled place. From its earliest days in the 1840s, Botany Bay man Mahroot acted as a tour guide and boatman for hotel patrons, a role Johnny Malone and his 'tribe' reprised in the 1860s. Local settlers maintained an Aboriginal cemetery within the hotel grounds that included the burials of Wingle, Mahroot, and possibly Mahroot's wife. These unmarked graves may still be present. In the 1880s, the hotel remodelled itself as a key venue in the popular foot racing ('pedestrianism') circuit, and race meets featured both Aboriginal runners and spectators. The site is preserved for its prominent role in the 19th-century leisure industry in Sydney, and throughout that time, Aboriginal people were part of its economic life. The Aboriginal economic entanglement with the Sir Joseph Banks Hotel also forms an important part of the back story to the enduring La Perouse Aboriginal settlement down the road.

Moving south again, we cross the bay to the so-called 'Birthplace of Modern Australia'; the site of Cook's landing in 1770, now within Kamay Botany Bay National Park at Kurnell.[8] Local Aboriginal people recognise Kurnell for its rich ancestral heritage as well as for symbolising Aboriginal dispossession, but for the past two centuries it has been managed and celebrated as European ground; a landscape literally dotted with monuments to every aspect of Cook's brief eight-day visit, and trees planted to commemorate numerous visiting dignitaries in the period since.[9] When Cook's Landing Place was recently renamed the Kurnell Meeting Place, the move was criticised by some as 'politically correct', but is in fact an appropriate description, given its entangled history.[10]

Under the mown grass of the foreshore lies an enormous Aboriginal campsite where generations of Aboriginal people cooked their catch from the bay, made fish hooks and other tools, and buried their dead.[11] As we have seen, Aboriginal people continued to live in the area alongside European families in the early to mid-19th century; minding their children, fishing the bay and leading hunting parties into the scrub. In the late 19th century, Aboriginal people were still coming to Kurnell to fish, and in the early 20th century, they crossed the bay from the La Perouse mission to gather shells and mangrove wood. These were fashioned into artefacts to sell to tourists near the mission.[12] Even the placement of some of the monuments to the brief visit of Cook's *Endeavour* in 1770 was guided by Aboriginal advice – they were after all the only eyewitnesses in Sydney to these events.[13] The footings of these monuments often dug into the remains of the ancient Aboriginal campsite below. Even in this most 'European' place, it seems that separating Aboriginal and European histories is an artificial exercise. As an example of the entangled nature of coastal Sydney, the Kurnell Meeting Place is indeed a historic site.

If we consider prominent places like Vaucluse House, the Sir Joseph Banks Hotel, and the Kurnell Meeting Place, we can clearly see that Sydney's Aboriginal history has never actually been hidden. Like many aspects of the past, it has been ignored and overlooked, but it has always been there. Just as the longstanding stigma surrounding convict origins saw this important aspect of Australia's history ignored and misunderstood for many years, there has been a structural forgetting of the histories and connections of Aboriginal people, particularly in densely populated colonial spaces like cities.[14] With persistence, these can be overcome. As in Sydney, there is a growing body of historical research in other Australian cities that explores how Aboriginal people attempted to remain in urban space.[15] These histories vary according to the particular ways in which each city developed, but in all cases patient research is revealing the rich, personal detail of Aboriginal connections, and the entangled nature of urban space.

The artificial divide between 'Aboriginal' and 'European' history has been torn down in academic circles, and with time will gain broader public acceptance. The sheer weight of evidence, and its increasing inclusion in published histories, makes this inevitable. Sydney is dotted with places that together represent the diverse experiences of Aboriginal people throughout the 19th century. Each place could reveal many more stories, and there are no doubt further places yet to be discovered, but it is my hope that this book provides an overall narrative that will help to make sense of them.

The future of the entangled past looks secure. Understanding the many layers of significance historic sites carry is the basic heritage principle that underpins how owners and managers look after them.[16] As long as places of Aboriginal history are preserved and remembered in this way, as long as ongoing Aboriginal attachments are acknowledged, and as long as Aboriginal people are involved in determining how this occurs, the entangled 19th century will never be overlooked. Iconic places like the Sydney Opera House could serve to remind millions of local and overseas visitors each year of this story. As they walk towards the glistening sails, they could be reminded of the government boatshed, the Aboriginal people who used it, the terrible legacy of government intervention that it spawned, and the perseverance of Aboriginal people to have lived through it. The descendants of some boatshed residents still live in coastal Sydney. They know and value that history. For them, and hopefully for an increasing number of others, history will continue to live in the landscape, in plain view for all who care to look.

Further reading

There are many good sources of information about Aboriginal history and culture. Those below provide further context to this book, and mostly concern the Sydney area, though they will also help point out where to find information about other places and topics.

For the most comprehensive account of pre-European Aboriginal life in Sydney see:

> Val Attenbrow, *Sydney's Aboriginal Past: Investigating the archaeological and historical records*, 2nd edn, UNSW Press, Sydney, 2010.

For Aboriginal places to visit in Sydney see:

> City of Sydney, *Barani Barrabugu: Yesterday Tomorrow: Sydney's Aboriginal Journey*, City of Sydney, Sydney, 2011.
> Melinda Hinkson, *Aboriginal Sydney: A Guide to Important Places of the Past and Present*, 2nd edn, Aboriginal Studies Press, Canberra, 2010.
> See also the 'Sites to Visit' section of Attenbrow's *Sydney's Aboriginal Past*.

For Aboriginal people and places in early colonial Sydney see:

> Grace Karskens, *The Colony: A History of Early Sydney*, Allen & Unwin, Sydney, 2009.
> <www.sydneybarani.com.au>

Further reading

For Aboriginal people in particular parts of coastal Sydney see:

Heather Goodall and Allison Cadzow, *Rivers and Resilience: Aboriginal People on Sydney's Georges River*, UNSW Press, Sydney, 2009.

Individual Heritage Group, *La Perouse: The place, the people and the sea: A collection of writing by members of the Aboriginal community*, Aboriginal Studies Press, Canberra, 1988.

Maria Nugent, *Botany Bay: Where histories meet*, Allen & Unwin, Sydney, 2005.

For the broader history of government and Aboriginal interactions in NSW see:

Anna Doukakis, *The Aboriginal People, Parliament & 'Protection' in New South Wales 1856–1916*, Federation Press, Sydney, 2006.

Richard Egan, *Neither amity nor kindness: government policy towards Aboriginal people of NSW 1788 to 1969*, Richard Egan Publishing, Sydney, 2012.

Heather Goodall, *Invasion to Embassy: Land in Aboriginal Politics in New South Wales, 1770–1972*, Allen & Unwin in association with Black Books, Sydney, 1996.

Image references

Figure number	Map point	Source
Front Cover		GE Peacock, 1847, *Port Jackson N.S.W. View in Double Bay S. Side Middle Head in the distance (near sunset)*, SLNSW, DG 37.
Figure 1.1		All objects from the collections of the Australian Museum. Top row – V Attenbrow, *Sydney's Aboriginal Past: Investigating the archaeological and historical records*, 2nd edn, UNSW Press, Sydney, 2010, Plate 19; middle left – Manly hatchet #iE086449+03; middle right – Kurnell fish hooks #iNP01059-42, #iNP01059-50 & #iNP01059-53; bottom left – Kurnell bone points #iNP01059-13+02, # iNP01059-17+01 & # iNP01059-25+02; bottom right – Kurnell shell scraper #iNP01059-01.
Figure 1.2	Image of Bennelong	Port Jackson Painter, c.1791, *Native name Ben-nel-long, as painted when angry after Botany Bay Colebee was wounded*, © The Trustees of the Natural History Museum, London, Watling Drawing No. 41.
	1	KV Smith, 'Bennelong among his people', *Aboriginal History* vol. 33, 2009, p. 7.
	2	Smith 2009, pp. 11–12.
	3	Smith 2009, p. 17.
	4	G Karskens, *The Colony: A History of Early Sydney*, Allen & Unwin, Sydney, 2009, pp. 383–5.
	5	Smith 2009, p. 17.
	6	Karskens 2009, pp. 389–90.
	7	Karskens 2009, p. 421.
	8	D Collins, *An Account of the English Colony in New South Wales: Volume 1*, ed. Fletcher, B, London, Cadell and Davies [AH & AW Reed, in association with the Royal Australian Historical Society, Sydney] 1798 [1975], pp. 439–40.
	9	Karskens 2009, pp. 380–423.
	10	Smith 2009, p. 19.
	11	Smith 2009, pp. 20–23.
	12	'Natives', *Sydney Gazette*, 17/3/1805, p. 3.
	13 & burial	Smith 2009, p. 21.
	Father's affiliation	Smith 2009, p. 10.
	Barangaroo's affiliation	Smith 2009, pp. 16–17.
	Goroobooroballo's association	Smith 2009, p. 17.

Image references

Figure number	Map point	Source
Figure 1.2	Boorong's affiliation	J Hunter, *An Historical Journal of the Transactions at Port Jackson and Norfolk Island*, ed. Bach, J, J Stockdale, London [Australian Facsimile Editions No. 148, Libraries Board of South Australia, Adelaide], 1973 [1968], p. 468. Extract of original image.
Figure 1.3	Image of Mahroot	Pavel Mikhailov, 1820, *Movat & Salamander*, © State Russian Museum, St Petersburg, Inv # P-29209.
	1	Testimony of Mahroot, in NSW Legislative Council, *Report from the Select Committee on the Condition of the Aborigines, with appendix, minutes of evidence and replies to a circular letter*, Government Printer, Sydney, 1845, p. 1 [question 1].
	2	BB Carter, *Journal on Anne and Hope 1798–1799*, SLNSW, MSS PMB769, frames 81–82.
	3	KV Smith, *Mari Nawi ('Big Canoes'): Aboriginal voyagers in Australia's maritime history, 1788–1855*, PhD thesis, Macquarie University, 2008, pp. 112–15.
	4	Testimony of Mahroot, 1845, p. 2 [questions 63–64].
	5	O West, 'Old and New Sydney: To the Editor of the *Herald*', *SMH*, 24/5/1882, p. 3.
	6	Smith 2008, p. 134.
	7	R Bourke, 'Governor's Minute no 1839 [re. Bosun Maroot] 17 April 1832', *Records of Boatswain Maroot, 1832–1851*, SANSW, NRS907, CSLIL [2/7914]; 'Testimony of Mahroot', 1845, pp. 3–4 [questions 116–132].
	8	'Governor's Memorandum 2 May 1832', 'Memorandum c.1834', *Records of Boatswain Maroot, 1832–1851*, SANSW, NRS907, CSLIL [2/7914].
	9 & 10	'Memorial of Maria Maroot 1/6/1837', *Records of Boatswain Maroot, 1832–1851*, SANSW, NRS907, CSLIL [2/7914].
	11	'Aboriginal Christmas Festivities', *The Australian*, 27/12/1844, p. 3.
	12	Testimony of Mahroot, 1845.
	13	'The Queen's Birthday', *SMH*, 26/5/1849, p. 2.
	14	'The Ring. Full Account of the Great Fight between Perry, the Black and George Hough', *Bell's Life in Sydney and Sporting Reviewer*, 13/10/1849, p. 2; 'Botany Bay', *SMH*, 28/1/1861, p. 5.
	15	GC Mundy, *Our antipodes, or, Residence and rambles in the Australasian colonies: with a glimpse of the gold fields*, vol. 1., Richard Bentley, London, 1852, p. 393.
	16	'Died', *SMH*, 2/2/1850, p. 5.
	Burial of Mahroot's father	R Hill & G Thornton, *Notes on the Aborigines of New South Wales: with personal reminiscences of the tribes formerly living in the neighbourhood of Sydney and the surrounding districts*, Government Printer, Sydney, 1892, p. 7.

Figure number	Map point	Source
Figure 1.3	Burial of Mahroot	E Knapp, 'Letter from E. Knapp, 30/9/1868', *Letters received, Miscellaneous Branch, Department of Lands*, SANSW, NRS8258, 68/4452 [2/1045]. Mahroot's wife was not definitely buried at the hotel but this appears likely as Mahroot tended her grave and was buried at the hotel; JP Townsend, *Rambles and Observations in New South Wales*, Chapman and Hall, London, 1849, p. 120.
	Mother's affiliation	Based on Mahroot's birth at the Cooks River and his mother's recorded movements with Mahroot's father around Botany Bay.
	Father's affiliation	Mahroot is described as the son of a 'chief' and as having an affiliation to Botany Bay, and his father Mahroot the Elder lived around Botany Bay; WA Miles, 'How did the natives of Australia become acquainted with the demigods and daemonia, and with the superstitions of the ancient races? And how have many oriental words been incorporated in their dialects and languages?', *Journal of the Ethnological Society of London*, vol. 3, 1854, pp. 4–5; Carter 1798–1799, frames 81–82.
Figure 1.4	Image of Tamara	GF Angas, 1845, *Old King Tamara: The Last of the Sydney Tribe. Aug. 15, 1845*, Angas Collection, South Australian Museum, Image AA8/4/2/3.
	1	O West, 'Old and New Sydney: To the Editor of the *Herald*', *SMH*, 24/5/1882, p. 3.
	2	'Baptism certificate of Gertrude 15/11/1827', NSW BDM Vol. 128 #924; 'Ordered 830, 28/4/1828', SANSW, NRS905, CSLR, 29/7059 [4/2045].
	3	'Ordered 830, 28/4/1828', SANSW, NRS905, CSLR, 29/7059 [4/2045].
	4	Based on receiving blankets in Sydney and the Illawarra.
	5	'List of Native Blacks who assembled at Wollongong, Illawarra on May 7th 1830', SANSW, NRS905, CSLR, 30/3673 with 29/7059 [4/2045].
	6	'Return of Aboriginal Natives, Taken at Parramatta, May 1836', SANSW, NRS905, CSLR, 36/6546 [4/2219.1].
	7	'Return of Aboriginal Natives, Taken at Sydney, 1836', SANSW, NRS905, CSLR [4/2302.1].
	8	M Organ (ed.), *Illawarra and South Coast Aborigines 1770–1850*, Aboriginal Education Unit, University of Wollongong, Wollongong, 1990, pp. 199–200.
	9	*Proclamation of Queen Victoria in N.S.W. 27 October 1837*; signed by Governor Bourke, members of the Executive Council, magistrates, clergy etc, SLNSW, MSS DLADD270.
	10	Organ 1990, pp. 223–5.
	11	Organ 1990, pp. 272–273.
	12	H Laracy, 'Leopold Verguet and the Aborigines of Sydney, 1845', *Aboriginal History*, vol. 4, no. 2, 1980, pp. 178–83.

Image references

Figure number	Map point	Source
Figure 1.4	13 & 14	'Aborigines', *SMH*, 20/4/1846, 2. Tamara is not specifically mentioned, but the fishing party included the 'whole [...] of the Sydney tribe', of which he was an acknowledged leader.
	15 & 16	JP Townsend, 'Journal, 21 July – 6 Dec. 1846', in *Joseph Phipps Townsend Papers 21 July 1846 – 24 Sep 1862*, SLNSW, MSS 1461/1 [CY2477]), frame 87.
	17	'Minutes for 8/9/1846', BSNSW, *Minutes of the Acting Committee*, Nov 1845 – Dec 1846, SLNSW, MSS A7174.
	Nanny Nellola's affiliation	'Baptism certificate of Gertrude 15/11/1827', NSW BDM Vol. 128 #924
Figure 1.6		A Earle, c.1826, *Portrait of Bungaree, a native of New South Wales, with Fort Macquarie, Sydney Harbour*, NLA, nla.obj-134114940.
Figure 2.1		R Westmacott, 1840–1846, *Botany Bay Heads from Newtown, New South Wales*, NLA, nla.obj-138707546.
Figure 2.2		American and Australasian Photographic Company 1870–1875, *Panorama of Moore Park and Surry Hills from the entrance gates to Moore Park*, SLNSW ON 4 Box 55 No 223. Extract of original image.
Figure 2.3		American and Australasian Photographic Company 1870–1875, *Gun emplacement and two artillerymen, Camp Cove & Watson's Bay*, SLNSW ON 4 Box 57 No 268. Extract of original image.
Figure 2.4		GF Angas, 1845, *Old Queen Gooseberry: Widow of Bungaree: Sydney, 1845*, Angas Collection, South Australian Museum, Image AA8/4/2/4.
Figure 2.5		*Tracing from Asst Surveyor Gorman's Plan illustrative of Mr JN Brown's Memorial*, SANSW, NRS 13886, Surveyor General's Sketch Books, [X764], Vol 6 Fol 45, Reel 2780, frame 93. Annotated extract of original.
Figure 2.6		H Campbell, c.1842, 'Scene on Double Bay', in *Sydney Views*, SLNSW, PXC 291f.35.
Figure 2.7		JS Prout, 1843, *In the Domain, Sydney, Decr. 15, '43*, NLA, nla.obj-134402199.
Figure 2.8		C Rodius, 1833. 'View from the Government Domain, Sydney', in *Views of Sydney and Parramatta*, SLNSW, PXA 997 f.2.
Figure 2.9	a	J Waterman, 'Recollections of Sydney', *JRAHS*, vol. 8, Supplement, 1923, p. 359.
	b	'Aboriginal Christmas Festivities', *The Australian*, 27/12/1844, p. 3 refers to the 'Woolloomooloo tribe'.
	c	H Laracy, 'Leopold Verguet and the Aborigines of Sydney, 1845', *Aboriginal History*, vol. 4, no. 2, 1980, pp. 178–83.

Figure number	Map point	Source
Figure 2.9	d	JP Townsend, 'Journal, 21 July – 6 Dec. 1846', in *Joseph Phipps Townsend Papers 21 July 1846 – 24 Sep 1862*, SLNSW MSS 1461/1 [CY2477]), frame 87.
	e	GF Angas, *Savage life and scenes in Australia and New Zealand: being an artist's impression of countries and people at the antipodes. Volume I: Sth Aust & New Zealand*, Smith, Elder & Co., London, 1847 (facs. edn, Johnson Reprint Corporation, New York, 1969), pp. 200–202.
	f	Testimony of Mahroot, in NSW Legislative Council, *Report from the Select Committee on the Condition of the Aborigines, with appendix, minutes of evidence and replies to a circular letter*, Government Printer, Sydney, 1845, p. 3 [questions 116–118].
	g	Testimony of Mahroot, 1845, p. 2 [questions 44, 52–3].
	h	W Houston, 'Notes of an Interview between W. Houston Esq., one of the Trustees of Captain Cook's Land Place (Kurnell) and Mr. Longfield, at Kurnell on Sunday the 22nd January 1905', CCLP, Box 12 Item 141, 1905, pp. 1–2, 5.
	i	'Petition of Jackey Gogey to the Governor General regarding purchase of a boat, 3/9/1850', SANSW, NRS905, CSLR, 50/7957 [4/2912].
	1	'Aboriginal Superstition', *The Australian*, 1/6/1844, p. 3; 'Aboriginal Christmas Festivities', *The Australian*, 27/12/1844, p. 3; 'Funeral of Mr Charles Smith', *Bell's Life in Sydney and Sporting Reviewer*, 25/1/1845, p. 3; 'The Aborigines', *SMH*, 20/11/1845, p. 3.
	2	Testimony of Mahroot, 1845.
	3	E Delessert, *Voyage dans les Deux Oceans Atlantique et Pacifique 1844 a 1847*, A Franck, Paris, 1848, pp. 169–177 [translated for author by Michael Wotodzo].
	4	'Aborigines', *SMH*, 20/4/1846, p. 2.
	5	'Whales', *SMH*, 1/11/1845, p. 2.
	6	'Receipts, 3/3/1844, 6/4/1844', SLNSW, Wentworth Papers MSS 8/1 Ser. 7; 'Receipts, December 1845', SLNSW, Wentworth Papers ML MSS 8/1 Ser. 8.
	7	'Incendiarism and its Effects', *SMH*, 22/1/1845, p. 3.
	8	'Inquest', *SMH*, 25/1/1845, p. 2.
	9	'Aborigines', *The Morning Chronicle*, 12/4/1845, p. 3.
	10	'The Aborigines', *SMH*, 9/4/1845, p. 3.
	a–11	Waterman 1923, p. 359.
	b–1	'Aboriginal Christmas Festivities', *The Australian*, 27/12/1844, p. 3.
	c–1	Laracy 1980, p. 179.
	d–1	Townsend 1846, frame 87.
Figure 3.1		WH Wells, 1843, *Map of the City of Sydney*, SLNSW, Map ZM2 811.17/1843/2. Extract of original map.
Figure 3.2		WG Mason, 1857, *View of the market, Sydney*, NLA, nla.obj-138449698.

Image references

Figure number	Map point	Source
Figure 3.3		JS Prout & J Rae, *Sydney illustrated (1842–1843)*, Tyrrell, Sydney, 1948, p. 83. Image courtesy SLNSW.
Figure 3.4		*Smart's Hotel, cnr Pitt & Market Sts, 21 May 1901*, City of Sydney Archives, CRS 51/94.
Figure 3.5		*Proclamation of Queen Victoria in N.S.W. 27 October 1837; signed by Governor Bourke, members of the Executive Council, magistrates, clergy etc*, SLNSW, MSS DLADD270. Extract of original document.
Figure 3.6		Anon., 1843, 'William Minam [Minan?] Walamata Port Aitken', in *Portraits of the Aborigines of New South Wales Sydney*, SLNSW, SAFE / PXA 74, Item 1.
Figure 3.7		C Rodius, 1848, '[Portrait of George R Nichols, the elder (possibly)]', SLNSW, P2/12.
Figure 4.1		WS Jevons, 1858 *[Possibly Double Bay]*, Copyright of the University of Manchester, JA/33/1/1, image number JRL023280tr.
Figure 4.2		NSW Government Printing Office, 1880, *Double Bay*, SLNSW, SPF/657.
Figure 4.3		J Hardwick, c.1853, 'The mendicant Blackfellow of Rose Bay, Sydney', in *Views in Victoria, New South Wales and Tasmania*, SLNSW, PXA 6925, Item 3.
Figure 4.4		Conrad Martens, *The Cottage, Rose Bay, 1857*, watercolour, gouache, black pencil, varnish, 46 x 66.1 cm, National Gallery of Australia, Canberra, purchased 1978.
Figure 4.5	a	'The Late Hon. R. Hill, MLC: A Sketch of His Career', *SMH*, 21/8/1895, p. 8.
	b	'Death of Ricketty Dick', *SMH*, 13/6/1863, p. 4; K Scherzer, 'Journal entry 15/11/1858', in *Journal of Dr Karl Scherzer, 1858* translated D.Clark (<www.uow.edu.au/~morgan/novara2.htm> (accessed 7/1/17), pp. 49–50.
	c	S Wentworth, 'Letter from Sarah Wentworth to Thomasine Fisher c late 1864', SLNSW, Wentworth Papers, MSS A868 [CY POS 725], frame 865.
	d	'Obituary: E.S. Hill', *SMH*, 25/2/1880, pp. 7–8.
	e	'Death certificate of Johnny Baswick alias Bankie 18/8/1880', NSW BDM 1880/3881.
	f	WH East, 'Sixty Years Ago. Transformation of Sydney', *SMH*, 15/2/1930, p. 13.
	g	'Water Police Court', *SMH*, 27/10/1875, p. 7.
	h	'Harry, the King of Kissing Point', *SMH*, 17/7/1880, p. 7.
	i	'Death certificate of Johnny Baswick alias Bankie 18/8/1880'.
Figure 4.6		American & Australasian Photographic Company 1870–1875, *Horse and cart at the tollgates, New South Head Road, Rushcutters Bay*, SLNSW, ON 4 Box 13 No 38.

Figure number	Map point	Source
Figure 4.7		WG Mason, 'William Beaumont, Sir Joseph Banks Hotel Zoological Gardens Botany', in *The Australian Picture pleasure book, illustrating the scenery, architecture historical events, natural history, public characters, Etc., of Australia*, J.R. Clarke, Sydney, 1857, p. 63. Image courtesy SLNSW.
Figure 5.1		C Rodius, 1844, *Ricketty Dick, Broken Bay tribe*, SLNSW, PXA 1005.
Figure 5.2		Left – *Statuette, 'Ricketty Dick', silver, gold and ebonised wood (base), Julius Hogarth, Sydney, New South Wales, Australia, c.1855*, Museum of Applied Arts and Sciences, 96/22/1, photo by Ryan Hernandez; Right – Julius Hogarth, c.1857, Commemorative silver inkwell, Sydney Living Museums, Museum of Sydney COL_MOS2007_0 033_1_6a.
Figure 5.3		Mrs AG Foster, *Aboriginal Cemetery*, Royal Australian Historical Society, Image #23204107.
Figure 5.5		C Bayliss, 1879–1882 *[Garden Palace]*, SLNSW, SPF/267.
Figure 5.6		'Sydney International Exhibition – Ethnological Court [1879]' in *Sydney International Exhibition photographic album volume 1*. SLNSW, Q606/S v.1. Image courtesy SLNSW.
Figure 5.7		*[The Fire King c.1866–1873]*, The Great Southern Card Publishers, Australia.
Figure 5.8	Image of Johnny Malone	*[Johnny Malone]*, NSW National Parks and Wildlife Service collection, Kurnell.
	1	Based on age in later records, and association of mother with Botany Bay area. Goodall & Cadzow suggest that Johnny may have been born at Weeney Bay on a block of land belonging to settler James Malone (his possible father), although there is no specific evidence that Johnny Malone or any Aboriginal people were associated with this land or with James Malone. See H Goodall & A Cadzow, *Rivers and Resilience: Aboriginal People on Sydney's Georges River*, UNSW Press, Sydney, 2009, pp. 67–9.
	2	G Thornton, '[Distribution of blankets in Sydney]. Letter to Colonial Secretary 13/10/1857', SANSW, NRS905, CSLR, 57/4140 with 58/1529 [4/3378].
	3	K Scherzer, 'Journal entry 1/12/1858', in *Journal of Dr Karl Scherzer, 1858*, translated D.Clark (<www.uow.edu.au/~morgan/novara2.htm> (accessed 7/1/17), pp. 71–73.
	4	'Circular – Sir Joseph Banks Hotel', *SMH*, 18/4/1862, p. 1.
	5	'Burglaries, Stealing from Premises', *NSWPG*, 22/4/1868, p. 124; 'Marriage certificate of John Bran and Elizabeth Malone 21/5/1884', NSW BDM 1884/3129.

Image references

Figure number	Map point	Source
Figure 5.8	6	'Wallaby Shooting at Port Hacking', *Australian Town & Country Journal*, 30/7/1870, p. 27; J Jervis & LR Flack, *A Jubilee History of the Municipality of Botany*, Botany Municipal Council, Botany, 1938, p. 304.
	7	Jervis & Flack 1938, p. 304; 'Death certificate Charles Golden 4/4/1919', NSW BDM 1919/5807.
	Mother's affiliation	Johnny's mother was described as being of the 'Sydney tribe', linking her to coastal Sydney. CC Greenway, T Honery, Mr McDonald, J Rowley, J Malone & Dr Creed, 'Australian Languages and Traditions', *The Journal of the Anthropological Institute of Great Britain and Ireland*, vol. 7, 1878, p. 262.
	Lizzie Malone's affiliation	Lizzie's death certificate gives her place of birth as Wollongong but her mother was said to be from the Shoalhaven. 'Elizabeth Golden (Malone) death certificate', NSW BDM #3492/1901; CC Greenway, T Honery, Mr McDonald, J Rowley, J Malone & Dr Creed, 'Australian Languages and Traditions', *The Journal of the Anthropological Institute of Great Britain and Ireland*, vol. 7, 1878, p. 263.
Figure 5.9	Image of Biddy Giles	Australian Indigenous Ministeries, 1880, *Last of the Georges River Tribe, NSW [workers on the Holt Sutherland Estate, 1880. Jim Brown, Joe Brown, Joey, Biddy Giles, Jimmy Lowndes]*, SLNSW, Australian Indigenous Ministries – pictorial collection – various historical photographs, c.1860–1909. PXA773, Series 3, Box 6, Image 42. Extract of original image.
	Birth	H Goodall & A Cadzow, *Rivers and Resilience: Aboriginal People on Sydney's Georges River*, Sydney, University of New South Wales Press, 2009, pp. 87–8. Her exact birthplace is not known but is likely to have been around Botany Bay.
	1	'Death certificate of Ellen Anderson 14/5/1931', NSW BDM 1931/7672; Goodall & Cadzow 2009, pp. 88–9, p. 301, note 20.
	2	MM Everitt, 'Letter to Mr Stephens 24 June 1901', in *Illawarra and South Coast Aborigines 1770–1900*, M Organ (compiler), Australian Institute of Aboriginal and Torres Strait Islander Studies, Canberra, 1993, p. 198; Woolla-Nora [pseud.], 'Old Times. A Day at Billy Giles' Home', *St George Call*, 17/8/1907, p. 3.
	3	SBJ Robinson, 'Small beer chronicles and chronicle small beer', *St George Call*, 8/4/1911, p. 6.
	4	Goodall & Cadzow 2009, pp. 94–100; D McGinley, 1983, 'An Aboriginal Tragedy at Port Hacking', *Sutherland Shire Historical Society Bulletin*, no. 44, pp. 41–2; One of the Old Sort [pseud.], 'A Reminiscence of the Sixties', *St George Call*, 11/5/1907, p. 3.
	5	'Sans Souci Celebrities', *St George Call*, 14/5/1904, p. 1; *The Last of the Dolls Point Aboriginals*, SLNSW, SPF/2703; Australian Indigenous Ministeries, 1880, *Last of the Georges River Tribe, NSW*, SLNSW, PXA773, Series 3, Box 6, Image 42.

Figure number	Map point	Source
Figure 5.9	6	'News of the Day', *SMH*, 10/1/1888, p. 7.
	7	'Black Biddy', *Australian Star*, 18/12/1888, p. 6; 'Death certificate of Biddy (Aboriginal) 25/12/1888', NSW BDM 1888/4712.
	Burragalong's affiliation	Goodall & Cadzow 2009, p. 301, note 20. Burragalong is almost exclusively documented residing in the Illawarra area and died there in 1877.
Figure 5.10		*G.R. Nichols – member of 1st Govt 1856, NSW*, Royal Australian Historian Society, Glass Slide Collection, Image #1098. Extract of original image; *George Hill (b. 1802 – d. 1883), date unknown*, City of Sydney Archives SRC18689; *Postmasters General [The Hon Daniel Egan, MP]*, National Archives of Australia, Ser C4078, N4064C. Extract of original image; *Alderman George Thornton, c.1850*, City of Sydney Archives SRC18750.
Figure 6.1		Public transport network information from S Fitzgerald, *Rising Damp, Sydney 1870–1890*, Oxford University Press, Melbourne, p. 56.
Figure 6.2		TG Glover, 1878, *La Perouse Botany Bay, N.S.W*, NLA, nla. obj-138860972.
Figure 6.3		American & Australasian Photographic Company, 1870–1875, *Looking across the Harbour from cottage on Blues Point Road towards Fort Macquarie and Government House*, SLNSW, ON 4 Box 80 No 8. Extracts from original image.
Figure 6.4		American & Australasian Photographic Company, 1870–1875, *Wharves near Fort Macquarie, Bennelong Point*, SLNSW, ON Box 60 No. 359.
Figure 6.5		H King, c.1886–1892, *Phillip St., Sydney: Circular Quay*. SLNSW, SPF764.
Figure 6.6		'Sydney Aboriginals, Past and Present', *The Illustrated Sydney News and New South Wales Agriculturist and Grazier*, 15/5/1880, p. 23. Image courtesy SLNSW.
Figure 6.7		Left – *Daniel & Janet Matthews, Paddy & Jenny Swift, London, 1889*, State Library of South Australia, PRG422/3/795. Extract of original image. Right – NSW Government Printing Office c.1896, *George Thornton*, SLNSW, Government Printing Office 1 - 08571.
Figure 6.8		'The Hon. Richard Hill, M.L.C.', *The Bulletin*, 15/1/1881, p. 1. Image courtesy SLNSW. Thanks to John Ruffels for locating the image.
Figure 6.9		AG Foster, c.1900–1914, '[Miss Hill's cottage, Bent Street]', in *Glass negatives of Sydney and suburbs, headstones in Devonshire Street Cemetery, Sydney ca. 1900–1914*, SLNSW, ON146/185.
Figure 6.10		A Collingridge, 1883, 'The Blacks at La Perouse', *Sydney Mail*, 27/1/1883, pp. 160, 168. Image courtesy SLNSW.
Figure 6.11		'Untitled plan with the application for the establishment of a public school at Sandringham, 28th December 1883', *School Files, Sandringham*, SANSW, NRS 3829 [5/17590.3].

Image references

Figure number	Map point	Source
Figure 7.1		'Mrs Golden, The Oldest Resident of the La Perouse Camp, and her Son', *Evening News*, 17/11/1900, p. 3S. Image courtesy SLNSW.
Figure 7.2		*La Perouse mission church c.1894*, Randwick & District Historical Society.
Figure 7.3		*[Emma Timbery at La Perouse]*, Woollahra Local History Collection, Woollahra Libraries, Robinson, Leo Whitby – personal papers WLHC MS 3.
Figure 7.4		*[Hut at La Perouse]*, Woollahra Local History Collection, Woollahra Libraries, Robinson, Leo Whitby – personal papers WLHC MS 3.
Figure 7.5	Image of William Rowley	*[William and Mary Ann Rowley]*, Randwick Library, Randwick Social History Project.
	1 & 2	'Baptism Record James William Rowley, 23 June 1857', SAG, *Church of England in Australia – Parish registers, 1839–1970*, SAG Reel 001, frame 1090.
	3	SJ Carruthers, EE Laycock, WA Macdonald & CH Bertie, 'Captain Cook and Botany Bay – comments', *JRAHS*, vol. 11, no. 1, 1925, p. 35.
	4	'Coroner's Inquests: Drowned in Botany Bay', *SMH*, 11/11/1885, p. 6; G Thornton, 'Aborigines: Report of the Protector to 31 December 1882', NSW VPLA 1883, vol. 3, Government Printer, Sydney, p. 899.
	5	'Household Returns for Census District no. 80 Heathcote Subdistrict B Holt Sutherland', *Collector's books, 1891 Census*, SANSW, NRS683, [2/8423]; J Murphy, 'Letter to Mr W Rowley 6 March 1893', SLNSW, *Holt Family Papers 1861–1933*, MSS 2170 Volume 9 [CY Reel 3958], frame 221; 'Found Dead in Bed', *SMH*, 25/5/1897, p. 5.
	6	W Carter, 'Links with the past – William Rowley of Salt Pan', *The Propeller*, 31/1/1935, p. 7.
	7	M Maloney, 'Letter to William Rowley of Sylvania, May 1899', SLNSW, *Holt family papers 1861–1933*, MSS 2170/10-11 [CY Reel 3972], frame 570.
	8	'Household Returns for Census District no. 38 Illawarra', *Collector's books, 1901 Census* SANSW, NRS683 [2/8448].
	9	'Marriage certificate for William Rollie and Mary Ann Steele', NSW BDM 1905/2652; 'Meeting minutes for 17/8/1911', *AWB Minute Books 9/3/1911–21/12/1911*, SANSW, NRS2 [4/7117]; '[Entry for William and Mary Ann Rowley]', *1913 State Electoral Roll: District of Randwick* <www.ancestry.com. Australia, Electoral Rolls, 1903–1980>.
	10	'Certificate of Title 6/4/1927, Lot 145 in Deposited Plan 11124', NSW Land Titles Office Volume 3989, Folio 6; Carter 1935, p. 7.

Figure number	Map point	Source
Figure 7.5	11	'[Entry for William and Mary Ann Rowley]', *1937 Australian Electoral Roll, Eden Monaro District, Nowra Sub-district*, (<www.ancestry.com> Australia, Electoral Rolls, 1903–1980); 'Death certificate of Mary Ann Rowley 25/9/1938', NSW BDM 1938/14669; 'News from Our Mission Stations: Roseby Park', *The United Aborigines' Messenger*, 1/9/1941, p. 4.
	Mother's affiliation	Rowley's mother's affiliation is not stated explicitly but is inferred by the fact that he was born at Kurnell and she lived her life in the area; 'Coroner's Inquests: Drowned in Botany Bay', *SMH*, 11/11/1885, p. 6; SJ Carruthers *et al.*, 'Captain Cook and Botany Bay', p. 35; W. Carter, 'Links with the past'.
	Mary Ann's affiliation	'Death certificate of Mary Ann Rowley 25/9/1938', NSW BDM 1938/14669.
Figure 7.7	Image of Ellen Anderson	Australian Indigenous Ministries, *'[Eight photos from an album showing Aboriginal people at various places including] Trida [and] Salt Pan Creek'*, SLNSW, Australian Indigenous Ministries – pictorial collection – various historical photographs, c.1860–1909. PXA773, Series 3, Box 1, Image 78. Extract of original image.
	1	'Death certificate of Ellen Anderson 14/5/1931', NSW BDM 1931/7672. The precise date of her birth is not known but was probably in the mid-1850s.
	2	JG Treseder, 1891, *Report by John G. Treseder of his visit to the Aboriginal mission station at Coomergunga and Warangesda*, SLNSW, Parkes Correspondence, vol. 40, p. 29.
	3	D Matthews *[Diary entries for 4/5/1881 & 9/7/1881]*, SLNSW, Daniel Matthews Papers 1861–1917, Volume 2 Part 1 No. 3. Diary 1878–1881.
	4	D Matthews, *Maloga Aboriginal Mission Annual Reports*, 1881–1889.
	5	'The Aborigines Camp at Kangaroo Valley', *School Files, Kangaroo Valley*, SANSW, NRS3829 [5/16418.2 Bundle A]; 'Aboriginal Mission', *Goulburn Herald*, 21/11/1889, p. 2; 'Treatment of the Aborigines', *SMH*, 8/12/1890, p. 5.
	6	Treseder 1891, p. 29; 'Household Returns for Census District no. 66 Deniliquin, Subdistrict', *Collector's books, 1891 Census*, SANSW, NRS683 [2/8423]; N Cato, *Mister Maloga*, University of Queensland Press, St Lucia, 1976, p. 196.
	7	CW Peck, 1933, *Australian Legends: Tales Handed Down from the Remotest Times By the Autocthonous Inhabitants of Our Land*, Lothian Publishing Company, Melbourne, p. 16.
	8	G Ardler, 1991, *The Wander of it All*, Darlinghurst, Burraga Aboriginal History and Writing Group Inc., pp. 19–20.
	9	'Death certificate of Hugh Anderson Jr', NSW BDM 1897/1870; 'Birth certificate of John Anderson', NSW BDM 1899/32276; see also *Maloga Aboriginal Mission Annual Reports*.

Image references

Figure number	Map point	Source
Figure 7.7	10	'Mrs Ellen Anderson: Death of Aged Aboriginal', *SMH*, 16/5/1931, p. 14; E Dickinson, 'Salt Pan Creek About 1913', *Bankstown Historical Society Newsletter*, vol. 8, no. 4, 1974; Recollections of David Cross in 'Salt Pan Creek Aborigines', *Hurstville Historical Society Newsletter*, vol. 2, no. 49, 1981.
	11	'Birth certificate of John Anderson Bundle 9/7/1917', NSW BDM 1917/39851.
	12	'Certificate of Title 3/12/1925, Lot 146 in Deposited Plan 11124', NSW Land Titles Office Volume 3808, Folio 215; H Goodall & A Cadzow, *Rivers and Resilience: Aboriginal People on Sydney's Georges River*, UNSW Press, Sydney, 2009, Chs 5 & 6.
	13	Peck 1933, pp. 9, 16.
	14	Goodall & Cadzow 2009, pp. 139–42.
	15	'Mrs Ellen Anderson: Death of Aged Aboriginal', *SMH*, 16/5/1931, p. 14; 'Death certificate of Ellen Anderson 14/5/1931', NSW BDM 1931/7672; 'Death certificate of Hugh Anderson 12/7/1928', NSW BDM 1928/11835.
	Mother's affiliation	Ellen said that her mother Biddy Giles came from the northern end of the Dharawal language area, and this fits with her being affiliated with Botany Bay; Peck 1933, p. 15.
	Father's affiliation	Goodall & Cadzow 2009, p. 301, note 20. Burragalong is almost exclusively documented residing in the Illawarra area and died there in 1877.
	Husband's affiliation	Hugh Anderson was from the Goulburn Valley area in Victoria; Goodall & Cadzow 2009, p. 113.

Abbreviations

ACEU	Australian Christian Endeavour Union
APB	Aborigines Protection Board
AWB	Aborigines Welfare Board
BDM	Births, Deaths and Marriages
BSNSW	Benevolent Society of New South Wales
CCLP	Captain Cook's Landing Place Trust Archives, Kamay Botany Bay National Park, Kurnell
CSLR	Colonial Secretary's Correspondence – Main Series of Letters Received
CSLIL	Colonial Secretary's Correspondence – Letters from Individuals Re. Land
HRA	Historical Records of Australia
HRNSW	Historical Records of New South Wales
JRAHS	*Journal of the Royal Australian Historical Society*
MSS	Manuscript
nd	No date
np	No page numbers in document
NLA	National Library of Australia
NSW	New South Wales
NSWPG	*New South Wales Police Gazette*
pers. com.	Personal communication
SAG	Society of Australian Genealogists
SANSW	State Archives and Records Authority of New South Wales
SLNSW	State Library of NSW (Mitchell Library)
SMH	*Sydney Morning Herald*
VPLA	NSW Legislative Assembly, Votes and Proceedings

Notes

Introduction: A gap in place and time
1. M Hinkson, *Aboriginal Sydney: A Guide to Important Places of the Past and Present* (2nd edn), Aboriginal Studies Press, Canberra, 2010; City of Sydney, *Barani Barrabugu: Yesterday Tomorrow: Sydney's Aboriginal Journey*, City of Sydney, Sydney, 2011.
2. This gap has been noted by others. See P Read, 'Book Review: *Aboriginal Darwin, A Guide to Exploring Important Sites of the Past and Present and Aboriginal Sydney, A Guide to Important Places of the Past and Present*', *Aboriginal History*, vol. 35, 2011, pp. 207–8. It can also be quantified. Of the fifty places in Hinkson's guide, the only places representing this period are two cemeteries and the La Perouse Aboriginal mission, though the 19th-century Aboriginal community at Blacktown in western Sydney is also briefly referenced. In the City of Sydney guide, the only places used between the 1820s and 1920s (out of 58 places described) are two Aboriginal settlements used up to the mid-19th century, and the Circular Quay Boatshed settlement of the late 1870s and early 1880s.
3. P Irish, 'The Salt Pan Creek Boondi', in S Brown, A Clarke & U Frederick (eds), *Object Stories: Artifacts & Archaeologists*, Left Coast Press, Walnut Creek, 2015, pp. 125–30.
4. G Karskens, *The Colony: A History of Early Sydney*, Allen & Unwin, Sydney, 2009.
5. Karskens 2009, p. 12.
6. H Goodall and A Cadzow, *Rivers and Resilience: Aboriginal People on Sydney's Georges River*, UNSW Press, Sydney, 2009, p. 8.
7. M Nugent, *Botany Bay: Where histories meet*, Allen & Unwin, Sydney, 2005.
8. Historians and a number of other scholars make this argument, drawing on the ideas of historian Patrick Wolfe. See the journal *Settler Colonial Studies*, vol. 3, no. 1, 2013 for a range of scholars articulating this view, and for further references to their recent work.
9. P Irish, *Hidden in Plain View: Nineteenth-Century Aboriginal People and Places in Coastal Sydney*, PhD thesis, UNSW, 2015. <http://handle.unsw.edu.au/1959.4/54313>.

1 Surviving the early colony (1788–1820s)
1. E Stockton, 'Archaeology of the Blue Mountains', in E Stockton & J Merriman (eds) *Blue Mountains Dreaming: the Aboriginal heritage*, 2nd edn, Blue Mountains Education & Research Trust, Sydney, 2009, pp. 41–72; V Attenbrow, *Sydney's Aboriginal Past: Investigating the archaeological and historical records*, 2nd edn, UNSW Press, Sydney, 2010a, pp. 18–21; AN Williams *et al.*, 'A glacial cryptic refuge in south-east Australia: human occupation and mobility from 36000 years ago in the Sydney Basin, New South Wales', *Journal of Quaternary Science*, vol. 29, no. 8, 2014, pp. 735–48.
2. Attenbrow 2010a, pp. 38, 55–56; PS Roy & EA Crawford, 'Holocene geological evolution of the southern Botany Bay – Kurnell region, central New South Wales', *Records of the Geological Survey of NSW*, vol. 20, no. 2, 1981, pp. 195–97.
3. Attenbrow 2010a, pp. 38–39; Roy & Crawford 1981, pp. 198–200.

4   RJ Haworth, RGV Baker & PJ Flood, 'A 6000-year-old Fossil Dugong from Botany Bay: Inferences about Changes in Sydney's Climate, Sea Levels and Waterways', *Australian Geographical Studies*, vol. 42, no. 1, 2004, pp. 46–59.
5   Attenbrow 2010a, pp. 56, 102–3, 117–19.
6   V Attenbrow, 'Aboriginal Fishing in Port Jackson, and the Introduction of Shell-fish Hooks in Coastal NSW, Australia', in D Lunney, P Hutchings & D Hochuli (eds), *The Natural History of Sydney*, Royal Zoological Society, Sydney, 2010b, pp. 16–34; S Bowdler, 'Hook, Line and Dilly Bag: An interpretation of an Australian coastal shell midden', *Mankind*, vol. 10, 1976, pp. 248–58; G Karskens, *The Colony: A History of Early Sydney*, Allen & Unwin, Sydney, 2009, pp. 40–1, 406–7.
7   For adornments see Attenbrow 2010a, pp. 108–9; P Irish, 'Bundeena Bling? Possible Aboriginal Shell Adornments from Southern Sydney', *Australian Archaeology*, vol. 64, 2007, pp. 46–9. The connection between *malgun* and fishing was stated by Botany Bay man Mahroot, though whether this was the sole reason is debated. Mahroot's testimony in NSW Legislative Council, *Report from the Select Committee on the Condition of the Aborigines, with appendix, minutes of evidence and replies to a circular letter*, Government Printer, Sydney, 1845, p. 5 [questions 181–184]; Attenbrow 2010a, p. 137; A Roberts & K Schilling, *Aboriginal women's fishing in New South Wales: a thematic history*, NSW Department of Environment, Climate Change and Water, Sydney, 2010, pp. 9–10.
8   Attenbrow 2010a, pp. 122–4; V Attenbrow *et al.*, 'Crossing the Great Divide: a ground-edged hatchet-head from Vaucluse, Sydney', *Archaeology in Oceania*, vol. 47, no. 1, 2012, pp. 47–52; V Attenbrow & C R Cartright, 'An Aboriginal shield collected in 1770 at Kamay Botany Bay: an indicator of pre-colonial exchange systems in south-eastern Australia', *Antiquity* vol. 88, 2014, pp. 883–95; P Grave *et al.*, 'Non-destructive pXRF of mafic stone tools', *Journal of Archaeological Science*, vol. 39, 2012, pp. 1674–86.
9   Attenbrow 2010a, pp. 156–7; A Ross, 'Tribal and linguistic boundaries: A reassessment of the evidence', in G Aplin (ed.) *A Difficult Infant: Sydney before Macquarie*, New South Wales University Press, Sydney, 1988, pp. 42–53.
10 M Powell & R Hesline, 'Making tribes? Constructing Aboriginal tribal entities in Sydney and coastal N.S.W. from the early colonial period to the present', *JRAHS*, vol. 96, no. 2, 2010, p. 117.
11 For a broader Australian discussion of these concepts, see P Sutton, *Country: Aboriginal boundaries and land ownership in Australia*, Aboriginal History Monograph 3, Aboriginal History Inc, Canberra, 1995; and for an example of the shifting links of inviduals to land, see F Myers, *Pintupi country, Pintupi self: sentiment, place and politics among Western Desert Aborigines*, Smithsonian Institute Press, Washington DC, 1986.
12 Attenbrow 2010a, pp. 22–30, 57–8. Other researchers have identified additional clans, but the evidence for these is inconclusive, as Attenbrow discusses. The suffix –'gal' refers to the men of the clan and 'galleon' refers to the women.
13 Attenbrow 2010a, p. 29.
14 Karskens 2009, p. 435.
15 Governor Phillip's 1788 estimate of fifteen hundred Aboriginal people was not for the whole Sydney region but the areas explored by that time, from Botany Bay north to Broken Bay and west to Prospect. See Attenbrow 2010a, p. 17. This area is of

similar size to coastal Sydney, and a population of around this number is therefore a reasonable estimate.
16 Karskens 2009, pp. 361–72.
17 DF Collins, *An Account of the English Colony in New South Wales: Volume 1*, London, Cadell and Davies, 1798 (facs. edn, BH Fletcher ed., A.H. & A.W. Reed in association with the Royal Australian Historical Society, Sydney, 1975), p. 496. The origins of the epidemic are not definitively known, but it most likely came from the Europeans at Sydney Cove. See a recent discussion of the theories in C Mear, 'The origin of the smallpox outbreak in Sydney in 1789', *JRAHS* vol. 94, no. 1, 2008, pp. 1–22.
18 Karskens 2009, p. 374.
19 A Phillip, 'Letter from Governor Phillip to Lord Sydney 13/2/1790', *HRNSW* vol. 1, no. 2, pp. 304–10.
20 Collins 1798 (1975), p. 497.
21 Recent examples include Attenbrow 2010a, p. 21; M Hinkson, *Aboriginal Sydney: A guide to important places of the past and present*, Aboriginal Studies Press, Canberra, 2001, p. xx; Karskens 2009, p. 377. For the naming of the third survivor as Caruey see KV Smith, *Eora Clans: A history of Indigenous social organisation in coastal Sydney, 1770–1890*, MA Thesis, Macquarie University, 2004, p. 105.
22 L Macquarie, 'New South Wales. The Governor's Diary and Memorandum book Commencing on Wednesday the 1st of March 1820 and Ending on Thursday 8th of March 1821', in *Journals of his Tours in New South Wales and Van Diemen's Land, 1810–1822*, vol. 13, SLNSW, A774–2, p. 256 (Reel CY301, fr672). For prior Aboriginal attachment see E Hall, 'Mr E.S. Hall to Sir George Murray 26 November 1828', *HRA* vol. 28, 1828, pp. 596–7.
23 Karskens 2009, Ch. 13.
24 P Hiscock, *Archaeology of ancient Australia*, Routledge, London and New York, 2008, pp. 14–16; Karskens, 2009, pp. 377–8.
25 Attenbrow 2010a, p. 30; Karskens 2009, p. 37.
26 Karskens 2009, p. 377; Smith 2004, pp. 156–9. Violent behaviour was not unprecedented but it was not an unchanged part of traditional culture, as some have argued. See, for example, I Clendinnen, *Dancing with Strangers*, Text, Melbourne, 2003, pp. 159–67.
27 DK Richter, *Facing East from Indian country: a Native history of early America*, Harvard University Press, Cambridge, Mass., 2001, p. 62.
28 J Beckett, 'Kinship, mobility and community among part-Aborigines in Rural Australia', *International Journal of Comparative Sociology*, vol. 6, no. 1, 1965, pp. 7–23; C Birdsall, 'All one family', in I Keen (ed.), *Being Black: Aboriginal Cultures in 'Settled' Australia*, Aboriginal Studies Press, Canberra, 1991, pp. 137–58.
29 Collins 1798 (1975), p. 497.
30 Karskens 2009, pp. 389, 424.
31 Smith 2004, p. 76.
32 Attenbrow 2010a, p. 54.
33 WA Miles, 'How did the natives of Australia become acquainted with the demigods and daemonia, and with the superstitions of the ancient races? And how have many oriental words been incorporated in their dialects and languages?', *Journal of the Ethnological Society of London*, no. 3, 1854, p. 5.
34 'Murder', *Sydney Gazette and NSW Advertiser*, 11/9/1838, p. 2; G Bennett,

Recollections of William Scott: The Port Stephens Blacks, The Chronicle Office, Dungog, 1929, pp. 7–8; M Bennett, *For a Labourer Worthy of His Hire: Aboriginal Economic Responses to Colonisation in the Illawarra and Shoalhaven, 1770–1900*, PhD thesis, University of Canberra, 2003, p. 156; AW Howitt, *The Native Tribes of Southeast Australia*, 1904, facs. edn, Aboriginal Studies Press, Canberra, 1996, pp. 495, 566–67.

35 Howitt 1904, pp. 82–3.
36 'Aborigines', *SMH*, 20/4/1846, p. 2.
37 His lack of local connection has been echoed by most since first proposed in 1966 by FD McCarthy, 'Bungaree (? – 1830)', *Australian Dictionary of Biography*. National Centre of Biography, Australian National University, <www.adb.anu.edu.au/biography/bungaree-1848/text2141>, published first in hardcopy 1966, viewed 27 October 2016. See, for example, Karskens 2009, p. 432; NSW Department of Education, *These are my people, this is my land – Bungaree: Aboriginal people and their culture, north of Sydney Harbour*, 1991; KV Smith, *King Bungaree, a Sydney Aborigine meets the Great South Pacific Explorers, 1799–1830*, Kangaroo Press, Sydney, 1992, p. 47.
38 M Dunn, *A Valley in a Valley: Colonial Struggles over land and resources in the Hunter Valley, NSW 1820–1850*, PhD thesis, University of New South Wales, 2015, pp. 64, 80–2, 103–4.
39 Cora was known as 'Queen of Sydney and Botany', see T Cleary, *Poignant Regalia: 19th century Aboriginal images and breastplates*, Historic Houses Trust, Sydney, 1993, pp. 107–9.
40 Historian KV Smith suggests that Matora was from the Central Coast, but the only reason suggested is that a similar-sounding word in the Central Coast/Newcastle language means 'snapper'. For this and Bowen Bungaree see KV Smith, *Mari Nawi: Aboriginal Odysseys*, Rosenberg Publishing, Sydney, 2010, pp. 135–41.
41 G Barratt, *The Russians at Port Jackson 1814–1822*, Australian Institute of Aboriginal Studies, Canberra, 1981, p. 34.
42 Annotation in J Walker, *1791–2. A Map of the Hitherto explored country contiguous to Port Jackson*, Mitchell Library, SLNSW, Printed map DL Q79/64.
43 Karskens 2009, Ch. 13.
44 J Piper, 'July 1822 Letter from John Piper to Governor Brisbane', SANSW, NRS897, Colonial Secretary's Papers 1788–1825, [4/1753], Reel 6052, p. 159; J Connell, *Letter to Governor Darling requesting blankets* [nd.], SLNSW MSS Aa84 (CY3583).
45 'Mr William Small', *Daily Telegraph*, 23/1/1888, p. 6.
46 Karskens 2009, pp. 352, 445.
47 L Ford, *Settler sovereignty: jurisdiction and indigenous people in America and Australia, 1788–1836*, Harvard University Press, Cambridge, Mass., 2010.
48 Karskens 2009, pp. 2, 193, 197; P Bridges, *Foundations of identity: building early Sydney 1788–1822*, Hale & Iremonger, Sydney, 1995, pp. 95ff.
49 Karskens 2009, p. 499.
50 J Brook & J Kohen, *The Parramatta Native Institution and the Black Town: A History*, UNSW Press, Sydney, 1991.
51 L Macquarie, 'Points to talk to the Natives upon at the Meeting on 28 Decr 1814', Lachlan Macquarie, 27 Dec 1814, SLNSW MSS ADD340.
52 Smith 1992, pp. 77–80, 121–2.

53 *Macquarie 1810–1822*, vol. 13, SLNSW, A774-2, p. 256 (Reel CY301, fr672); G Karskens, 'Naked Possession: Building and the Politics of Legitimate Occupation in Early New South Wales', in C Shammas (ed.), *Investing in the Early Modern Built Environment: Europeans, Asians, Settlers and Indigenous Societies*, Brill Academic Publishers, Leiden, 2012, pp. 325–57.

54 Brook & Kohen 1991.

55 B Reece, 'Feasts & Blankets: The history of some early attempts to establish relations with the Aborigines of New South Wales, 1814–1846', *Archaeology & Physical Anthropology in Oceania*, vol. 2, 1967, pp. 190–206; M Smithson, 'A misunderstood gift: the annual issue of blankets to Aborigines in New South Wales, 1826–48', *Push (Armidale, NSW)*, vol. 30, 1992, pp. 73–108.

2   Living to fish (1830s–1840s)

1 W Proctor, *Journal on the John Craig [1834]*, SLNSW MSS B1126:122 (CY1518), pp. 118–22 [fr71–73]. Though *gunyahs* are not described, it seems most likely that these were the 'bushes' described by Proctor, and again a decade later by George French Angas. Camp Cove Beach Park, between Victoria Street and the beach, approximates the course of the tidal creek.

2 Proctor 1834, p. 122 [fr 73].

3 'Distribution of Blankets to the Aborigines', *SMH*, 27/5/1850, p. 2.

4 There are no precise records but figures from the 1841 and 1846 censuses suggest a European population of this order, and certainly not significantly more; R Mansfield, *Analytical view of the census of New South Wales for the year 1841: with tables showing the progress of the population during the previous twenty years*, Kemp and Fairfax, Sydney, 1841; R Mansfield, *Analytical view of the census of New South Wales for the year 1846: with tables showing the progress of the population during the previous twenty-five years, and an appendix*, Kemp & Fairfax, Sydney, 1847.

5 S Cumming, 'Chimneys and Change: Post-European environmental impact in Green Square', in G Karskens & M Rogowsky (eds), *Histories of Green Square: Waterloo, Alexandria, Zetland, Beaconsfield, Rosebery*, School of History, University of New South Wales, Sydney, 2004, pp. 31–2; S Fitzgerald, *Sydney 1842–1992*, Hale & Ironmonger, Sydney, 1992, p. 30.

6 G Karskens, *The Colony: A History of Early Sydney*, Allen & Unwin, Sydney, 2009, p. 404.

7 See, for example, the 'Sites to Visit' section of V Attenbrow, *Sydney's Aboriginal Past: Investigating the archaeological and historical records*, 2nd edn, UNSW Press, Sydney, 2010; P Stanbury & J Clegg, *A Field Guide to Aboriginal Rock Engravings*, Oxford University Press, Melbourne, 1990.

8 Archaeological and historical records confirm the species diversity and richness of the fishing grounds in these areas; V Attenbrow, 'Aboriginal Fishing in Port Jackson, and the Introduction of Shell-fish Hooks in Coastal NSW, Australia', in D Lunney, P Hutchings & D Hochuli (eds), *The Natural History of Sydney*, Royal Zoological Society of NSW, Sydney, 2010, p. 20; NSW Government, *Report of the Royal Commission upon the actual state and prospects of the fisheries of this Colony 1879–1880*, Government Printer, Sydney, 1880, pp. 48–9.

9 R Derricourt, 'Watson's Bay', *The Sydney Journal*, vol. 1, no. 2, 2008, pp. 117–25.

10   A Murray, 'Letter to the Australian Museum 18th February 1909 from Aubrey Murray, Compiling Branch, Lands Department', Australian Museum Archives, Series 9 Correspondence M7/1909. Women are not specifically mentioned fishing at Camp Cove due to the masculine bias of the observers, but they undoubtedly fished from their *nowie*, as they continued to do elsewhere.

11   G Angas, *Savage life and scenes in Australia and New Zealand: being an artist's impression of countries and people at the antipodes. Volume I: Sth Aust & New Zealand*, Smith, Elder & Co., London, 1847 (facs. edn, Johnson Reprint Corporation, New York, 1969), pp. 200–2.

12   Angas 1847 (1969), p. 202; GF Angas, 'Hunting for Hieroglyphics', *Colonies and India*, April 21, 1877, vol. 244, p. 5.

13   R Bourke, 'Governor's Minute no 1839 [re. Bosun Maroot] 17 April 1832', in *Records of Boatswain Maroot, 1832–1851*, SANSW, NRS 907, CSLIL [2/7914].

14   R Bourke, 1832; ED Thomson, 'Letter from Colonial Secretary E. Deas Thomson to Surveyor General 24 September 1838', *Copies of letters to the Surveyor General, the Land Board, Assistant Surveyors and the Commissioners for Apportioning the Colony, 6 October 1826 – 8 October 1856*, SANSW, NRS 1001 [4/3920]. For Maria see Maria Maroot, 'Memorial of Maria Maroot [1837]', in *Records of Boatswain Maroot, 1832–1851*, SANSW, NRS 907, CSLIL [2/7914]. For gardening see Mahroot's testimony in NSW Legislative Committee Votes and Proceedings, *Report from the Select Committee on the Condition of the Aborigines, with appendix, minutes of evidence and replies to a circular letter*, Government Printer, Sydney, 1845, p. 4 [questions 129–132]. The bay has been reclaimed as a Government Bus Depot and container storage facility but the line of the beach shown in Figure 2.5 is approximated by a stormwater channel immediately east of the depot.

15   Testimony of Mahroot 1845, pp. 3 & 4 [questions 108–114 & 131]. At this time, carpenters and masons earned just over one pound per week, and it was estimated that this was also the amount required to feed and house a family with three children; see 'To The Editor', *SMH*, 21/8/1846, p. 3. A couple without children, not paying rent and growing some of their own food could survive on substantially less. Mahroot's phrase 'I threw it away along with my people' signifies this distribution and his obligations to kin, rather than wastage.

16   Testimony of Mahroot 1845, p. 3 [questions 121, 124].

17   Sydney District Council, *Assessment Book, Parishes of Alexandria and Botany*, SLNSW MSS D66 [CY1413 fr37-131], 1843–1846?, Appendix 5. This states that five men were living in 'small slab huts' on Mahroot's land in the 1840s. See also Mahroot's testimony 1845, p. 4 [questions 126–128].

18   H Laracy, 'Leopold Verguet and the Aborigines of Sydney, 1845', *Aboriginal History*, vol. 4, no. 2, 1980, pp. 178–83. The western end of Double Bay was closest to Verguet's lodgings at Woolloomooloo, and as Verguet mentions that he was able to 'run back to the house by myself and return to the rock with my paper and crayons', it seems most likely that the shelter was at this end of the bay (p. 181).

19   Laracy 1980; 'Baptism certificate of Gertrude 15/11/1827', NSW BDM Vol. 128 #924.

20   JP Townsend, 'Journal, 21 July – 6 Dec. 1846', in *Joseph Phipps Townsend Papers 21 July 1846 – 24 Sep 1862*, SLNSW MSS 1461/1 (CY2477), Frame 87. Townsend mentions 'King Tamarin' but this is almost certainly Tamara, who was also known

as King Tamara or Thomas Tamara. There are no other people named in this area at this time with a similar name, and the names of most of those given status such as 'King' by Europeans are recorded.

21 'Aborigines', *SMH*, 20/4/1846, p. 2; Townsend 1846, Frame 87.
22 Laracy 1980, pp. 179, 181.
23 T Bonyhady, *Images in opposition: Australian landscape painting 1801–1890*, Oxford University Press, Oxford, 1985, p. 24; B Smith, *European vision and the South Pacific*, 2nd edn, Oxford University Press, Oxford, 1985, p. 235. This view is being challenged; G Karskens, 'Red coat, blue jacket, black skin: Aboriginal men and clothing in early New South Wales', *Aboriginal History*, vol. 35, 2011, p. 26.
24 SLNSW, *George Edwards Peacock in the Picture Gallery: guide*, nd, p. 12 (image 11 caption).
25 Historian Stephen Gapps has come to a similar view. See S Gapps, *Cabrogal to Fairfield City: A history of a multicultural community*, Fairfield City Council, Fairfield, 2010, p. 153.
26 L Ford, *Settler sovereignty: jurisdiction and indigenous people in America and Australia, 1788–1836*, Harvard University Press, Cambridge, Mass., 2010.
27 Karskens 2009, p. 531.
28 'The Blacks', *Sydney Gazette*, 17/5/1842, p. 2
29 s49, *Licensed Publicans Act* (No 2) 1838, <www.austlii.edu.au/au/legis/nsw/num_act/lpa21838n22226/> (viewed 12 October 2016). For its ineffectiveness see B Bridges, *Aboriginal and White Relations in New South Wales, 1788–1855*, Masters thesis, Sydney University, 1966, pp. 880–1.
30 See, for example, 'Police Court Business', *SMH*, 29/12/1843, p. 2; 'Police Court Business', *SMH*, 15/4/1844, p. 2; 'Central Police Court – Thursday', *SMH*, 30/3/1855, p. 4; 'Central Police Court – Tuesday', *SMH*, 25/6/1856, p. 4.
31 'Conflicting Evidence', *Empire*, 9/8/1860, p. 5.
32 See, for example, 'The Aborigines', *The Colonist*, 19/12/1840, p. 3; 'The Blacks', *The Australian* 26/10/1842, p. 3; 'Original Correspondence', *SMH*, 23/2/1853, p. 2.
33 NSW *Vagrancy Act* 1835 s2, <www.austlii.edu.au/au/legis/nsw/num_act/va1835n11131.pdf> (viewed 12 October 2016). For exclusion of Aboriginal people see Bridges 1966, pp. 877–8; P Edmonds, *Urbanizing Frontiers: Indigenous Peoples and Settlers in 19th-Century Pacific Rim Cities*, UBC Press, Vancouver, 2010, p. 137.
34 J Broadbent, 'The Push East: Woolloomooloo Hill, the first suburb', in M Kelly (ed.), *Sydney: City of Suburbs*, New South Wales University Press, Sydney, 1987, pp. 12–29.
35 G Karskens, 'Naked Possession: Building and the Politics of Legitimate Occupation in Early New South Wales', in C Shammas (ed.), *Investing in the Early Modern Built Environment: Europeans, Asians, Settlers and Indigenous Societies*, Brill Academic Publishers, Leiden, 2012, pp. 327–9.
36 KV Smith, *King Bungaree, a Sydney Aborigine meets the Great South Pacific Explorers, 1799–1830*, Kangaroo Press, Sydney, 1992, pp. 136, 143, 147.
37 For blankets see J Meredith, *The Last Kooradgie: Moyengully, Chief Man of the Gundungurra People*, Kangaroo Press, Sydney, 1989, p. 68; J Smith, *Aborigines of the Burragorang Valley, 1830–1960*, Privately Published, Sydney, 1991, p. 2. For Werriberri see W Russell, *My Recollections*, Camden News Office, Camden, 1914, p. 21. George's sister Fanny was also sympathetic to Aboriginal people,

	understanding that agressive settlers were to blame for much of the apparent Aboriginal violence on the frontier; see J Hughes, B Earnshaw & L Davidson, *Fanny to William: the letters of Frances Leonora Macleay 1812–1836*, Historic Houses Trust of NSW, Sydney, 1993, p. 63.
38	The latest reference found to the use of the specific Elizabeth Bay area is in 1838; see 'Murder', *Sydney Gazette and NSW Advertiser*, 11/9/1838, p. 2.
39	D Byrne, 'Segregated landscapes: the heritage of racial segregation in New South Wales', *Historic Environment – Islands of Vanishment,* vol. 17, no. 1, 2003, p. 14.
40	Karskens 2009, p. 209; KV Smith, *Mari Nawi: Aboriginal Odysseys*, Rosenberg Publishing, Sydney, 2010, pp. 54, 57–8; J Waterman, 'Recollections of Sydney', *JRAHS*, vol. 8, Supplement, 1923, p. 359.
41	The hut is documented from a sketch by artist John Skinner Prout in 1843. The original image does not reference Aboriginal people, but an annotation on its mounting (not in Prout's hand) reads 'Blackfellows Hut / in the Domain / Sydney' and both the condition of the mounting and terminology of the annotation suggest its addition in the mid- to late 19th century. Several figures are clearly shaded as having darker coloured skin but the designation as a 'Blackfellows hut' could not reasonably be made on this basis alone and suggests some prior information from the artist which has subsequently been lost. Thanks to Andrew Sergeant (Reference Librarian, NLA) and Richard Neville (Mitchell Librarian) for their thoughts on the provenance and content of this image. Aboriginal people also lived near Serpentine or Centipede Rock, a sandstone outcrop near the current site of the Art Gallery of NSW.
42	Maria Maroot 1837.
43	J Galloway, 'Letter from Surveyor James Galloway to Surveyor General 11 February 1843', in *Records of Boatswain Maroot, 1832–1851*, SANSW, NRS 907, CSLIL [2/7914].
44	'Memorandum from Governor 4 & 5 May 1843', in *Records of Boatswain Maroot, 1832–1851*, SANSW, NRS 907, CSLIL [2/7914].
45	TL Mitchell, 'Letter from Surveyor General T.L. Mitchell to Boatswain Mahroot 2 March 1841', Surveyor General's Papers – *Copies of letters sent to private persons and officials, 1822–1853*, SANSW, NRS 13762 [2/2219].
46	'Letter from Boatswain Maroot to Colonial Secretary 11 March 1841', in *Records of Boatswain Maroot, 1832–1851*, SANSW, NRS 907, CSLIL [2/7914]; ED Thomson, 'Letter from Colonial Secretary to Boatswain Maroot 24 March 1841', *Copies of letters to individuals, organisations etc re Land, 2 January 1827–17 November 1856*, SANSW, NRS 945 [4/3580].
47	See, for example, 'The Aborigines', *SMH*, 14/12/1842, p. 2; 'To the Editors of the Sydney Morning Herald', *SMH*, 23/2/1853, p. 2.
48	D Byrne & M Nugent, *Mapping Attachment: A spatial approach to Aboriginal post-contact heritage*, Department of Environment and Conservation, Sydney, 2004, pp. 123–7.
49	Waterman 1923, p. 359; Smith 1992, p. 147.
50	'Coroner's Inquest', *SMH*, 2/3/1853, p. 2; 'Inquest', *SMH*, 18/8/1858, p. 3.
51	H Goodall & A Cadzow, *Rivers and Resilience. Aboriginal People on Sydney's Georges River*, UNSW Press, Sydney, 2009, pp. 28–30, 280–1.

Notes

3 Cross-cultural relationships (1790s–1840s)

1. 'Domestic Intelligence', *The Sydney Herald*, 11/6/1838, p. 2; KCS Robertson, 'Original Correspondence – Colonial Hospital', *The Sydney Herald*, 7/6/1838, p. 3; JE Tenison-Woods, *Fish and fisheries of New South Wales*, Government Printer, Sydney, 1882, p. 81.
2. N Oldham, *Letter: Journal*, 1840–1841, NLA MS9048.
3. KV Smith, 'Bennelong among his people', *Aboriginal History*, vol. 33, 2009, p. 11.
4. G Karskens, *The Colony: A History of Early Sydney*, Allen & Unwin, Sydney, 2009, p. 468. Aboriginal people who adopted European names should be distinguished from those who were given names by Europeans, such as adopted Aboriginal children.
5. Karskens 2009, p. 436; I McBryde, '"Barter … immediately commenced to the satisfaction of both parties": cross-cultural exchange at Port Jackson, 1788–1828', in R Torrence & A Clark (eds), *The Archaeology of Difference*, Routledge, London, 2000, pp. 238–77.
6. Karskens 2009, p. 449.
7. C Liston, 'The Dharawal and Gandangara in Colonial Campbelltown, New South Wales, 1788–1830', *Aboriginal History*, vol. 12, no. 1, 1988, pp. 51–2.
8. Quoted in Karskens 2009, p, 432. See also pp. 387–90, 431–7.
9. G Karskens, 'Naked Possession: Building and the Politics of Legitimate Occupation in Early New South Wales', in C Shammas (ed.), *Investing in the Early Modern Built Environment: Europeans, Asians, Settlers and Indigenous Societies*, Brill Academic Publishers, Leiden, 2012, p. 327.
10. JM MacKenzie, *The empire of nature: hunting, conservation, and British imperialism*, Manchester University Press, Manchester, 1988, Ch. 2.
11. A O'Brien, *Philanthropy and Settler Colonialism*, Palgrave Macmillan, Basingstoke, 2015; *The Australian Aborigines Protection Society: Instituted 1838*, James Spilsbury, Sydney, 1838.
12. 'Vox Populi – Vox Dei', *The Australian*, 20/11/1838, p. 2; 'Legislative Council: Wednesday: Aboriginal Natives' Evidence Bill', *SMH*, 29/6/1849, pp. 2–3.
13. D Denholm, *The Colonial Australians*, Penguin Books Australia, Ringwood, 1979, p. 168.
14. P Cunningham, *Two years in New South Wales*, 1927 (facs. edn, D.S. Macmillan ed., Angus & Robertson in association with the Royal Australian Historical Society, Sydney, 1966), p. 187.
15. For John Wentworth see H Goodall & A Cadzow, *Rivers and Resilience: Aboriginal People on Sydney's Georges River*, UNSW Press, Sydney, 2009, p. 53.
16. R Broome, '"There were vegetables every year Mr Green was here": Right behaviour and the struggle for autonomy at Coranderrk Aboriginal reserve', *History Australia*, vol. 3, no. 2, 2006, pp. 43.1–43.16.
17. B Reece, 'Feasts & Blankets: The history of some early attempts to establish relations with the Aborigines of New South Wales, 1814–1846', *Archaeology & Physical Anthropology in Oceania*, vol. 2, 1967, p. 205; M Smithson, 'A misunderstood gift: the annual issue of blankets to Aborigines in New South Wales, 1826–48', *Push (Armidale, NSW)*, vol. 30, 1992, pp. 86, 104.
18. R Mansfield, *Analytical view of the census of New South Wales for the year 1841: with tables showing the progress of the population during the previous twenty years*, Kemp and Fairfax, Sydney, 1841.

19 G Aplin, 'The Rise of Suburban Sydney', in M Kelly (ed.), *Sydney: City of Suburbs*, New South Wales University Press, Sydney, 1987, p. 198; J Broadbent, 'The Push East: Woolloomooloo Hill, the first suburb', in M Kelly (ed.), *Sydney: City of Suburbs*, New South Wales University Press, Sydney, 1987, p. 14.
20 S Fitzgerald, *Sydney 1842–1992*, Hale & Iremonger, Sydney, pp. 34–5.
21 Karskens 2009, p. 533.
22 JS Prout and J Rae, *Sydney Illustrated (1842–1843): With extended collection of early Sydney paintings*, DMK Publishing, Cabarita Beach, 2011.
23 Prout and Rae 2011, pp. 64–5.
24 G Karskens, 'The dialogue of townscape: the Rocks and Sydney, 1788/1820', *Australian Historical Studies*, vol. 27, no. 108, 1997, p. 89.
25 For proliferation of public houses see J Hood, *Australia and the East: being a Journal Narrative of a Voyage to New South Wales, &c., in the Years 1841 and 1842*, vol. 8, Murray, London, 1843, p. 87; C Wilkes, *Narrative of the United States Exploring Expedition during the years 1838, 1839, 1840, 1841, 1842*, vol. 2, Lea and Blanchard, Philadelphia, 1844, p. 164. For a resident's nuanced perspective see E Walker, 'Old Sydney in the 'Forties: Recollections of Lower George Street and "the Rocks" [Transcribed by SK Johnstone]', *JRAHS*, vol. 16, no. 4, 1930, pp. 298–9.
26 D Byrne, 'Segregated landscapes: the heritage of racial segregation in New South Wales', *Historic Environment – Islands of Vanishment*, vol. 17, no. 1, 2003, pp. 14–15.
27 J Waterman, 'Recollections of Sydney', *JRAHS*, vol. 8, Supplement, 1923, p. 359.
28 G Karskens, 'Red coat, blue jacket, black skin: Aboriginal men and clothing in early New South Wales', *Aboriginal History*, vol. 35, 2011, p. 26.
29 'Stabbing', *SMH*, 19/5/1849, p. 2; 'Disorderly Conduct', *Empire*, 18/5/1852, p. 2; 'Furious Driving', *The Sydney Gazette and New South Wales Advertiser*, 24/3/1840, p. 2.
30 For details of Smith's life see KR Binney, *Horsemen of the first frontier (1788–1900) and the Serpent's legacy*, Volcanic Productions, Sydney, 2005.
31 'Death of Mr Charles Smith', *The Parramatta Chronicle*, 25/1/1845, p. 3.
32 'Sydney Blacks', *The Australian*, 2/11/1844, p. 3.
33 'The Blacks', *Sydney Gazette*, 17/5/1842, p. 2; 'News of the Day: Street Acting – A Black Joke', *Sydney Monitor*, 19/11/1840, p. 2; 'Domestic Intelligence – The Aborigines', *Sydney Herald*, 7/9/1841, p. 2; JP Townsend, 'Journal, 21 July – 6 Dec. 1846', in *Joseph Phipps Townsend Papers 21 July 1846 – 24 Sep 1862*, SLNSW ML MSS 1461/1 (CY2477), Frame 87.
34 Old Chum [JM Forde], 'Old Sydney. Some Old-Time Inns', *Truth*, 28/8/1910, in JM Forde, 1903–28 *Old Sydney: Truth Articles: Volume A*, SLNSW, p. 125.
35 'Queen Gooseberry', *SMH*, 31/7/1852, p. 8; Old Chum [JM Forde] *Truth*, 6/4/1919 in Forde, J.M. 1903–28 *Old Sydney: Truth Articles: Volume C*, SLNSW, pp. 101–2. The Sydney Arms was at 224 Castlereagh Street, now the site of a skyscraper.
36 Old Chum [JM Forde] 1910. The cemetery was located at what became Central Railway Station, and her grave was moved to Botany Cemetery ahead of its construction.
37 'Death of an Aboriginal', *SMH*, 14/4/1849, p. 3.
38 'Inquests', *The Australian*, 8/9/1846, p. 3; 'Inquests', *Sydney Chronicle*, 9/9/1846, p. 3.
39 Barron Field in Karskens 2009, p. 432.
40 Anon, 'Blacks', *The Australian*, 2/11/1842.

Notes

41 'The Municipal Elections', *The Australian*, 2/11/1842, p. 2.
42 B Reece, *Aborigines and Colonists: Aborigines and Colonial Society in New South Wales in the 1830s and 1840s*, Sydney University Press, Sydney, 1974, Ch. 5; J Mitchell, *In Good Faith? Governing Indigenous Australia Through God, Charity and Empire, 1825–1855*, Aboriginal History Monograph 23, ANU E Press, Canberra, 2011, pp. 173–91.
43 J Ferry, 'The Failure of the New South Wales Missions to the Aborigines before 1845', *Aboriginal History*, vol. 3, no. 1, 1979, pp. 25–35. As historian Jessie Mitchell has argued, the accepted historical view of these ventures as 'failures' masks the complexity of the effects of these places on Aboriginal people, Mitchell 2011, pp. 191–4.
44 For example, three young orphaned children were sent from northern New South Wales by the Commissioner of Crown Lands to Sydney Normal School in 1841, see 'Aboriginal Children', *Sydney Monitor*, 26/11/1841, p. 2. For Aboriginal convicts see K Harman, *Aboriginal convicts: Australian, Khoisan and Maori exiles*, UNSW Press, Sydney, 2012; 'Humanity', *The Colonist*, 20/5/1840, p. 2. Of around eighty Aboriginal prisoners identified in the records of Sydney gaols between 1839 and 1849, almost all were from regions some distance from Sydney; see 'Entrance Books 1819–1849', *Sydney & Darlinghurst Gaol Records*, SANSW, NRS 2514 & 2519 [4/6438–4/6441].
45 J Hirst, 'Historical reconsiderations 1: Keeping colonial history colonial: the Hartz thesis revisited', *Historical Studies*, vol. 21, no. 82, 1984, pp. 87–8; A O'Brien, 'Kitchen fragments and garden stuff': poor law discourse and indigenous people in early colonial New South Wales', *Australian Historical Studies*, vol. 39, no. 2, 2008, p. 162.
46 See Reece 1967, pp. 200–3.
47 Smithson 1992, pp. 101–2. For the context of other policies in this period see Mitchell 2011; Reece 1974.
48 A Curthoys, *Race and Ethnicity: A Study of the response of British Colonists to Aborigines and Chinese and non-British Europeans in New South Wales 1856–1881*, PhD thesis, Macquarie University, 1973, p. 175.
49 'The Aborigines' Petition', *The Australian*, 29/7/1842, p. 2. For relationship to Bulkabra see J Connell, 'Letter to Governor Darling requesting blankets [nd]', SLNSW MSS Aa84 (CY3583).
50 Records suggest that there may have been two William Annans, perhaps father and son. A 'William and Ann' was first noted as a young man in Sydney in 1797 by David Collins, and would have been born in the 1780s, making him around 50 by the early 1830s. However, at this time, Annan and blanket returns state his age as 25, and this appears more in line with the sketch in Figure 3.6 from 1843. It is possible therefore that the original William and Ann was the later William Annan's father. DF Collins, *An Account of the English Colony in New South Wales: Volume 2*, Cadell and Davies, London, 1802 (facs. edn, BH Fletcher ed., AH & AW Reed in association with the Royal Australian Historical Society, Sydney, 1975), pp. 40–1; N Plomley (ed.), *Friendly Mission: The Tasmanian Journals and Papers of George Augustus Robinson 1829–1834*, 2nd edn, Queen Victoria Museum and Art Gallery/Quintus Publishing, Hobart, 2008, pp. 505–6; *Papers dealing with issue of blankets etc. and including returns of the native population in the various districts, 1833–35*, SANSW, NRS 905 [4/6666B.3], Reel 3706, frame 65.

51 For quote see 'Recontre', *The Australian*, 16/7/1828, p. 3. Also, 'Bushrangers', *Sydney Gazette and New South Wales Advertiser*, 25/7/1828, p. 3; '[No Title – Williminan]', *The Australian*, 1/8/1828, p. 3.
52 For continued fishing see Tenison-Woods 1882, p. 81. For seeking donations see 'The Aborigines' Petition', *The Australian*, 29/7/1842, p. 2. It is assumed that this petition to the governor was written by Annan, though no trace of the original document has been found.
53 See, for example, 'News of the Day', *Sydney Monitor and Commercial Advertiser*, 28/4/1841, p. 2.
54 'Sudden Death of an Aboriginal Native', *The Australian*, 31/5/1844, p. 3.
55 'The Sydney Aborigines', *Morning Chronicle*, 8/6/1844, p. 2.
56 G Nichols, 'The Aborigines of Sydney', *The Australian Daily Journal*, 5/6/1844, p. 2.
57 K Mills, 'George Robert Nichols (1809–1857): Forgotten Patriot and Lawmaker', *Journal of Australian Colonial History*, vol. 11, 2009, pp. 101–28.
58 'Sydney', *Sydney Gazette*, 12/5/1805, pp. 2–3; see references in note 51.
59 'The Sydney Blacks', *SMH*, 28/12/1844, p. 3; Townsend 1846, fr. 87. For Townsend's 'Tamarin' as Tamara see ch. 2, note 20.
60 'Aboriginal Superstition', *The Australian*, 1/6/1844, p. 3.
61 'Aboriginal Christmas Festivities', *The Australian*, 27/12/1844, p. 3. 'Boatswain' was the name Europeans often gave to Mahroot. Tarban may be Thomas Tamara, though this is not certain. For number of attendees see 'The Late Mr Charles Smith', *Bell's Life in Sydney and Sporting Reviewer*, 20/12/1845, p. 2.
62 'Funeral of Mr Charles Smith', *Bell's Life in Sydney and Sporting Reviewer*, 25/1/1845, p. 3.
63 H Goodall, *Invasion to Embassy: Land in Aboriginal Politics in New South Wales, 1770–1972*, Allen & Unwin in association with Black Books, Sydney, 1996, pp. 44–87.
64 B Bridges, *Aboriginal and White Relations in New South Wales, 1788–1855*, Masters thesis, Sydney University, 1966, p. 673; NSW Legislative Committee Votes and Proceedings, *Report from the Select Committee on the Condition of the Aborigines, with appendix, minutes of evidence and replies to a circular letter*, Government Printer, Sydney, 1845.
65 Karskens 2009, p. 522.
66 Bridges 1966, pp. 673–4.
67 'Aborigines', *SMH*, 20/4/1846, p. 2.
68 GR Nichols *et al.*, 'Letter to Colonial Secretary 19/4/1847', SANSW, NRS 905, CSLR, 47/3360 with 58/1129 [4/3378].
69 J Long Innes *et al.*, 'Letter to Colonial Secretary 27/11/1848', SANSW, NRS 905, CSLR, 48/13283, [4/2820]; J Gogey, 'Petition of Jackey Gogey to the Governor General regarding purchase of a boat, 3/9/1850', SANSW, NRS 905, CSLR, 50/7957 [4/2912].

4 Entangled lives (1850s–1870s)
1 WH East, 'Sixty Years Ago. Transformation of Sydney', *SMH*, 15/2/1930, p. 13.
2 NSW Government, *Census of 1871 Consisting of Report, Summary Tables and Appendix*, Thomas Richards, Government Printer, Sydney, 1873.

Notes

3   G Wotherspoon, 'Buses', *Dictionary of Sydney*, 2008, <www.dictionaryofsydney.org/entry/buses> (viewed 27 October 2016).

4   'Distribution of Blankets to the Aborigines', *SMH*, 27/5/1850, p. 2; 'Blankets for the Aborigines. Returns 1857–1861', *VPLA 1862*, vol. 5, Government Printer, Sydney, 1862, pp. 1171–4. The Aboriginal population was certainly greater than the ten Aboriginal people recorded in the 1871 census, which may not have included part-Aboriginal people or perhaps focussed only on those living with Europeans. It entirely ignored the Aboriginal people living at Botany at this time, for example; see NSW Government 1873, *Census of 1871*.

5   'Watson's Bay', *SMH*, 27/12/1859, p. 4; 'The Late Melancholy Yacht Accident', *Illawarra Mercury*, 30/12/1864, p. 2; TR Roe, *Plan of the town of Watson's Bay*, Allen & Wrigley, Sydney, 1857.

6   The idea was most influentially articulated in N Thomas, *Entangled objects: exchange, material culture, and colonialism in the Pacific*, Harvard University Press, Harvard, 1991.

7   Quote in 'Incendiarism and its Effects', *SMH*, 22/1/1845, p. 3; and see 'Domestic Intelligence – The Bushrangers', *The Sydney Herald*, 14/2/1842, p. 2; 'Receipts, 3 March 1844, 6/4/1844', SLNSW, Wentworth Papers, MSS 8/1 Ser. 7; 'Receipts, December 1845', SLNSW, Wentworth Papers, MSS 8/1 Ser. 8.

8   'Incendiarism and its Effects', *SMH*, 22/1/1845, p. 3; 'Praiseworthy Conduct', *SMH*, 24/1/1845, p. 4.

9   'Rickety Dick', *SMH*, 16/6/1863, p. 4.

10 For relationship see annotation on JH Flynn, *Ethnology: Original Sketches with reference to Sydney: Aboriginals and their homes &c.*, [c.1880s], SLNSW, PXA618, image 5. For travels with Cora see J Waterman, 'Recollections of Sydney', *JRAHS*, vol. 8, Supplement, 1923, p. 359; Old Chum [JM Forde], 'Old Sydney: Some Old-Time Inns', *Truth*, 28/8/1910, in JM Forde 1903–28 *Old Sydney: Truth Articles:Volume A*, SLNSW, p. 125.

11 JA Dowling, 'Recollections of New South Head Road and Woollahra', *JRAHS*, vol. 10, no. 1, 1925, pp. 54–5. Though Warrell may have lived both outside Rose Bay cottage, as stated in this source, and further east over the years, the latter location seems most likely, as is mentioned by several sources. This area is now entirely built over.

12 'Death of Old Ricketty Dick', *Empire*, 16/6/1863, p. 4. Cooper is also said to have provided for Warrell; see K Scherzer, *Journal of Dr Karl Scherzer*, 1858 (Transcribed by Mrs Dymphna Clark, January–February 1995), <www.uow.edu.au/~morgan/novara2.htm> (viewed 27 October 2016).

13 'Return of Mr W.C. Wentworth', *SMH Supplement*, 19/4/1861, p. 5.

14 S Wentworth, 'Letter from Sarah Wentworth to Thomasine Fisher c. late 1864', SLNSW, Wentworth family papers, MSS A868 (CY POS 725), frame 685.

15 'Obituary E.S. Hill', *Town and Country Journal*, 3/4/1880, p. 648.

16 'The Late Hon. R. Hill, MLC. A Sketch of His Career', *SMH*, 21/8/1895, p. 8.

17 'Death certificate of Johnny Baswick alias Bankie 18/8/1880', NSW BDM #1880/3881; Council of Education, 'Application for the establishment of a Provisional School at North Huskisson and New Bristol, 1871', *Council of Education, Miscellaneous Letters Received, 1867–1875*, SANSW, NRS 2621, Volume 143 [1/875].

18   BT Dowd & W Foster (eds), *The History of the Waverley Municipal District*, The Council of the Municipality of Waverley, 1959, p. 139; 'Coroner's Inquest', *SMH*, 16/12/1873, p. 6; 'Harry, the King of Kissing Point', *SMH*, 17/7/1880, p. 7.
19   East 1930, p. 13. Baswick's group are not specifically named as the fishermen, but are the only Aboriginal residents of the Rose Bay area described elsewhere in the article.
20   'Death of a Young Aboriginal Female', *SMH*, 5/10/1876, p. 5; NSW Legislative Council, '30 June 1880', in *Parliamentary Debates Session 1879–1880*. First Series, Vol. 3, Government Printer, Sydney, pp. 3115–16; APB, 'Protection of the Aborigines: Report of Board for 1891', *VPLA 1892–93*, vol. 7, Government Printer, Sydney, p. 21.
21   'Sydney News', *Maitland Mercury & Hunter River General Advertiser*, 22/9/1859, p. 3. The settlement is described in several different locations within a fairly small area over the years. Another possible location is immediately south of New South Head Road at the northern end of what is now the NSW Lawn Tennis association grounds.
22   East 1930, p. 13; A Gelding, 'The Reminiscences of Alfred Gelding, 1937', in C Silas-Smith (ed.), *The Reflective Gardener* <www.reflectivegardener.blogspot.com.au/2012/08/the-reminiscences-of-alfred-gelding.html> (viewed 27 October 2016).
23   See, for example, 'Sydney News', *Maitland Mercury & Hunter River General Advertiser*, 14/2/1863, p. 3; 'Accidents and Offences', *SMH*, 25/11/1878, p. 8; Gelding 1937.
24   East 1930, p. 13. East also recalled that Aboriginal people had fought with indentured South Pacific labourers nearby at Double Bay. This has the air of local legend, but Double Bay resident Robert Towns did transport labourers to his properties in northern Queensland in the 1860s and it is possible that some transited through his property, Cranbrook.
25   E Wait, *The Migration of People of Aboriginal Ancestry to the Metropolitan Area and their Assimilation*, BA Honours thesis, University of Sydney, 1950, p. 15.
26   ADMB, 'Seven Shilling Beach: A Quaint Story', *SMH*, 5/4/1941, p. 9. For a slightly different version see J Jervis & V Kelly, *The History of Woollahra: A record of Events from 1788 to 1960 and a Centenary of Local Government*, The Municipal Council of Woollahra, 1960, p. 44. Gurrah and Nancy's hut was built in what is now the public garden immediately east of the house.
27   Jervis & Kelly 1960, p. 44.
28   R Waterhouse, 'Bare-knuckle prize fighting, masculinity and nineteenth century Australian culture', *Journal of Australian Studies*, vol. 26, no. 73, 2002, pp. 101–10, 236–8.
29   For the exodus elsewhere, see H Goodall, *Invasion to Embassy: Land in Aboriginal Politics in New South Wales, 1770–1972*, Allen & Unwin in association with Black Books, Sydney, 1996, pp. 57–66.
30   J Fletcher, *Clean, Clad & Courteous: A History of Aboriginal Education in New South Wales*, Southward Press Pty Ltd, Sydney, 1989, pp. 35–8. National Education Office, 'Minutes of Meeting 23/3/1853', *Board of National Education Fair Minute Books*, SANSW, NRS637 [1/331], p. 560.
31   M Parsons, 'The tourist corroboree in South Australia to 1911', *Aboriginal History*, vol. 21, 1997, p. 48.
32   See, for example, 'The Pleasures of Botany', *Bell's Life in Sydney and Sporting Reviewer*, 23/2/1850, p. 2.

Notes

33 'The Ring: Full Account of the The Great Fight between Perry, the Black and George Hough', *Bell's Life in Sydney and Sporting Reviewer*, 13/10/1849, p. 2; 'Died', *SMH*, 2/2/1850, p. 5; GC Mundy, *Our antipodes, or, Residence and rambles in the Australasian colonies: with a glimpse of the gold fields*, Richard Bentley, London, 1852, p. 393.
34 'Botany Bay', *SMH*, 28/1/1861, p. 5.
35 E Knapp, 'Letter from E. Knapp, 30/9/1868', *Letters received, Miscellaneous Branch, Department of Lands*, SANSW, NRS8258, 68/4452 [2/1045].
36 Testimony of Mahroot in NSW Legislative Committee Votes and Proceedings, *Report from the Select Committee on the Condition of the Aborigines, with appendix, minutes of evidence and replies to a circular letter*, Government Printer, Sydney, 1845, p. 4 [question 142].
37 Scherzer 1858, pp. 71–2.
38 'Circular – Sir Joseph Banks Hotel', *SMH*, 18/4/1862, p. 1.
39 'Burglaries, Stealing from Premises', *NSWPG*, 22/4/1868, p. 124. Their daughter Elizabeth was born there; see 'Marriage certificate of John Timbery and Elizabeth Brand', NSW BDM #1910/6400.
40 'Wallaby Shooting at Port Hacking', *Australian Town & Country Journal*, 30/7/1870, p. 27.
41 H Goodall & A Cadzow, *Rivers and Resilience: Aboriginal People on Sydney's Georges River*, UNSW Press, Sydney, 2009, pp. 87–91.
42 'Reports of Crime: District of Liverpool', *NSWPG*, 4/8/1857, p. 1; 'Public Notice', *Empire*, 18/5/1872, p. 1. A settler reminiscence in the *St George Call* newspaper in 1904 incorrectly stated that the owner was Dr Alexander Cuthill, but Alexander lived in the city up until his death in 1854, and these references and parish maps show the owner of the Mill Creek land was James Ferrier Cuthill.
43 Woolla-Nora [pseud.], 'Old Times. A Day at Billy Giles' Home', *St George Call*, 17/8/1907, p. 3. The boys living with Biddy do not appear to have been her own children. They are described as 'two waifs who had found a home' with Biddy and Billy.
44 Goodall & Cadzow 2009, pp. 94–100, quote on p. 100.
45 Old Ned, 'When our Beards Were Black', *Sydney Sportsman*, 17/6/1903, p. 3.
46 For wallbungers see 'Wallaby Shooting at Port Hacking', *Australian Town & Country Journal*, 30/7/1870, p. 27; Goodall & Cadzow 2009, p. 101. For Biddy and Mahroot's prowess see 'Botany Bay', *SMH*, 28/1/1861, p. 5; Goodall & Cadzow 2009, pp. 95–6.
47 For Malone's knowledge of areas south of Sydney see J Ensor, 'National Park Caves', *SMH*, 26/7/1905, p. 6.
48 For the booming trade see A Coote, 'Science, Fashion, Knowledge and Imagination: Shopfront Natural History in 19th-Century Sydney', *Sydney Journal*, vol. 4, no. 1, 2013, 1–18. For Aboriginal participation see GAC Kennedy, 'To the Editor of the Herald', *SMH*, 16/2/1861, p. 6; 'Death from Disease, Accelerated by Intemperance', *Empire*, 18/8/1858, p. 5. Biddy's ex-husband Paddy also participated in this trade in the Illawarra; 'Rara Avis', *SMH*, 21/8/1858, p. 7.
49 E Delessert, *Voyage dans les Deux Oceans Atlantique et Pacifique 1844 a 1847*, A Franck, Paris, 1848, pp. 169–70 [trans. Michael Wotodzo].
50 Goodall & Cadzow 2009, pp. 100, 108.
51 'Obituary E.S. Hill', *Town and Country Journal*, 3/4/1880, p. 648.

52   See, for example, E Hill, 'Marriage of an Aboriginal Black with an Englishwoman', *SMH*, 21/5/1864, p. 2.
53   Examples include 'The Aborigines of Australia', *Empire*, 16/7/1861, p. 5; JE Tenison-Woods, *Fish and fisheries of New South Wales,* Government Printer, Sydney, 1882; SW Macarthur, 'Specimens of Woods Indigenous to the Southern Districts', in *Catalogue of Natural and Industrial Products: New South Wales International Exhibition*, Government Printer, Sydney, 1861. Thanks to John Ruffels for pointing these out.
54   Scherzer 1858, p. 72.
55   M Horsburgh, 'The apprenticing of dependent children in New South Wales between 1850 and 1885', *Journal of Australian Studies*, no. 7, 1980, pp. 33–54; I Walden, *Aboriginal Women in Domestic Service in New South Wales, 1850–1969*, BA Honours thesis, University of NSW, 1991; S Robinson, 'Regulating the race: Aboriginal children in private European homes in colonial Australia', *Journal of Australian Studies*, vol. 37, no. 3, 2013, pp. 302–15; V Haskins, *One Bright Spot*, Palgrave Macmillan, Basingstoke, 2005.
56   W Macdonald, 'Forby Sutherland's Grave at Kurnell', *JRAHS*, no. 19, 1928, p. 286.
57   J Connell, 'Letter to Governor Darling requesting blankets [nd]', SLNSW MSS Aa84 (CY3583), nd; W Houston, 'Notes of an Interview between W. Houston Esq., one of the Trustees of Captain Cook's Land Place (Kurnell) and Mr. Longfield, at Kurnell on Sunday the 22nd January 1905', CCLP Archives, Box 12 Item 141, p. 5.
58   For death of Thomas Snr see 'Coroner's Inquest', *Empire*, 2/3/1853, p. 2. For Thomas Jnr as servant see 'Central Police Court – Thursday', *Empire*, 4/1/1868, p. 2. No specific document has been found to link the elder and younger Thomas, but no others are known by this name and it is highly unlikely that they lived in the same area if they were not closely related.
59   S Wentworth 1864; L Wentworth, 'Letter from Laura Wentworth to Thomasine Fisher 15 July (1864?)', in SLNSW, Wentworth family papers, MSS A868 (CY POS 725), frame 908.
60   For Emma and George see Wait 1950, p. 10; 'Queen Emma Dead. Last Monarch of La Perouse', *Sunday Times*, 3/12/1916, p. 26. The Mrs Edward Hill mentioned may have been Richard's sister in law but is more likely a mistaken reference to his own wife, Henrietta. Other servants of Richard Hill included Billy Malone (most likely a relative of Johnny Malone and therefore local to Sydney) and an Aboriginal woman from within the coastal zone at Newcastle, who worked for him for over thirty years and provided him with Aboriginal language information. See 'Five Pounds Reward', *SMH*, 4/4/1856, p. 1; R Hill, 'Aboriginal Names', *SMH*, 24/5/1890, p. 6.
61   'Central Police Court – Friday: Stealing', *Empire*, 3/3/1855, p. 6.
62   'Record #439 & #452 (1/3/1855 – 2/3/1855), #1354 & #1618 (21/6/1855, 24/7/1855)', *Darlinghurst Gaol Entrance Books 1853–1855*, SANSW, NRS 2134, [5/1892]; 'Record #1288 & #2397 (1856)', *Sydney Gaol and Darlinghurst Gaol Description Books 1855–1860*, SANSW, NRS 2523 [4/6304].
63   'Inquests', *SMH*, 15/4/1857, p. 5.
64   For asylum history see RW Rathbone, *A Very Present Help; Caring for Australians since 1813: The History of the Benevolent Society of New South Wales*, State Library of New South Wales Press, Sydney, 1994. For deaths see P Jalland, *Australian ways*

of death: a social and cultural history, 1840–1918, Oxford University Press, Oxford, 2002, Ch. 11. The building was demolished to make way for Central Station around 1900.

65 'Minutes for 8/9/1846', *Minutes of the Acting Committee Nov 1845 – Dec 1846*, SLNSW, BSNSW collection, 1813–1996, A7174; 'minutes for 21/11/1848', *Minutes of the Acting Committee Sep 1848 – Apr 1850*, SLNSW, BSNSW collection, 1813–1996, A7176. Tamara was recommended by Police Superintendent WA Miles after he visited Tamara at Vaucluse in 1846. Warrell was recommended by John Dalley, who was the father of WD Dalley of Vaucluse. For Warrell's refusal to return see 'Death of Old Rickety Dick', *Empire*, 16/6/1863, p. 4.

66 'Burglaries, Stealing from Premises', *NSWPG*, 22/4/1868, p. 124.

67 JB Martin, 'Letter to Colonial Secretary from Camden Police Office 21/2/1862', SANSW, NRS 905, CSLR, 62/925 [4/3465].

68 J Gogey, 'Petition of Jackey Gogey to the Governor General regarding purchase of a boat, 3/9/1850', SANSW, NRS 905, CSLR, 50/7957 [4/2912]; J Goggey, 'Petition to the Governor General, 18/11/1857', *Department of Lands and Public Works Correspondence, Letters Received, 1856–1866*, SANSW, NRS 7933, 57/4196 [5/3581].

69 Goodall & Cadzow 2009, pp. 56–61. Goodall and Cadzow state that the takeover of Goggey's land was undertaken by John Rowley's nephew of the same name, and contrast his actions with the more benevolent stance of his uncle, but it was the elder John Rowley in both instances. The younger John Rowley had died at Liverpool a year and a half before Jonathan Goggey wrote to the government about the eviction.

70 'John Rowley, 1842', *Insolvency files*, SANSW, NRS 13654, 00571 [2/8717]; 'John Rowley (Snr), 1858', *Insolvency files*, SANSW, NRS 13654, 04340 [2/8961].

71 Goggey 1857; 'Letter from N.S.W. Surveyor-General, 16/1/1858', *Department of Lands and Public Works Correspondence, Letters Received, 1856–1866*, SANSW, NRS 7933, 57/4196 [5/3581].

72 'John Rowley (Snr), 1858', *Insolvency files*, SANSW, NRS 13654, 04340 [2/8961]; Goodall & Cadzow 2009, p. 175.

73 R Baker, *Land is Life: From Bush to Town: The Story of the Yanyuwa People*, Allen and Unwin, Sydney, 1999, p. 179; Goodall 1996, p. 67.

74 Bennelong Point on the eastern side of Circular Quay is a much earlier example of this, in recognition that Bennelong occupied a hut built there for him on Governor Phillip's orders in 1790, but there are few examples in coastal Sydney in the interim.

75 ADMB, 'Seven Shilling Beach: A Quaint Story', *SMH*, 5/4/1941, p. 9.

76 For Sophia's Spring see Jervis & Kelly 1960, p. 44. For Black Gin Beach see W Barracluff, 'Letter to the Editor', *The Courier*, 13/9/1960, in *Waverley Local Studies Collection*, p. 4.

5 Strangers in their own land (1850s–1870s)

1 'Distribution of Blankets to the Aborigines', *SMH*, 27/5/1850, p. 2.

2 For a clear and considered exploration of how these ideas developed, see D Byrne, 'Deep nation: Australia's acquisition of an indigenous past', *Aboriginal History*, vol. 20, 1996, 82–107.

3 For Bennelong see 'Sydney', *Sydney Gazette*, 9/1/1813, p. 2. For Bungaree see 'Boongarie', *The Australian*, 3/12/1830, p. 3.

4   Examples include E Dortins, 'The many truths of Bennelong's tragedy', *Aboriginal History*, vol. 33, 2009, pp. 53–75; KV Smith, 'Bennelong among his people', *Aboriginal History*, vol. 33, 2009, pp. 7–30; <www.findingbennelong.com/perspectives-bennelong> (viewed 28 October 2016); M Dunn, *A Valley in a Valley: Colonial Struggles over land and resources in the Hunter Valley, NSW 1820–1850*, PhD thesis, University of New South Wales, 2015, pp. 64, 80–2, 103–4; KV Smith, 'Bungaree', Dictionary of Sydney, 2011, <www.dictionaryofsydney.org/entry/bungaree> (viewed 28 October 2016).
5   E Furniss, 'Timeline history and the Anzac myth: Settler narratives of local history in a North Australian town', *Oceania*, vol. 71, no. 4, 2001, p. 288.
6   R Foster, 'Tommy Walker walk up here …', J Simpson & L Hercus (eds), *History in portraits: biographies of nineteenth century South Australian Aboriginal people*, Aboriginal History Monograph 6, Canberra, Aboriginal History Inc., 1998, pp. 217–18.
7   'Domestic Intelligence – Billy Worrall', *The Colonist*, 22/12/1840, p. 2. By 1844 he was also known as Ricketty Dick; see reference for Figure 5.1.
8   K Scherzer, *Narrative of the circumnavigation of the globe by the Austrian frigate Novara (commodore B. Von Wullerstorf-Urbair) undertaken by order of the Imperial Government in the years 1857, 1858 & 1859*, vol. 3, Saunders, Otley & Co., London, 1863, p. 17. See also P Mukhanov, '"Sydney", Translated from the Russian of Pavel Mukhanov by Verity Fitzhardinge', *JRAHS*, vol. 51, no. 4, 1965, pp. 296–316; GF Angas, 'On the Aboriginal inhabitants of N. S. Wales', *Australian Almanac and Country Directory*, 1858, p. 59.
9   E Czernis-Ryl, 'Early Australian silver statuette: a story of Julius Hogarth and Ricketty Dick', *The Australian Antiques & Fine Art Dealer's Fair catalogue*, 1996, pp. 6–10. Samuel Cook, who received the Hogarth inkwell, lived in Sydney and worked for the *Sydney Morning Herald* in the 1850s.
10 'An Australian Ruin', *Empire*, 29/12/1860, p. 4.
11 'Rickety Dick', *SMH*, 16/6/1863, p. 4; 'Death of Old Rickety Dick', *Empire* 16/6/1863, p. 4.
12 'Botany Bay', *SMH*, 28/1/1861, p. 5; WJ Molony, 'Letter to J.B. Wilson Minister of Lands 26/8/1868', *Letters Received Lands Department Miscellaneous Branch*, SANSW, NRS8258, 68/4452 [2/1045]. Mahroot's wife was not definitely buried at the hotel but this appears likely as Mahroot elsewhere described tending her grave and was probably buried with her.
13 T Griffiths, *Hunters and Collectors: The Antiquarian Imagination in Australia*, Cambridge University Press, Melbourne, 1996, p. 112.
14 Czernis-Ryl 1996, p. 10; B Hornshaw, 'Ricketty Dick', *Mankind*, August, 1933, pp. 162–3. For presence of Aboriginal people see 'Intercolonial Exhibition', *SMH*, 25/4/1873, p. 6.
15 For the Sydney tribe, see 'The Sydney Blacks', *SMH*, 28/12/1844, p. 3; 'Legislative Council', *SMH*, 27/6/1844, p. 2; H Laracy, 'Leopold Verguet and the Aborigines of Sydney, 1845', *Aboriginal History*, vol. 4, no. 2, 1980, p. 181; 'Aborigines', *SMH*, 20/4/1846, p. 2. For Warrell see 'Rickety Dick', *SMH*, 16/6/1863, p. 4; WH Fernyhough, c.1836, 'Bill Worrall, Five Island Tribe', in *Profiles of the Aborigines of New South Wales*, SLNSW, PXA616, Image 4; Figure 5.1.
16 'Summary of Monthly News from 20th January to 18th February, 1863,' *SMH*,

19/2/1863; 'Sydney News', *Maitland Mercury & Hunter River General Advertiser*, 14/2/1863, p. 3.
17 GC Mundy, *Our antipodes, or, Residence and rambles in the Australasian colonies: with a glimpse of the gold fields*, vol. 1, Richard Bentley, London, 1852, pp. 392–3.
18 Mukhanov 1965, pp. 303, 307.
19 'Mr Craig's Exhibition', *SMH*, 6/2/1862, p. 5; E Hamilton-Smith & B Finlayson, *Beneath the surface: a natural history of Australian caves*, UNSW Press, Sydney, 2003, pp. 156–8.
20 A Coote, 'Science, Fashion, Knowledge and Imagination: Shopfront Natural History in 19th-Century Sydney', *Sydney Journal*, vol. 4, no. 1, 2013, pp. 8–9. Other examples included the 1864 display of the skull of 'Black Jack' at the 'Phrenological Museum' and the 'native mummy' on display in the Chamber of Horrors at the Wax Works in 1867; 'Phrenological Museum', *SMH*, 29/12/1864, p.1; 'Terrible Novelty – The New Wonder. The mysterious Queensland Native Mummy', *SMH*, 9/2/1867, p. 4.
21 'Second Fight', *Bell's Life in Sydney and Sporting Reviewer*, 13/7/1850, p. 2; 'Malcolm's Circus', *Empire*, 22/5/1852, p. 2; 'Public Amusements. Our Lyceum', *Empire*, 26/1/1857, p. 1.
22 'Colonial and Intercolonial News', *SMH*, 1/9/1866, p. 4; R Harcourt & DJ Mulvaney, *Cricket walkabout: the Aboriginal cricketers of the 1860s*, 3rd edn, Golden Point Press, Melbourne, 2005, pp. 31–2.
23 'The Cricket Match', *Empire*, 23/2/1867, p. 4.
24 'An Aboriginal Exhibition – A Good Idea', *Australian Town & Country Journal*, 8/3/1879, p. 17.
25 For the Sydney artefacts see V Attenbrow, *Sydney's Aboriginal Past: Investigating the archaeological and historical records*, UNSW Press, Sydney, 2010, p. 86.
26 'The Sydney International Exhibition', *Australian Town & Country Journal*, 31/1/1880, p. 7.
27 'Sydney News', *Maitland Mercury & Hunter River General Advertiser*, 14/2/1863, p. 3. Emphasis added, but it is clear from the context that the intended meaning was 'mine' not 'yours'.
28 'George's River', *SMH*, 8/8/1870, p. 2.
29 For Shoalhaven visitors see 'Murder', *Sydney Gazette and NSW Advertiser*, 11/9/1838, p. 2; A Berry, 'Recollections of the Aborigines', 1838, in M Organ (ed.), *Illawarra and South Coast Aborigines 1770–1850*, Aboriginal Education Unit, University of Wollongong, 1990, pp. 229–40; M Bennett, *For a Labourer Worthy of His Hire: Aboriginal Economic Responses to Colonisation in the Illawarra and Shoalhaven, 1770–1900*, PhD thesis, University of Canberra, 2003, pp. 81, 96, 113, 151–2, 156, 164, 177, 199; F Cridland, 'Illawarra Scenery', *SMH*, 22/1/1925, p. 6. Visitors from Eden appear to have largely stayed on their boat, though one article suggests 'Sydney' Aboriginal people were involved in a regatta at Eden at this time, which suggests that these groups were making contact; see 'Aboriginal Sailors', *The Australian*, 8/4/1844, p. 2; 'Vessels in Harbour', *The Australian*, 29/5/1845, p. 2.
30 'Minutes of Aborigines Protectorate Board Meeting 26/4/1894', *Aborigines Protection Board Minute Books 1890–1901*, SANSW, NRS 2 [4/7108]. This suggests that free travel had existed for some time.

31 See various letters in this period to the colonial secretary from local police, magistrates and others regarding the annual issue of blankets. See also 'Distribution of Blankets to the Aborigines', *SMH*, 27/5/1850, p. 2; 'Blankets for the Aborigines. Returns 1857–1861', *VPLA 1862*, vol. 5, Government Printer, Sydney, 1862, pp. 1171–4.

32 'The Aborigines', *Empire*, 15/4/1856, p. 4; Angas 1858, p. 59; 'Blankets for the Aborigines. Returns 1857–1861', *VPLA 1862*, vol. 5, Government Printer, Sydney, 1862, pp. 1172–3; G Thornton, '[Distribution of blankets in Sydney]. Letter to Colonial Secretary 13/10/1857', SANSW, NRS 905, CSLR, 57/4140 with 58/1529 [4/3378].

33 G Thornton, 'Letter to Colonial Secretary 13/2/1868', SANSW, NRS 905, CSLR, 68/1002 [4/619].

34 'Gathering of the Blacks', *SMH*, 12/3/1868, p. 4; 'Cundletown', *Manning River News*, 21/3/1868, p. 3; 'Aborigines Feast', *SMH*, 12/3/1868, p. 8.

35 'Attempted Assassination of The Duke of Edinburgh', *Empire*, 27/3/1868, p. 2. The event is briefly mentioned in J Milner & OW Brierly, *The Cruise of H.M.S. Galatea: Captain H.R.H. The Duke of Edinburgh, K.G. In 1867–1868*, W.H. Allen, London, 1869. Accounts of other legs of the trip in Australia were much more detailed.

36 LF Mann, 'Early Neutral Bay', *JRAHS*, vol. XIX, no. 5, 1932, p. 196. A similar rehearsal appears to be the basis for an anecdote in M Levy, *Wallumetta: A history of Ryde and Its District 1792–1945*, W.E. Smith, Sydney, 1947, p. 8.

37 For return home see, 'The Attempted Assassination of The Prince: Further Particulars', *Empire*, 14/3/1868, p. 4. For ceremony see J Jervis & V Kelly, *The History of Woollahra: A record of Events from 1788 to 1960 and a Centenary of Local Government*, The Municipal Council of Woollahra, 1960, p. 44.

38 CC Greenway, T Honery, Mr McDonald, J Rowley, J Malone, & Dr Creed, 'Australian Languages and Traditions', *The Journal of the Anthropological Institute of Great Britain and Ireland*, vol. 7, 1878, pp. 262–263; H Goodall & A Cadzow, *Rivers and Resilience: Aboriginal People on Sydney's Georges River*, UNSW Press, Sydney, 2009, p. 69.

39 Goodall & Cadzow 2009, pp. 83–8.

40 See, for example, S Furphy, *Edward M. Curr and the tide of history*, ANU E Press, Canberra, 2013.

41 'Supreme Criminal Court', *Sydney Gazette*, 12/8/1834, p. 2.

42 'Thursday July 26, 1849. Legislative Council', *SMH*, 26/7/1849, p. 2.

43 GR Nichols *et al.*, 'Letter to Colonial Secretary 19/4/1847', SANSW, NRS 905, CSLR, 47/3360 with 58/1129 [4/3378].

44 For 1844 committee see G Nichols, 'The Aborigines of Sydney', *The Australian Daily Journal*, 5/6/1844, p. 2. For boat repairs see J Long Innes *et al.*, 'Letter to Colonial Secretary 27/11/1848', SANSW, NRS 905, CSLR, 48/13283 [4/2820].

45 See, for example, G Hill, GR Nichols & D Egan, 'Letter to Colonial Secretary 30/5/1850', SANSW, NRS 905, CSLR, 50/5239 [4/2902]; GR Nichols, G Thornton & D Egan, 'Letter to Colonial Secretary 1/5/1855', SANSW, NRS 905, CSLR, 55/4117 [4/3274].

46 B Reece, 'Feasts & Blankets: The history of some early attempts to establish relations with the Aborigines of New South Wales, 1814–1846', *Archaeology & Physical Anthropology in Oceania*, vol. 2, 1967, p. 196.

Notes

47 For non-evangelism see A Curthoys, 'Good Christians and Useful Workers – Aborigines, Church and State in NSW 1870–1883', in Sydney Labour History Group (eds), *What rough beast?: the state and social order in Australian history*, George, Allen & Unwin, Sydney, 1982, pp. 45–6. For prior contact with Aboriginal people see L Bowen, *Early Coogee and Randwick: Evidence from the St Jude's case 1861–1862*, Randwick & District Historical Society, Randwick, 1998, p. 33; 'The Aboriginal Names of Places', *SMH*, 28/3/1896, p. 7; 'Kangaroo Hunting', *Bell's Life in Sydney and Sporting Reviewer*, 19/8/1848, p. 2.
48 GR Nichols, G Thornton & D Egan, 'Letter to Colonial Secretary 1/5/1855', SANSW, NRS 905, CSLR, 55/4117 [4/3274].
49 G Thornton, '[Distribution of blankets in Sydney]. Letter to Colonial Secretary 13/10/1857', SANSW, NRS 905, CSLR, 57/4140 with 58/1529 [4/3378].
50 G Hill & D Egan, 'Letter to Colonial Secretary 21/4/1858', SANSW, NRS 905, CSLR, 58/1538 [4/3378].
51 G Thornton, 'Letter to colonial secretary 27/4/1858', SANSW, NRS 905, CSLR, 58/1529 [4/3378]. Bill Worrell was William Warrell (Ricketty Dick).
52 Margin notes of the colonial secretary in G Thornton, 'Letter to Colonial Secretary 27/4/1858', SANSW, NRS 905, CSLR, 58/1529 [4/3378].
53 'Blankets for the Aborigines: Returns 1857–1861', *VPLA 1862*, vol. 5, Government Printer, Sydney, 1862, pp. 1171–4; G Hill & D Egan, 'Letter to Colonial Secretary 4/4/1860', SANSW, NRS 905, CSLR, 60/1451 [4/3451]. This letter is missing but Register records demonstrate its content.
54 G Hill, 'Letter to Colonial Secretary 16/5/1870', SANSW, NRS 905, CSLR, 70/3918, with 70/5265 [4/698].
55 Registers to the colonial secretary's papers at SANSW show a number of letters written from George Thornton seeking assistance or reimbursement for expenses in relation to Aboriginal people at Jervis Bay, though most original records are missing. One surviving example is G Thornton, 'Letter to Colonial Secretary 13/11/1867', SANSW, NRS 905, CSLR, 67/6667 [4/607].

6 Intervention (1870s–1880s)

1 JB Gribble, 'The Condition of the Aborigines', *SMH*, 13/5/1880, p. 3. Gribble was referring to the Rushcutters Bay settlement. The term 'Double Bay' was a general name for this part of the eastern suburbs.
2 JH Bell, *The La Perouse Aborigines*, PhD thesis, University of Sydney, 1960, pp. 84–6, 96; B Bridges, *Aboriginal and White Relations in New South Wales, 1788–1855*, Masters thesis, Sydney University, 1966, p. 745; A Curthoys, *Race and Ethnicity: A Study of the response of British Colonists to Aborigines and Chinese and non-British Europeans in New South Wales 1856–1881*, PhD thesis, Macquarie University, 1973, pp. 50, 230–1.
3 The idea was first fully articulated by historian Ann Curthoys in 1982; see A Curthoys, 'Good Christians and Useful Workers – Aborigines, Church and State in NSW 1870–1883', in Sydney Labour History Group (eds), *What rough beast?: the state and social order in Australian history*, George, Allen & Unwin, Sydney, 1982, pp. 49–50. For later citations see H Goodall, 'New South Wales', in A McGrath (ed.) *Contested Ground: Australian Aborigines under the British Crown*, Allen &

Unwin, Sydney, 1995, pp. 72–3; H Goodall, *Invasion to Embassy: Land in Aboriginal Politics in New South Wales, 1770–1972*, Allen & Unwin in association with Black Books, Sydney, 1996, pp. 75, 89; M Nugent, *Botany Bay: Where histories meet,* Allen & Unwin, Sydney, 2005, pp. 46–7; A Doukakis, *The Aboriginal People, Parliament & 'Protection' in New South Wales 1856–1916*, Federation Press, Sydney, 2006, pp. 8, 41–4; R Egan, *Neither amity nor kindness: government policy towards Aboriginal people of NSW 1788 to 1969*, Richard Egan Publishing, Sydney, 2012, p. 95.

4   'Blankets for the Aborigines. Returns 1857–1861', *VPLA 1862,* vol. 5, Government Printer, Sydney, 1862, pp. 1171–4; 'Aborigines. Distribution of Blankets to During 1880', *VPLA, 1879–80*, vol. 5, Government Printer, Sydney, 1880, p. 1239. Figures taken for Wollongong, Ulladulla, Shoalhaven, Moruya, Kiama, Eden and Bega. In 1861 Kiama figures are not provided, so these were taken from 1860.

5   Gribble 1880, p. 3; D Matthews, *Seventh Report Maloga Aboriginal Mission*, Colonial Publishing Society Ltd, Sydney, 1881–82, p. 7. Gribble's 'Double Bay' is the Rushcutters Bay settlement, while Matthews' North Shore and Lavender Bay refers to several locations around North Sydney. Rose Bay was mentioned by parliamentarian John Robertson; see NSW Legislative Council, '30 June 1880', in *Parliamentary Debates Session 1879–1880*. First Series, vol. 3, Government Printer, Sydney, pp. 3115–16.

6   Matthews refers to the 'scrub near Lavender Bay', local resident Livingston Mann refers to camps on the ridge between the bays and a number of locations around both sides of Neutral Bay, and Agnes Bennett described a settlement at Cremorne Reserve on the next point to the east in the 1870s and/or early 1880s; Matthews 1881–82, p. 7; LF Mann, 'Early Neutral Bay', *JRAHS*, vol. XIX, no. 5, 1932, p. 196; C Manson & C Manson, *Doctor Agnes Bennett*, Michael Joseph, London, 1960, p. 11.

7   Mann 1932, p. 196. Mann was born in 1860 and came to live in the area in 1863.

8   Many of the references to the Manly settlement are vague reminiscences or retellings, so details are difficult to determine. Resident Arthur Lowe, for example, discusses his grandmother knowing a local Aboriginal woman in the 1840s as well as Aboriginal residents during his own childhood in the 1880s; AM Lowe, *Surfing, surf-shooting and surf-life-saving pioneering*, Self-published, Manly, 1958, np. Several published reminiscences recall Aboriginal people living at Manly in the 1860s and possibly 1870s; see 'Official jubilee souvenir to commemorate the 50th anniversary of the incorporation of the Municipality of Manly, 1877–1927', *Manly Daily*, Sydney, 1927, np; 'Manly In the Old Days (By an Old Boy)', *SMH*, 31/12/1935, p. 6. For the Aboriginal use of the broader area see I Jacobs, *A History of the Aboriginal Clans of Sydney's Northern Beaches*, Northside Printing, Sydney, 2003, pp. 52–4.

9   G Thornton, 'Aborigines: Report of the Protector to 31 December 1882', *VPLA 1883*, vol. 3, Government Printer, Sydney, 1883, p. 893; 'Good Work at La Perouse', *Evening News*, 6/9/1879, p. 4. The latter reference shows that Aboriginal people were already established at La Perouse by 1879.

10 Emma Timbery's maiden name was Walden after her European father. She was later known as Lowndes after her stepfather; see M Nugent, 'Timbery, Emma (1842–1916)', *Australian Dictionary of Biography*, National Centre of Biography, Australian National University, 2005, <www.adb.anu.edu.au/biography/timbery-emma-13218/text23935> (viewed 28 October 2016).

Notes

11 Report of Sub-Inspector John Donohoe 29/1/1881 in G Thornton, 'Aborigines: Report of the Protector to 31 December 1882', *VPLA 1883*, vol. 3, Government Printer, Sydney, 1883, p. 893. Donohoe stated that Aboriginal people had been at the boatshed for two years prior to his report. In early 1879 an Aboriginal man was present at dawn in the area when he discovered a body floating in the water, suggesting he was living nearby; see 'Coroner's Court', *Evening News*, 27/3/1879, p. 3. The boatshed has previously been said to have been located on the western side of the quay, but careful research by City of Sydney historians Lisa Murray and Laila Ellmoos confirmed its location at Bennelong Point.

12 LA Gilbert, *The Royal Botanic Gardens, Sydney: a history 1816–1985*, Oxford University Press, Melbourne, 1986, pp. 103, 106.

13 For numbers see various reports in Thornton, 'Aborigines: Report of the Protector to 31 December 1882'; '[Joseph Bundle]', *Daily Telegraph*, 9/7/1881, p. 5. For work see D Matthews, 'Diary entry for 4/5/1881', *Daniel Matthews Papers: Volume 2 Part 1 No 3. Diary 1878–1881*, SLNSW, MSS A3384; 'Death of an Aboriginal Boy', *Evening News*, 8/7/1881, p. 3. For the adoption of shellwork by Aboriginal people see M Nugent, '"You really only made it because you needed the money": Aboriginal Women and Shellwork Production, 1870s to 1970s', *Labour History*, vol. 101, 2011, pp. 71–90. There is no evidence for historian Heather Goodall's assertion that residents came there 'demanding fishing boats and land', Goodall 1996, p. 75.

14 'Coroner's Court', *Evening News*, 27/3/1879, p. 3; D Matthews, 'Diary entry for 4/5/1881', SLNSW MSS A3384.

15 'Frank Foster death certificate', NSW BDM 180116/2005; '[Frank Foster]', *Daily Telegraph*, 29/4/1880, p. 2. For birth of Joseph see 'Death of an Aboriginal Boy', *Evening News*, 8/7/1881, p. 3.

16 Thornton, 'Aborigines: Report of the Protector to 31 December 1882'.

17 S Fitzgerald, *Red tape gold scissors: the story of Sydney's Chinese*, rev. edn, Halstead in association with the City of Sydney, Sydney, 2008, pp. 23–8; 'News of the Day', *SMH*, 9/4/1880, p. 5; L Johnson, *Gaslight Sydney*, George Allen & Unwin, Sydney, 1984, pp. 90–2.

18 Curthoys 1982, pp. 50–1; Nugent 2005, pp. 48, 63; Doukakis 2006, p. 43.

19 G Thornton, 'Letter to Colonial Secretary 27/4/1858', SANSW, NRS 905, CSLR, 58/1529 [4/3378]; G Thornton, 'Letter to Colonial Secretary 18/1/1881', SANSW, NRS 905, CSLR, 81/446 [1/2510]).

20 Thornton, 'Letter to Colonial Secretary 18/1/1881', SANSW, NRS 905, CSLR, 81/446 [1/2510]).

21 G Thornton, 'Letter to Colonial Secretary 21/2/1881', in *Autograph Letters of Notable Australians*, SLNSW, MSS A69 [CY1133], frame 48–50.

22 Prince Little report with John Donohoe letter 29/1/1881 in Thornton, 'Aborigines: Report of the Protector to 31 December 1882', p. 894. See also other reports in this document.

23 Thornton, 'Letter to Colonial Secretary 21/2/1881'. See also Curthoys 1982, p. 50.

24 G Thornton, 'Letter to Henry Parkes 6/5/1881', in *Sir Henry Parkes – Papers, 1833–1896*, SLNSW, MSS A910, pp. 128–31.

25 Curthoys 1982, pp. 37–45; D Matthews, 'Diary entries for April 1881 to August 1881', *Daniel Matthews Papers: Volume 2 Part 1 No 3. Diary 1878–1881*, SLNSW, MSS A3384.

26 D Matthews, 'Diary entries for 16/6/1881, 17/6/1881 and 14/7/881', *Daniel Matthews Papers: Volume 2 Part 1 No 3. Diary 1878–1881*, SLNSW, MSS A3384.
27 D Matthews, 'Our Aborigines', *SMH*, 25/6/1881, p. 7.
28 'Death of an Aboriginal Boy', *Evening News*, 8/7/1881, p. 3; '[Joseph Bundle]', *Daily Telegraph*, 8/7/1881, p. 3; '[Joseph Bundle]', *Daily Telegraph*, 9/7/1881, p. 5.
29 Memo of Edmund Fosbery 8/7/1881 and Report of Sub-Inspector Donohoe 8/7/1881 in Thornton, 'Aborigines: Report of the Protector to 31 December 1882', p. 895.
30 Report of Sub-Inspector Donohoe 12/7/1881 in Thornton, 'Aborigines: Report of the Protector to 31 December 1882', p. 896.
31 Report of Sub-Inspector Donohoe 15/7/1881 in Thornton, 'Aborigines: Report of the Protector to 31 December 1882', p. 896.
32 Report of Sub-Inspector Donohoe to Water Police Magistrate 24/8/1881 in Thornton, 'Aborigines: Report of the Protector to 31 December 1882', p. 896.
33 Both Catholics and Presbyterians were active in the area; see 'Good Work at La Perouse', *Evening News*, 6/9/1879, p. 4; Rev. TJ Curtis, '[Letter to the editor]', *SMH*, 6/1/1883, p. 7.
34 For distribution of supplies at La Perouse by the Hills see J McElhone, 'The Aborigines: To the Editor of the Herald', *SMH*, 10/1/1883, p. 5. For employment of the Timberys see E Wait, *The Migration of People of Aboriginal Ancestry to the Metropolitan Area and their Assimilation*, BA Honours thesis, University of Sydney, 1950, p. 10; Daniel Matthews refers to George Timbery as a 'black boy' in his diary, implying that he was an employee of Hill's. See D Matthews, 'Diary entry for 14/6/1881', *Daniel Matthews Papers: Volume 2 Part 1 No 3. Diary 1878–1881*, SLNSW, MSS A3384.
35 George Timbery showed Matthews around at La Perouse and accompanied him to the boatshed settlement, D Matthews, 'Diary entries for 4/5/1881 and 14/6/1881', *Daniel Matthews Papers: Volume 2 Part 1 No 3. Diary 1878–1881*, SLNSW, MSS A3384.
36 D Matthews, 'Diary entry for 2/8/1881', *Daniel Matthews Papers: Volume 2 Part 1 No 3. Diary 1878–1881*, SLNSW, MSS A3384.
37 D Matthews, 'Diary entry for 2/8/1881', *Daniel Matthews Papers: Volume 2 Part 1 No 3. Diary 1878–1881*, SLNSW, MSS A3384.
38 Report of Sub-Inspector Byrne 17/1/1883 in Thornton, 'Aborigines: Report of the Protector to 31 December 1882', pp. 897–8.
39 D Matthews, 'Diary entry for 2/8/1881', *Daniel Matthews Papers: Volume 2 Part 1 No 3. Diary 1878–1881*, SLNSW, MSS A3384.
40 G Thornton, 'Letter to Henry Parkes 19/12/1881', in *Sir Henry Parkes – Papers, 1833–1896*, SLNSW, MSS A929, pp. 48–51; H Parkes, 'Governor's Minute no 18310 28/12/1881', SANSW, NRS 905, CSLR, M18310, filed with 82/98 [1/2530].
41 Curthoys 1982, pp. 50–1.
42 G Thornton, 'Letter to Colonial Secretary 4/1/1882', SANSW, NRS 905, CSLR, 82/98 [1/2530].
43 G Thornton, 'Aborigines. Report of Protector 14/8/1882', *VPLA 1882*, Vol 4, Government Printer, Sydney, 1882, pp. 1525–7.
44 Nugent 2005, pp. 51–2.
45 G Thornton, 'The Blacks at Botany', *Evening News*, 9/1/1883, p. 3.

Notes

46 Thornton, 'Aborigines: Report of the Protector to 31 December 1882', p. 891.
47 J McElhone, 'The Aborigines: To the Editor of the Herald', *SMH*, 10/1/1883, p. 5.
48 J McElhone, 'Letter to Treasury Department 4/1/1883', SANSW, NRS 905, CSLR, 83/122 [1/2532].
49 NSW Legislative Assembly, '4/1/1883', in *Parliamentary Debates Session 1883*. First Series, Vol. 8. Sydney, Government Printer, pp. 29–32; Curthoys 1982, pp. 51–3; Rev. TJ Curtis, '[Letter to the editor]', *SMH*, 6/1/1883, p. 7.
50 Curthoys 1982, pp. 52–4; APB, 'Protection of the Aborigines. Report of the Board 10/3/1884', *VPLA, 1883–4,* Vol XI, p. 939. Though Thornton retained an interest in Aboriginal affairs, he was never again formally involved with the Protection Board.
51 Matthews 1881–82; D Matthews, *Eighth Report of the Maloga Aboriginal Mission School, Murray River, New South Wales*, RG Foyster, Echuca, 1883. Gussie Davis (15), Kate Smith (19) and Emma Jane Arrabin (39) all died within months of arriving, followed by teenage sisters Harriet (15) and Lettie (13) Oney in 1883. Matthews noted their existing sickness and weakness, though their cause of death is not known. Bill Foot was back at La Perouse by 20/1/1883 where he signed a letter; see Thornton, 'Aborigines. Report of the Protector to 31 December 1882', p. 899. Matthews lists the thirteen people who returned home in 1883 as 'Maitland Blacks' but his labels are often unreliable and the lower Hunter area in any case was part of the affiliated coastal zone. The fact that the Sydney affiliated people mentioned do not appear on the mission roll after this time suggests that they were among these thirteen people. Reverend John Gribble also mentions that by 1888 people had returned to La Perouse after being at Maloga and Warangesda for 'years': JB Gribble, 'The Aborigines', *SMH*, 2/2/1888, p. 7.
52 S Fitzgerald, *Rising Damp: Sydney 1870–1890*, Oxford University Press, Melbourne, 1987, p. 18; G Aplin, 'From Colonial Village to World Metropolis', in J Connell (ed.), *Sydney: the emergence of a world city*, Oxford University Press, Oxford, 2000, p. 58.
53 See, for example, discussion by Protection Board member and MP John Chanter in NSW Legislative Assembly, '11/10/1900', in *Parliamentary Debates Session 1900*. First Series, Vol. 106, Government Printer, Sydney, pp. 3891–2.
54 There are many references to Aboriginal people in the city from 1882 onwards, for example, 'Apprehensions &c.', *NSWPG*, 20/9/1882, p. 367; '[Nellie Bungin]', *Evening News*, 12/8/1882, p. 3; Report of Senior Constable Byrne, Police Station Botany 17/1/1883 in Thornton, 'Aborigines. Report of the Protector to 31 December 1882', p. 897.
55 For the nature of the Board see Goodall 1996, pp. 90–1. A ban on free travel is implied by reports of Aboriginal people being fined during the week for travel without a ticket; see 'Police', *SMH*, 8/10/1887, p. 9, but other articles demonstrate the discretion of the conductor, such as C Paul, 'The Aboriginals', *SMH*, 26/9/1888, p. 6.
56 D Matthews, *Thirteenth Report of the Maloga Aboriginal Mission School, Murray River, New South Wales*, Mackay & Foyster, Echuca, 1888, p. 3; D Matthews, *Fifteenth and Sixteenth Reports: The Story of the Maloga Aboriginal Mission*, Rae Bros, Melbourne, 1892, p. 50; Report of Senior Constable Byrne, Police Station Botany 17/1/1883 in Thornton, 'Aborigines: Report of the Protector to 31 December 1882'.
57 For example, 'Robbing an Aboriginal', *Evening News*, 23/12/1882, p. 3; 'Our Letter

Box', *Evening News*, 16/1/1889, p. 8; '[Thomas Ryan]', *Evening News*, 26/1/1893, p. 2; 'Drunken Aborigines', *Evening News*, 29/10/1894, p. 4.
58 Wait 1950, pp. 12, 14–15.
59 Nugent 2005, pp. 49, 53.
60 Thornton, 'Aborigines: Report of the Protector to 31 December 1882', pp. 898–9. For 'village' see 'A Visit to the Blacks Camp at La Perouse', *SMH*, 16/1/1883, p. 5. For hut descriptions see GH Hyam, 'Re: State of Aborigines at La Perouse 29/9/1887. Report from Sub-inspector G.H. Hyam to Inspector General of Police', SANSW, NRS 905, CSLR, 87/10724 with 88/1253 [1/2687].
61 The Board repeatedly placed advertisements for boats of this kind in the 1880s, suggesting they had a preferred type of vessel; for example, 'Wanted', *SMH*, 9/1/1888, p. 1. David Payne of the Australian National Maritime Museum kindly decoded these descriptions and described the capabilities of such craft.
62 'A Visit to the Blacks Camp at La Perouse', *SMH*, 16/1/1883, p. 5.
63 For hiring out boats see Thornton, 'Aborigines: Report of the Protector to 31 December 1882', p. 893. For other goods and work see 'Yesterday's brevities', *Evening News*, 3/8/1893, p. 6; APB, 'Protection of the Aborigines: Report of Board for 1890', in *VPLA 1891–92*, Vol. 7, Government Printer, Sydney, 1892, p. 7; Nugent 2005, p. 49.
64 See various reports in Thornton, 'Aborigines: Report of the Protector to 31 December 1882'; APB, 'Protection of the Aborigines: Report of Board for 1890', Appendix E.
65 H Goodall & A Cadzow, *Rivers and Resilience: Aboriginal People on Sydney's Georges River*, UNSW Press, Sydney, 2009, p. 72; 'Metropolitan Quarter Sessions', *SMH*, 17/12/1881, p. 8; 'Inmates Journal entry 2/3/1886', in *BSNSW Inmates Journal October 1883 to December 1886*, SLNSW, MSS A7236; F Holt, 'Letter to Colonial Secretary 8/2/1886', SANSW, NRS 905, CSLR, 86/1559 with 86/3031 [1/2582]. The use of tents is suggested by a lack of references to other huts, and contemporary photos showing their use around this time; see *The last of the Dolls Point Aboriginals*, SLNSW Image SPF/2703, nd; B Earnshaw, *The Land Between Two Rivers: The St George District in Federation times*, Kogarah Historical Society, Sydney, 2001, p. 86.
66 It is mentioned in APB annual reports in between 1884 and 1890. See also APB, 'Tabulated Expenditure Kogarah 1887', *Aborigines Protection Board Expenditure 1887–1890*, SANSW, NRS13 [7/3641].
67 Goodall & Cadzow 2009, p. 72.
68 This is likely to be the settlement indicated by census entries for the 'Paddington' or 'Double Bay' areas in APB annual reports for 1896, 1898, 1899 and 1901.
69 'Native Nuisances: A Black Camp in a Church: Old St. Mark's, Darling Point', *Evening News*, 22/2/1895, p. 3.
70 Recollections of elderly La Perouse resident Charley Wells in 1950 in Wait 1950, pp. 14–15.
71 R Hill, 'Letter to Colonial Secretary 30/9/1887', SANSW, NRS 905, CSLR, 87/10724, with 88/1253 [1/2687].
72 Wait 1950, p. 11. Wait identifies her informant as 'Mrs N', an elderly woman residing in Redfern. From other information included by Wait (such as the identity of her stepfather, and the origin of her husband), it can be ascertained that this was

Notes

Harriet Neville (c.1880–1962).

73 GH Hyam, 'Re: State of Aborigines at La Perouse 29/9/1887. Report from Sub-inspector G.H. Hyam to Inspector General of Police', SANSW, NRS 905, 87/10724, with 88/1253 [1/2687].

7 New links and old ways (1890s–1930s)

1 'The La Perouse Blacks: A Visit to the Camp, their projected removal, a wish to remain at Botany Bay, reasons why they should go', *Evening News*, 14/11/1900, p. 2.

2 Based on Protection Board records of ration recipients (usually about half of the residents), meeting minutes, and annual census figures in the 1890s, as well as detailed resident lists from 1887 and 1900; see GH Hyam, 'Re: State of Aborigines at La Perouse 29/9/1887. Report from Sub-inspector G.H. Hyam to Inspector General of Police', SANSW, NRS 905, CSLR, 87/10724, with 88/1253 [1/2687]; APB, 'Letter to Colonial Secretary 5/10/1900', SANSW, NRS 905, CSLR, 00/19552 with 00/23677 [5/6574].

3 M Nugent, *Botany Bay: Where histories meet*, Allen & Unwin, Sydney, 2005, pp. 56, 63.

4 'News of the Day', *SMH*, 11/2/1886, p. 9; 'Inmates Journal entry 2/3/1886', in *BSNSW Inmates Journal October 1883 to December 1886*, SLNSW, MSS A7236; F Holt, 'Letter to Colonial Secretary 8/2/1886', SANSW, NRS 905, CSLR, 86/1559 with 86/303 [1/2582].

5 B Dickey, *No Charity There: A Short History of Social Welfare in Australia*, Allen & Unwin, Sydney, 1987, pp. 59–64; N Parry, 'Such a longing: black and white children in welfare in New South Wales and Tasmania, 1880–1940', PhD thesis, University of New South Wales, 2007, p. 122 and see also pp. 118–83.

6 Holt, 'Letter to Colonial Secretary 8/2/1886', SANSW, NRS 905, CSLR, 86/1559 with 86/303 [1/2582].

7 'Inmates Journal entry 6/4/1886 and 10/4/1886', in *BSNSW Inmates Journal October 1883 to December 1886*, SLNSW, MSS A7236; 'William Fussell Death Certificate', NSW BDM 1886/9166. Lily was a domestic servant in Sydney by the late 1890s; see 'Entry for Lily Fussel 22/7/1901', *Photographic description books – Bathurst Gaol*, SANSW, NRS 1998 [3/13073], p. 280.

8 Albert was recorded in the 1891 Census, and is most likely the man aged 40–60 consistently referred to in Protection Board annual reports between 1891 and 1899. Another Aboriginal man died there in 1894; see New South Wales Government, 'Household Returns for Census District no. 99 Kogarah and Rockdale Subdistrict C Scarborough Ward', *Collector's books, 1891 Census*, SANSW, NRS683, [2/8428]; 'An Unidentified Aboriginal', *SMH*, 30/1/1894, p. 5.

9 As shown in Board minutes for the 1890s.

10 APB, 'Protection of the Aborigines. Report of the Board for 1892', *VPLA 1892–93*, vol. 7, Government Printer, Sydney, 1893, p. 7.

11 For complaint and Board response see 'Aborigines Protection Board. The Tribe of Wild Blacks', *SMH*, 1/9/1893, p. 7; 'Minutes of Aborigines Protectorate Board Meetings 31/8/1893', *APB Minute Books 1890–1901*, SANSW, NRS 2 [4/7108]. For busking see 'Old Sydney: Visitor's Memories. A Philanthropic Mission', *SMH*, 7/10/1932, p. 8. The exact location of their settlement is not clear as Watsons Bay

was a broad name for the area east of Vaucluse, and included Parsley Bay where the Aboriginal performers at Watsons Bay were said to have been living.

12 'Native Nuisances: A Black Camp in a Church: Old St. Mark's, Darling Point', *Evening News*, 22/2/1895, p. 3; 'Minutes of Aborigines Protectorate Board Meeting 21/2/1895', *APB Minute Books 1890–1901*, SANSW, NRS 2 [4/7108]. The building was the former stone coach house of the Mona Estate which was used as the Chapel of St Marks in the 1840s. Other articles describe the camp as being in 'two old cottages' but this is likely also to be a reference to the coach house and perhaps an adjacent building; see 'Meetings: Board for Protection of Aborigines', *SMH*, 22/2/1895, p. 6.

13 'Meetings: Board for Protection of Aborigines', *SMH*, 22/2/1895, p. 6; 'Native Nuisances: A Black Camp in a Church: Old St. Mark's, Darling Point', *Evening News*, 22/2/1895, p. 3.

14 Nugent 2005, p. 55; M Berry, *A History of Col. Thomas Rowe F.R.I.B.A. Architect*, Honours thesis, University of New South Wales, 1969, p. 19.

15 E Telfer, *Amongst Australian Aborigines: Forty Years of Mission Work, The Story of the United Aborigines Mission*, Fraser & Morphet Pty Ltd, Sydney, 1939, p. 31, A Longworth, *Was it worthwhile?: an historical analysis of five women missionaries and their encounters with the Nyungar people of south-west Australia*, PhD thesis, Murdoch University, 2005, pp. 11–32.

16 For mission house see ACEU, 'Our Mission House', *Golden Link*, 1/12/1894, p. 58, *Australian Christian Endeavour Union records 1892–1998*, SLNSW, MSS 8088 Box 9; 'The La Perouse Aboriginals. Opening of a Mission-Hall', *SMH*, 19/11/1894, p. 3. For formation of committee see Telfer 1939, pp. 23–8.

17 This can be seen regularly in the Board minutes from this period. For example, 'Minutes of Aborigines Protectorate Board Meetings 10/11/1892, 8/6/1893, 7/12/1893 and 28/12/1893', *APB Minute Books 1890–1901*, SANSW, NRS 2 [4/7108]; 'Minutes of Aborigines Protectorate Board Meeting 27/12/1894', *APB Minute Books 1890–1901*, SANSW, NRS 2 [4/7109].

18 The photo was found among Leo's personal papers.

19 'Queen Emma Dead. Last Monarch of La Perouse', *Sunday Times*, 3/12/1916, p. 26; 'Boat for the La Perouse Aborigines', *Sunday Times*, 19/7/1903, p. 3; 'La Perouse Aborigines: To the Editor of the Herald', *SMH*, 29/3/1928, p. 8.

20 APB, 'Protection of the Aborigines: Report of Board for 1891', *VPLA 1892–93*, vol. 7, Government Printer, Sydney, 1893, p. 8.

21 'Plan of La Perouse Reserve #28358, notified 30th March 1895', *Register of Aboriginal Reserves, 1875–1904*, SANSW, NRS 23 [2/8349].

22 'The Late Richard Hill MLC', *The Daily Telegraph*, 23/8/1895, p. 5; E Waugh (ed.), *The Frank Baker Letters*, Randwick & District Historical Society Inc., Randwick, 1989, pp. 8–9; '[Cricket match at Coogee]', *Referee*, 27/3/1895, p. 8.

23 'The La Perouse Blacks: A Visit to the Camp, their projected removal, a wish to remain at Botany Bay, reasons why they should go', *Evening News*, 14/11/1900, p. 2.

24 'Minutes of Aborigines Protectorate Board Meeting 3/5/1894', *APB Minute Books 1890–1901*, SANSW, NRS 2 [4/7108]; 'Aborigines Protection Board. La Perouse Blacks', *SMH*, 20/4/1894, p. 3.

25 Rowley's mother was most likely from the Botany Bay area as she gave birth to him there and continued to live in the area until her death in 1885. His European father

Notes

lived at Weeney Bay where he gathered shells for sale to produce lime; see 'Baptism Record James William Rowley, 23 June 1857', SAG, Church of England in Australia – Parish registers, 1839–1970, SLNSW, SAG Reel 001, frame 1090. Anthropologist Esther Wait wrote in 1950 that Rowley was the nephew of Ellen Anderson based on information from La Perouse community members, and though her writings show that she did not always interpret genealogical information correctly, she is most likely correct that they were related in some way. See E Wait, *The Migration of People of Aboriginal Ancestry to the Metropolitan Area and their Assimilation*, BA Honours thesis, University of Sydney, 1950, p. 26.

26 For eviction see M Maloney, 'Letter to Mr Rowley of Sylvania, May 1899', *Holt Family Papers 1861–1933, Volume 9, Business Papers 1861–1933*, SLNSW, MSS 2170.

27 D Matthews, *Seventh Report Maloga Aboriginal Mission*, Colonial Publishing Society Ltd, Sydney, 1881–2, p. 17.

28 For speaking tours see D Matthews, *Eleventh Report of the Maloga Aboriginal Mission School, Murray River, New South Wales*, Mackay & Foyster, Echuca, 1886, p. 6. For early political activity at Cumeragunja see H Goodall, *Invasion to Embassy: Land in Aboriginal Politics in New South Wales, 1770–1972*, Allen & Unwin in association with Black Books, Sydney, 1996, pp. 77–9.

29 For settlement see 'Country News: Kiama', *SMH*, 2/5/1889, p. 5; 'The Aborigines Camp at Kangaroo Valley', in *Kangaroo Valley School Files 1876–1927*, SANSW, NRS3829 [5/16418.2 Bundle A]. For leaving the valley, see 'Treatment of the Aborigines', *SMH*, 8/12/1890, p. 5.

30 H Goodall & A Cadzow, *Rivers and Resilience: Aboriginal People on Sydney's Georges River*, UNSW Press, Sydney, 2009, p. 144. For origin of Paddy Swift see 'Marriage certificate for Paddy Swift and Jenny Johnston', NSW BDM 1886/001322.

31 'Aborigines' Mission', *Evening News*, 20/7/1896, p. 7.

32 Telfer 1939, pp. 26–8.

33 ACEU, 'New South Wales Aborigines' Mission', *Golden Link*, 2/10/1899, p. 33, *Australian Christian Endeavour Union records 1892–1998*, SLNSW, MSS 8088, Box 9.

34 For John Bundy see ACEU, 'Another Aboriginal Society', *Golden Link*, 1/3/1899, p. 95; *Australian Christian Endeavour Union records 1892–1998*, SLNSW, MSS 8088, Box 9; 'Kiama', *SMH*, 11/1/1899, p, 7. For Emma Timbery see 'La Perouse Aborigines Mission', *SMH*, 20/2/1899, p. 8. This refers only to a 'Mrs Timbery'. It was most likely Emma, who was active with the mission, but it may have been her daughter-in-law Jane, who was also involved; Individual Heritage Group, *La Perouse: The place, the people and the sea: A collection of writing by members of the Aboriginal community*, Aboriginal Studies Press, Canberra, 1988, p. 33.

35 'Charles Golden death certificate', NSW BDM 4572/1899; 'Barber/Foster marriage certificate', NSW BDM 8545/1906; C Anderson, 'Letter to Retta Long 13/5/1907 from Sackville Mission House', *Australian Indigenous Ministries Further Records 1904–1930*, SLNSW, MSS 7244/1/5.

36 DD Johnson, *Sacred waters: the story of the Blue Mountains gully traditional owners*, Halstead Press, Sydney, 2006, pp. 129–36. The mission was not part of the New South Wales Aborigines Mission.

37 Individual Heritage Group 1988, p. 33.

38 APB, 'Re: Aboriginals camped at head of Lavender Bay: Letter to Colonial Secretary 6/5/1886', SANSW, NRS 905, CSLR, 86/4620 [1/2587]; TJ Cotter, 'Report

from Sub-inspector T.J. Cotter to Inspector General of Police 5/5/1886', SANSW, NRS 905, CSLR, 86/4620 [1/2587].

39   '[Aborigines Protection Board]', *SMH*, 2/7/1892, p. 8. Other locations in this vicinity may have been used at other times.

40   'Carrington Athletic Grounds First Grand Handicap of £525', *Australian Town and Country Journal*, 4/12/1886, p. 41; 'Sir Joseph Banks Handicap', *SMH*, 31/8/1886, p. 10. For a general context of Aboriginal involvement in 'pedestrianism' see C Tatz, *Obstacle race: Aborigines in sport*, rev. ed., UNSW Press, Sydney, 1996, Ch. 6.

41   'Sir Joseph Banks Handicaps', *SMH*, 27/7/1886; 'Native Nuisances: A Black Camp in a Church: Old St. Mark's, Darling Point', *Evening News*, 22/2/1895, p. 3. The sprinters mentioned may have been locally affiliated people but could also have been the people who were there from the Macleay River area on the mid-north coast.

42   G Blades & K Edwards, 'Samuels, Charles (1864–1912)', *Australian Dictionary of Biography*, National Centre of Biography, Australian National University, 2005 <www.adb.anu.edu.au/biography/samuels-charles-13183/text23865> (viewed 28 October 2016).

43   'Minutes of Aborigines Protectorate Board Meetings 5/3/1891', *APB Minute Books 1890–1901*, SANSW, NRS 2 [4/7108]; '[Centennial Park]', *Referee*, 18/2/1891, p. 3; '[Aborigines Protection Board]', *SMH*, 2/7/1892, p. 8.

44   RW Rathbone, *A Very Present Help; Caring for Australians since 1813: The History of the Benevolent Society of New South Wales*, State Library of New South Wales Press, Sydney, 1994.

45   I have omitted Minnie's surname to preserve some degree of anonymity in case she has descendants who are not yet aware of it, as this information has only recently come to light. 'Inmates Journal entries for 5/6/1897 and 2/8/1897', *BSNSW Inmates Journal December 1886 to May 1889,* SLNSW, MSS A7243; 'Inmates Journal entries for 5/1/1900, 14/2/1900, 23/2/1900, 28/2/1900, 3/7/1900', *Inmates Journal May 1889 to February 1901*, SLNSW, MSS A7244.

46   For legislation see H Goodall, 'New South Wales', in A McGrath (ed.), *Contested Ground: Australian Aborigines under the British Crown*, Allen & Unwin, Sydney, 1995, pp. 75–80. For child removals see APB, 'Aborigines, Report of Board of Protection of, for year 1913', *Joint Volume of papers presented to the Legislative Council and Legislative Assembly, 1914/15*, vol. 2, Government Printer, Sydney, p. 890; I Walden, '"That was slavery days": Aboriginal domestic servants in New South Wales in the Twentieth Century', *Labour History*, vol. 69, 1995, pp. 196–209.

47   Walden 1995, pp. 196, 200; APB, 'Aborigines, Report of Board of Protection of, for the period of 1st January, 1919, to 30th June 1920', *Joint Volume of papers presented to the Legislative Council and Legislative Assembly, 1920/21*, vol. 2, Government Printer, Sydney, p. 885.

48   Walden 1995, pp. 199; Wait 1950, pp. 116–22; M Tucker, *If everyone cared: Autobiography of Margaret Tucker M.B.E.*, Grosvenor, Melbourne, 1983.

49   Walden 1995, p. 206; Wait 1950, p. 43; H Ireland, *Urban Fragments: Tracing Aboriginal Presence in Sydney through Criminal Justice Records*, Honours thesis, University of NSW, 2011, p. 39.

50   Wait 1950, p. 57.

Notes

51 For locations, occupations and activism, see J Maynard, *Fight for liberty and freedom: the origins of Australian Aboriginal activism*, Aboriginal Studies Press, Canberra, 2007, pp. 17–19; Wait 1950, pp. 42–3; Ireland 2011, pp. 43–49; D Plater (ed), *Other Boundaries: Inner-city Aboriginal Stories*, Leichhardt Municipal Council, Sydney, 1993, pp. 80–2. For urban identities see H Ireland, 'The Case of Agnes Jones. Tracing Aboriginal presence in Sydney through criminal justice records', *History Australia*, vol. 10, no. 3, 2013, pp. 245–51.

52 Based on around 1000 Aboriginal people in coastal Sydney in 1788 and estimates of around 2500 Aboriginal people in a slightly bigger area by 1945; see Wait 1950, p. 7.

53 Goodall 1995, pp. 85–6; Commonwealth Bureau of Census and Statistics (Australia), *Census of the Commonwealth of Australia, 30th June, 1933: Part I, New South Wales – population: Detailed tables for local government areas*, Commonwealth Government Printer, Canberra, 1933, pp. 100–9.

54 SC Smith & B Sykes, *Mum Shirl: an autobiography*, Heinemann Educational, Richmond Vic., 1981, p. 18. See also Wait 1950, p. 1; Ireland 2013, pp. 62–4.

55 JH Bell, 'Some Demographic and Cultural Characteristics of the La Perouse Aborigines', *Mankind*, vol. 5, no. 10, 1961, pp. 433–4; P Nixon, *The Integration of a half-caste community at La Perouse, NSW*, Masters thesis, University of Sydney, 1948, pp. 109–22.

56 Individual Heritage Group 1988, p. 15.

57 Nugent 2005, pp. 119–25; Goodall & Cadzow 2009, pp. 136–7.

58 A detailed account of the settlement can be found in Goodall & Cadzow 2009, pp. 114–64. Reminiscences of several local European residents date the establishment of the settlement to around the early 1910s; see 'Mrs Ellen Anderson. Death of Aged Aboriginal', *SMH*, 16/5/1931, p. 14; E Dickinson, 'Salt Pan Creek About 1913', *Bankstown Historical Society Newsletter*, vol. 8, no. 4, 1974, pp. 25–6; Recollections of David Cross in 'Salt Pan Creek Aborigines', *Hurstville Historical Society Newsletter*, vol. 2, no. 49, 1981, pp. 3–4. For purchase of land by Ellen Anderson and William Rowley respectively, see 'Certificate of Title dated 3/12/1925 for Lot 146 in Deposited Plan 11124', Land Titles Office Volume 3808, Folio 215; 'Certificate of Title dated 6/4/1927 for Lot 145 in Deposited Plan 11124', Land Titles Office Volume 3989, Folio 6.

59 Goodall & Cadzow 2009, pp. 125–33; Peakhurst School of Arts, *Tales from the Old Barn*, Peakhurst School of Arts, Sydney, 2005, p. 44.

60 For Hannon see Peakhurst School of Arts 2005, pp. 44, 63; 'Certificate of Title dated 3/12/1925 for Lot 146 in Deposited Plan 11124', Land Titles Office Volume 3808, Folio 215. For attempted eviction see Goodall & Cadzow 2009, p. 153.

61 Maynard 2007, Goodall & Cadzow 2009, pp. 147–51.

62 Goodall 1996, pp. 169–70; J Anderson, 'King Burraga to Professor A.P. Elkin, President, Association for the Protection of Native Races, 16 January 1936', in B Attwood & A Markus (eds), *The struggle for Aboriginal rights: a documentary history*, Allen & Unwin, Sydney, 1999, pp. 74–5.

63 J Horner & M Langton, 'The Day of Mourning', in B Gammage & P Spearritt (eds), *Australians 1938*, Syme & Weldon, Sydney, 1987, pp. 28–35; *The Australian Abo Call*, no. 2, May 1938, p. 1.

64 *The Australian Abo Call*, no. 1, April 1938, p. 2.

65 Goodall & Cadzow 2009, pp. 153–64.

Epilogue: In plain view

1 P Jones, *Ochre and Rust: Artefacts and Encounters on Australian Frontiers*, Wakefield Press, Kent Town, 2008, p. 1.
2 D Hayden, *The Power of Place: Urban Landscapes as Public History*, The MIT Press, Cambridge, Mass., 1999, p. 9.
3 R Griffin, 'Graven Images on the Wentworth Estate', *Insites, Newsletter of the Historic Houses Trust of New South Wales*, Autumn 2006, pp. 6–7. Other engravings that were once on the grounds of the estate are now located within private homes further upslope; P Irish & M Ingrey, *Aboriginal Connections to Vaucluse House and Elizabeth Bay House: Research Report*, Unpublished report to Historic Houses Trust of NSW, pp. 30–1.
4 V Attenbrow & D Steele, 'Fishing in Port Jackson, New South Wales – more than met the eye', *Antiquity*, vol. 69, no. 262, 1995, pp. 50–1.
5 '[Cricket match at Coogee]', *Referee*, 27/3/1895, p. 8.
6 '[Cricket match at Coogee]', *Referee*, 27/3/1895, p. 8; E Waugh (ed.), *The Frank Baker Letters*, Randwick & District Historical Society Inc., Randwick, 1989, pp. 8–9.
7 Shayne Williams pers. comm. 31/3/11. Shayne is the son of Tom and Iris.
8 It is known locally as this, as reflected by some historians; see M Hutton Neve, *Kurnell: birthplace of a nation*, NSW Shire Pictorial Publications, Caringbah, 1969; D Salt, *Kurnell: Birthplace of modern Australia – A pictorial history*, Southwood Press, Marrickville, 2000.
9 For Aboriginal significance see M Nugent, *Botany Bay, Where Histories Meet*, Allen & Unwin, Sydney, Ch. 7. For European monuments see M Nugent, *A contextual history of Botany Bay National Park (Kurnell Section)*, Unpublished report to the NSW NPWS, 2005, p. 25; G Eldershaw, *The Captain Cook's Landing Place Tree Register: An Investigation into the commemorative tree planting programme*, NSW National Parks & Wildlife Service, 2006.
10 J McDonald, 'Rock art and cross-cultural interaction in Sydney: How did each side perceive the other?', in P Veth, P Sutton & M Neale (eds), *Strangers on the Shore: Early Coastal Contacts in Australia*, National Museum of Australia, Canberra, 2008, pp. 94–6.
11 P Irish, *Final Report on Aboriginal Archaeological Monitoring and Salvage Excavations Meeting Place Precinct, Botany Bay National Park, Kurnell*, NSW, Australian Archaeological Consulting Monograph Series vol. 3, Australian Association of Consulting Archaeologists Inc., Sydney 2010; JVS Megaw, 'Excavations at the Captain Cook's landing place historic site, Kurnell 1968–1971', *Australian Society for Historical Archaeology Newsletter*, no. 1, 1972, pp. 7–8.
12 For fishing see 'Botany', *NSWPG*, 3/3/1886, p. 66. For artefacts and shells see Individual Heritage Group, *La Perouse: The place, the people and the sea: A collection of writing by members of the Aboriginal community*, Aboriginal Studies Press, Canberra, 1988, pp. 13, 24.
13 C Healy, *From the ruins of colonialism: history as social memory*, Cambridge University Press, New York, 1997, pp. 23–4; W Macdonald, 'Forby Sutherland's Grave at Kurnell', *JRAHS*, no. 19, 1928, p. 286; M Nugent, 'Historical encounters: Aboriginal testimony and colonial forms of commemoration', *Aboriginal History* vol. 30, 2006, pp. 33–47.
14 C Healy, *Forgetting Aborigines*, UNSW Press, Sydney, 2008.

Notes

15 Some examples include R Kerkhove, *Aboriginal Campsites of Greater Brisbane: An Historical Guide*, Boolarong Press, Salisbury Qld, 2015; P Edmonds, *Urbanizing Frontiers: Indigenous Peoples and Settlers in 19th-Century Pacific Rim Cities*, UBC Press, Vancouver, 2010; R Broome, *Aboriginal Victorians: A History Since 1800*, Allen & Unwin, Sydney, 2005; T Gara, *Aboriginal Fringe Camps in Adelaide, 1836–1911*, paper presented to the Royal Geographical Society of South Australia, 28 June 2001. Revised version, 5 August 2008; T Gara, 'The life and times of Mullawirraburka ('King John') of the Adelaide tribe', in J Simpson & L Hercus (eds), *History in portraits: biographies of nineteenth century South Australian Aboriginal people*, Aboriginal History Monograph 6, Aboriginal History Inc., Canberra, 1998, pp. 88–132; N Green, 'Survival against all odds: The Indigenous population of metropolitan Perth, 1829–2001', C Hansen & K Butler (eds) *Exploring urban identities and histories*, AIATSIS Research Publications, Canberra, 2013, pp. 133–52; D Cook, *'That was my home': Voices from the Noongar camps in Perth's western suburbs*, PhD thesis, Murdoch University, 2016.

16 Australia ICOMOS, *The Burra Charter: The Australia ICOMOS Charter for Places of Cultural Significance*, 2013, p. 4, Article 6. This principle has underpinned all state and federal heritage laws and practice since the 1970s.

Index

Pictures are indexed by caption number in italics, e.g. Bennelong *1.2*

A

Aboriginal clans and bands
  bands 18
  Botany tribe 34, 104
  Burragorang tribe 34
  Cadigal (clan) 17, 21
  clan names 17
  Five Islands tribe 34
  as form of social and economic organisation 17–18
  Georges River tribe 34
  inland/western Sydney people 6, 16–17, 24, 128, 133–134
  Macquarie's administration and tribal divisions 29–31
  Port Hacking tribe 34, 61–62
  Port Stephens tribe 34, 96, 102, 110, 112, 123
  primary rights and responsibilities 18–19
  regrouping following smallpox epidemic 20–27, 87
  secondary rights 18
  Sydney tribe 21, 28–29, 34, 44, 62–63, 90, 101
  Wanngal (clan) 23
  Wollongong tribe 34, 102
Aboriginal settlements
  accommodation of by Europeans 67–73
  affiliation to settlements 84, 129–130
  fishing as basis for 36–41, 45–46
  strategic distance from city 47–50
  type of dwellings 33
Aborigines Progressive Association 141–142
Aborigines Protection Act 1909 (amended 1915) 137
Aborigines Protection Association (APA) 113–114, 119
Aborigines Protection Board
  approach to settlements 126–127, 136
  closure of reserves 139
  continuing Aboriginal beats in late 1800s 120–123
  effect on settlements 125
  establishment 8, 119
  legal powers 137
  opposition to 141, 142
  removal of children 137
Aborigines Protection Society 54
Aborigines Welfare Board 142
Adelaide 74
affiliated coastal zone *1.5 see also* beats or runs; blanket distribution
  1800s (end) changes to 124
  1800s (late) continuing beats 120–123
  area defined 5–6
  exodus to missions 111–112, 115–116
  migration myths 107–111
  movement influenced by missionaries 131–134
  movement of evicted Circular Quay boatshed residents 115–116
  ongoing connections to 84, 94, 98–99, 123, 129–130
  relationship to prior cultural practice 25–27
  smallpox epidemic, regrouping

Index

following 20–21
statements of affiliation 94
Albert (at Sans Souci) 126
alcohol consumption 10
alcohol supply 42–43, 100–101
Alfred, Prince 96–98, 109, 136
Allen, Reverend William 127–128
Anderson (née Davis), Ellen *7.7*, 81, 110, 130, 131–132, 140
Anderson, Clara 134
Anderson, Hugh 131–132, 140
Anderson, Joe 141
Angas, George French 37, 38
Annan, William *3.6*, 51, 58, 61, 81
Appin massacre 53
Arabanoo 19–20
assimilation policy 142
The Australian 55, 62
Australian Aboriginal Progressive Association 141
Australian Party 62

B

backyard zone settlements 48
Baker, Harriet 127–128
bands *see* Aboriginal clans and bands
Barani Barrabugu Yesterday Tomorrow (City of Sydney) 2
Barber, Wes 134
bark *nowie* (canoes) *see* canoes (*nowie*)
Baswick, Freddy 71
Baswick, Johnny ('Bankey') 71, 145
Baswick [?], Rachael 71, 145
beats or runs 23–25, 33–34, 78, 94 *see also* affiliated coastal zone; blanket distribution
Bellbrook, Macleay Valley 134
Benevolent Society Asylum 82, 125, 136–137
Bennelong *1.2*, 20, 21, 23–24, 30, 52, 88, 89
Bennelong Point settlement *see* Circular Quay government boatshed settlement
Berry, Alexander 95
Billy (Hunter Valley man) 104
Black Gin Beach 85
Blacktown (Richmond Road) settlement 128

blanket distribution
centres of 95–96
by government 30–31, 34, 36, 56
south coast centres 108
by Sydney Aborigines Committee 62–63, 65, 86
Thornton's influence 101–105
winding back 61, 65
boats
gifts of 30, 36, 41, 63, 77, 83, 101, 104, 112, 118, 122, 128–129
replacing canoes 37, 74
used for fishing 36, 37, 39, 40–41, 63, 64, 109, 122, 129
used for guiding 32, 37, 75–76
used for travel 40, 48, 53, 64, 122
Bobby (servant to Wentworth family) 70–71, 80
boomerangs 40, 48, 57
Boorong 23, 24
Borton, Edward *5.3*, 43, 59, 90
Botany Bay 4 *see also* Sir Joseph Banks Hotel
in 1840s *2.1*
bark shield collected by Cook 16
First Fleet 12
during last ice age 14
Botany Bay lease to Mahroot *2.5*, 38–39, 48
Botany Heads 38
Botany Reserve 76
Botany settlement 36, 76, 79, 84, 109, 116, 122
Botany tribe 34, 104
bough shelter (*gunyah*) 32
Bourke, Governor Richard 38
brickfielder sandstorms *2.2*, 34
Broken Bay 13–14, 26–27
Broome, Richard 56
Brownlow Hill 45
Bulkabra 62
bunan (initiation) ceremony 26
Bundle, Joe 110–111, 114
Bundle, Joseph 110–111, 114, 142
Bundy, John 133
Bungaree *1.6*, 26–27, 30, 44, 45, 52, 70, 88, 89–90

Bungaree, Bowen (son) 27, 48
Bunnerong Creek 2.5, 38
Burdekin, Sydney 128
burial sites 5.3, 59, 70, 76, 89–90, 147
Burns, Mary Ann 81–82
burra (shell fish hooks) 1.1, 12, 15, 16, 35
Burragalong (Paddy Davis) 77, 110
Burragorang tribe 34
Burragorang Valley settlement 132, 134, 140
bushrangers 62
Byrne, Denis 45, 48, 57

C
Cadigal (clan) 17, 21
Camp Cove settlement 2.3, 32–33, 36–38, 45, 48, 68
canoes (*nowie*) 12, 15, 16, 35 *see also* boats
Carrington Ground 136
Caruey 21, 24
Castlereagh River 99
census 117, 123, 126
ceremonies 78
    bunan (initiation) ceremony 26
    Kurnell 78
    malgun (finger removal) 16, 25–26, 35
    planned corroboree for Prince Alfred 96–97
    ritual combats 28–29, 42, 57, 69–70
    Rushcutters Bay 72
Chapman, James 60
children 54, 61, 74, 79–80
    child removal 137
    children's homes 137
Chinese migration 111
Chit-Chat, Bob 48
Christian Endeavour Union 127, 133
Christian ethic 132
Christian religion 115 *see also* missionaries
Christmas feast 63–64
Circular Quay 6.5
Circular Quay government boatshed settlement 6.3, 6.4, 109–116
clans *see* Aboriginal clans and bands
Clarke family 71
Cliffbrook (Coogee) 129
climate change 13–14

Clontarf 97
coastal Sydney (definition) 5–6, 24 *see also* affiliated coastal zone
coastal Sydney people (definition) 7
Colebee 21, 24
Collins, David 20
Connell, John 28, 80
Cook, Lieutenant James 12, 14–15, 16, 147–148
Cooper, Daniel 4.4, 70, 71
Cooper family 55
Cootamundra Girls Home 137
Cowra 139
Craig, Thomas 91
Cricketers Arms 3.4, 43, 59
cross-cultural relationships 51–65
    colonial indifference 60–65
    early relationships 52–56
    in eastern suburbs 4.5
Cumeragunja 131–132, 134, 141
Curthoys, Ann 61, 117
Curtis, Thomas 119
Cuthill, James 77

D
Dalley, William Bede 71
Darling Harbour 51, 56
Darling Point 4.1, 4.2, 39, 123
Davis (later Anderson), Ellen 7.7, 81, 110, 130, 131–132, 140
Davis, Harry 120
Davis, Paddy (Burragalong) 77, 110
Day of Mourning Conference 141, 142
Delessert, Eugène 78
Denholm, David 55
Depression (1930s) 139, 140
Dixon, Retta 133
Domain settlement 2.7, 45–46, 48–49, 110
domestic service 79–81, 136–138
Donohoe, Sub-Inspector John 114–115
Double Bay 4.2, 73, 98
Double Bay settlement 2.6, 4.1, 33, 39–41, 45, 48–49, 68, 106 *see also* Seven Shillings Beach settlement
Duke of Edinburgh (Prince Alfred) 96–98, 109, 136
Durand's Alley slum 82

Index

E
East, WH 72
economic opportunity 138
Eden 95
Egan, Daniel *5.10*
   assistance to Aboriginal people 60
   background 54
   member of Sydney Aborigines Committee 65, 86, 100, 102–104
Elizabeth Bay settlement 21, 44–45, 56 *see also* Gurrajin fishing village
Ellesmere estate 122
Ellesmere House 122
engravings 16, 35, 38, 78, 146
entanglement (concept) 69 *see also* cross-cultural relationships
ethnological interests 78–79
Europeans 7 *see also* trade with Europeans
   acceptance of Aboriginal people 27–31, 50, 122–123
   attempts to evict Aboriginal people 41–47, 52, 83–85
   beliefs about Aboriginal people 12–13, 86–91
   complaints to Protection Board 126–128
   fishing economy 36
   food production 34
   laws 41, 42, 82–83
   recognition of Aboriginal connections 27–31, 99–100
   sympathisers with Aboriginal people 5, 44–45, 128–129, 141. *see also* Sydney Aborigines Committee
evangelical movement 127–128 *see also* Christian Endeavour Union; missionaries

F
Ferguson, Bill 141
Field, Judge Barron 53, 60
Fire King (steamer) *5.7*
First Fleet 17, 19
fish hooks (*burra*) *1.1*, 12, 15, 16, 35
fish hooks, metal 36
fish stocks 39, 40
fishing, importance of 35–41

fishing and hunting guides 32, 33, 74, 76–78
fishing spears (*garrara*) 15, 35, 37, 40
FitzRoy, Governor Charles 65
Five Islands tribe 34
Foot, Bill 120
Foot, Kate 81, 110–111, 114, 120, 139
foot racing 136, 147
Ford, Lisa 29
Fosbery, Edmund 114, 126
Foster, Adelaide 134
Foster, Emma Jane 134
Foster, Frank 110, 131, 132
Foster, Tom 141, 142
foster care (boarding out) system 125–126
frontier violence 46, 53, 61, 135
Fussell, Henry 125–126
Fussell, Lily 125–126
Fussell, Theresa 122, 125
Fussell, William 122, 125–126

G
Garden Palace *5.5*, 93
garrara (fishing spears) 15, 35, 37, 40
Gelding, Alfred 72
George Street Market Buildings 58
Georges Head 30
Georges River 14, 33, 49, 53, 77, 94, 99
Georges River tribe 34
Giles, Biddy *5.9*, 24, 76–78, 98–99, 110
Gipps, Governor George 46–47, 60–61
Goat Island 23
Goggey, Jackey 83–84
Golden (formerly Malone), Lizzie *7.1*, 76, 98, 109, 124
Golden, Charles *7.1*, 124, 128, 134
goldfields 67, 74
Gooseberry, Cora *2.4*, *5.3*, 27, 37, 38, 43, 45, 48, 59, 88, 90
Gorooboorooballo 23
Gorton government 146–147
government
   Aboriginal affairs expenditure review 61
   Aboriginal representation 141
   intervention issue 106–107, 112 *see also* Aborigines Protection Board

government rations 111, 112, 115, 118, 121, 122
Greenwich Pier Hotel 127
Greycliffe House *6.9*, 146
Gribble, Reverend John 106, 113
Griffiths, Tom 90
ground-stone hatchet (*mogo*) 15
guerrilla war 22
Gully Mission Katoomba 134
Gundagai 135
Gundungurra 83
gunyah (bough shelter) 32
Gurrah (and Nancy) 73, 84–85, 94
Gurrajin fishing village 21, 30, 44–45
Gweagal 17

H
Hacking River 77
Hannon, John 140–141
Harris, Jack 70, 90, 94, 103
Harris Creek settlement, Liverpool 83–84
Hayden, Delores 145
Hayden, John 62
Hill, Edward Smith 71, 76, 78–79, 104–105
Hill, George *5.10*
   assistance to Aboriginal people 60, 64–65, 77, 104, 129, 146
   background 54
   member of Sydney Aborigines Committee 86, 100, 102
   William Annan and 51, 63
Hill, George (son of Richard) 129, 146
Hill, James 129
Hill, Richard *6.8*
   assistance to Aboriginal people 71, 81, 116
   background 54
   death 129
   Emma Timbery and 128–129
   Greycliffe House *6.9*, 146
   La Perouse Aboriginal settlement 118–119
   as Protection Board chair 119, 123, 126, 129
Hill, William 129
Hill family 55, 71
historic houses 145

Hogarth, Julius 89, 90
Holt, Frederick 126
Holt Sutherland Estate 122, 130
hotel keepers 43, 59
Hunter region 26, 96, 100, 104, 110, 115
hunting *see* fishing and hunting guides
Hyde Park 28–29, 42, 48, 57

I
ice age 13–14
Illawarra (district) 24, 26, 48–49, 79, 110
Illawarra Steamship Company 129–130
immigration 58, 67, 120
Individual Heritage Group, La Perouse 4
Ingrey, Michael 5
inland/western Sydney people *see under* Aboriginal clans and bands
Ireland, Haidee 138

J
Jackey (Wong-ko-bi-kan) 100
Jervis Bay 102, 104
Jibbon Head 78
Johnson, 'King' Mickey 132, 133
Johnson, Rosie 133
Jones, Phillip 145

K
Kamay Botany Bay National Park 147
Kangaroo Valley 131–132
Karskens, Grace 19, 29, 53, 57
Kissing Point settlement 23, 24, 28
Kurnell Meeting Place 147–148
Kurnell settlement 33, 76, 78, 80, 130, 148

L
La Perouse *6.2*, 33, 91, 109
La Perouse settlement
   in 1883 *6.10*
   in 1890s *7.4*
   in 1900 124
   attachment to 129–130
   Botany camp moves to 116
   early residents 109, 116
   economy 122, 123, 128–129
   gazetted as Aboriginal Reserve (1895) 129

Index

government intervention issue 106–107
government rations begin 115
as Mission 7.2, 8–9, 128, 131, 132, 133–134, 139–140
as permanent village 121–122
population 123, 125
Protection Board and 120–121, 128–130
Thornton and 118–119
tramline 120
as urban Aboriginal centre 142–143
Laing, Edward 36–37
Lake Illawarra 133
Lake Macquarie mission 60
Lambert, Charlie 110
land animal population decrease 36
languages 25, 78, 98
'last of the tribe' 86–87, 90–91
Lavender Bay 109
Laycock, Elias Connell 80
Laycock family 80
Licensed Publicans Act 1838 42–43
Little, Constable 113
Little, John 60
Lock family 134
Lowndes, Anna 122–123
Lowndes, Jimmy 99

M

Macarthur family 94–95
McElhone, John 119
Macleay, Alexander 44–45
Macleay, George 45
Macquarie, Governor Lachlan 21, 44, 52
 administration of Aboriginal people 29–31
Mahroot ('Boatswain')
 affiliations *1.3*, 24
 Botany Bay settlement 2.5, 38–39, 48
 burial sites 90
 European attempts to evict 46–47, 52
 as fishing guide 75
 at Smith's Christmas feast 63–64
 as tribal celebrity 88, 90–91
 witness to *Select Committee on Aborigines* (1845) 64
Maloga Mission, Echuca 7.6, 111, 113, 114, 115–116, 120, 131, 132, 134, 141
Malone (later Golden), Lizzie 7.1, 76, 98, 109, 124
Malone, Agnes 122–123
Malone, Johnny
 affiliations 5.8, 75–76, 98–99
 Botany and Sans Souci settlements 79, 84, 109, 122
 Edward Smith Hill and 79
 reports theft of goods 83
 Thornton and 103
Malone family 109, 139
Manly settlement 109, 115, 116
Mann, Livingston 97
marriage
 polygamy 23
 shortage of women 24
Matora 27, 70
Matthews, Daniel 6.7, 111–116, 120
Matthews, Janet 113
Maynard, Fred 141
mental maps 57–58
metal hooks 36
Mettymong, Sally 80
middens 16
Miles, WA 37, 49
Mill Creek settlement 77
Minnie (from Mudgee) 137
missionaries 108, 119, 124, 142
 evangelical movement 127–128 *see also* Christian Endeavour Union
 influence on Aboriginal movement 7.6, 131–134
mogo (stone hatchet) 15
Mona Estate 127
Moore Park settlement 136
Moyse, Vickers 76
Mukhanov, Pavel 91
Mundy, Godfrey Charles 90–91
Murray, Aubrey 37, 38
Myall Creek massacre 54–55, 61

N

names, personal 52, 56, 62
Nanbaree 21
Nancy (and Gurrah) 73, 84–85, 94
Native American tribal territories 17, 22–23

Native Institution, Parramatta 29, 30
Nellola, Nanny 24, 39, 63
Neutral Bay settlement *see* North Shore settlement
Neville, Harriet 121, 123
New South Wales Aborigines Mission 7.6, 133–134, 142
Newcastle 26, 110
Newcastle Steamship Company 129–130
Newtown 67
Nichols, Benjamin 62, 63
Nichols, George Robert ('Bob') 3.7, 5.10
   assistance to Aboriginal people 62–65
   background 54–55
   member of Sydney Aborigines Committee 86, 100
Nichols, Isaac 64
Nielsen Park 146
North Shore settlement 108–109, 115, 135–136
nowie (canoes) 12, 15, 16, 35 *see also* boats
Nugent, Maria 4, 48, 118, 121, 125

O
Oatley, James 54, 77, 80, 104–105

P
Pannerong (ritual combat ground) 69–70
Parkes, Sir Henry 112–113, 114–115, 117, 119
Parramatta annual feasts 29, 44
Parsons, Michael 74
pedestrianism 136, 147
Pemulwuy 22
Petersham Congregational Church 128
Phillip, Governor Arthur 12, 14–15, 23, 52
Piper, Captain John 28
Pittwater 27
pleasure ground hotels 67, 75
Plough Inn 43
Point Piper 28, 69, 71, 79
police trackers 62
political activism 132–133, 138, 141–142
Poor Law 1834 (British) 61
population
   Aboriginal people 33, 34–35, 67–68, 139

   of Aboriginal settlements 125
   Europeans 19, 34, 54, 56, 67, 120, 139
   first Aboriginal census 117
   of La Perouse settlement 123, 125
Port Hacking 13–14, 76
Port Hacking tribe 34, 61–62
Port Kembla 130
Port Phillip (Victoria) 61
Port Stephens tribe *see under* Aboriginal clans and bands
possum skin cloaks 36
Potallick, Thomas 48, 80
Potallick, Thomas (father) 80
Prescott family 43
press 33, 111
Proctor, William 32–33, 38
Protectors of Aborigines 60–61, 117–119
Prout, John Skinner 57

R
Rachael [possibly Baswick] 71, 145
Rae, John 57
rail network 6.1, 120, 135
Randwick 67
rations, non-government 116 *see also* government rations
Rawlingson, George 70, 89
reciprocal exchange 53, 56, 118–119
Redfern 139, 142–143
Redleaf House 73
regrouping following smallpox epidemic 20–27, 87
right behaviour 55–56, 62–65, 71, 79, 81, 118
Robinson, Eliza 128
Robinson, Leo 128
Rose Bay 66
Rose Bay Cottage 4.4, 70
Rose Bay settlement 69–70, 71–72, 84, 94, 108
Roseby Park Aboriginal station 130
Rowe, Trescoe 127
Rowley, John 83–84
Rowley, Mary Ann 130, 140
Rowley, William 7.5, 81, 109, 130, 132, 140
Royal National Park 76, 77
Rum Rebellion 29

Index

Rushcutters Bay settlement *4.6*, 69, 72–73, 84, 90, 94, 108, 110–111, 121, 123, 127–128
Russell, William (Werriberri, 'Billy') 45, 83

S
Salamander 32
Salt Pan Creek settlement 3–4, 130, 132, 140–141, 142
Samuels, Charlie 136
Sans Souci Hotel 125
Sans Souci settlement *6.11*, 79, 84, 109, 122–123, 125–126
Scherzer, Karl von 79, 89
sea levels 13–14
segregation policy 142 *see also* Aborigines Protection Board
Select Committee on Aborigines (1845) 64
Seven Shillings Beach settlement 73, 84–85, 94
shell fish hooks *see* fish hooks (*burra*)
shell-encrusted ornaments (shellwork) 110, 114, 120, 122
Shingleman 43
Shoalhaven (district) 71, 80, 95, 110, 112
Shoalhaven River 130
Simms, Wesley 141
Sir Joseph Banks Hotel *4.7*, 75, 76, 90, 136, 147
Small, William 28
smallpox epidemic 20–21, 22
Smidmore, Thomas 60
Smith, Charles 51, 58, 63–64
Smith, Shirley ('Mum Shirl') 139
Sophia's Spring settlement 73, 85
steamships *5.5*, *5.7*, 95, 97, 98
Stewart, Jack 43
Stewart, Mrs *5.3*
stone hatchet (*mogo*) 15
stone implements *1.1*, 15, 16–17
Surry Hills *2.2*, 34
Sutherland, Forby 80
Swift, Paddy 132
Sydney (town and city)
    in 1790s 22
    in 1800s 28–29
    in 1830s 42
    in 1840s 34–35
    in 1840s: Aboriginal activities *2.9*
    in 1843 *3.1*
    in 1880: popular imaginings of Aboriginal people *6.6*
    1890s–1930s: Aboriginal arrivals 135–138
    Aboriginal strategic distance to 47–50
    Aboriginal use of 53–54, 56–60, 121
    heritage 144–149
    slums 81–82
    suburban expansion 44–47, 120
    Sydney plain exploration 22
    urban Aboriginal communities 139–143
Sydney Aborigines Committee *5.10*, 62–65, 71, 81, 100, 104, 119 *see also* Aborigines Protection Board
Sydney Arms Hotel 43
Sydney Cove (Warrane) 19, 21
Sydney Harbour 13–14, 27, 36
Sydney Intercolonial Exhibition (1873) 90
Sydney International Exhibition (1879) *5.5*, *5.6*, 93, 110
Sydney Markets *3.2*, 58
Sydney municipal elections 60
Sydney Opera House 149
Sydney region (term) 6
Sydney Rowing Club *6.3*, 112
Sydney Tribe 28–29
Sydney tribe *see under* Aboriginal clans and bands
Sydneysiders (term) 7

T
Tamara, Gertrude 40
Tamara, Thomas
    affiliations *1.4*, 24
    Benevolent Asylum 82
    Double Bay settlement 39–40, 48–49, 68, 73
    fishing 63
    presumed lost 26, 64
    signs allegiance to Queen Victoria *3.5*, 60
    at Vaucluse 70

Tarban 63
technological change *1.1*, 15–17, 36
Thornton, George *5.10*, *6.7*
   Circular Quay government boatshed 111–115
   La Perouse Aboriginal settlement 118–119
   Prince Alfred, planned corroboree for 96–97
   as Protector of Aborigines 117–119
   views about Aboriginal people 100, 101–105, 107, 108
Timbery, Emma (née Waldron/Lowndes) *7.3*, 81, 109, 116, 128–129, 133
Timbery, George ('Trimmer') 109, 116
Timbery, Joseph 141
Timbery family 139
track racing 136, 147
trade networks 16
trade with Europeans 48–49, 66, 74–81 *see also* Europeans
   eucalyptus gum 40
   fish 36, 39, 40
   labour and services 53
   shell-encrusted ornaments (shellwork) 110, 114, 120, 122
trams *6.1*, 120–121
tribal celebrities 87–91
tribes *see* Aboriginal clans and bands

U
urban Aboriginal communities 139, 143

V
Vagrancy Act 1835 43–44, 72, 113, 114
Vaucluse Estate 55, 70–71, 146
Vaucluse settlement 40, 69
Verguet, Leopold 39–40
Victoria, Queen 60
Victorian Aboriginal cricketers 92

W
Walker family 73, 84–85
wallbungers *see* fishing and hunting guides
Wanngal (clan) 23
Warangesda Mission *7.6*, 106, 113
Warrane (Sydney Cove) 19, 21

Warrell, William ('Ricketty Dick') *4.3*, *5.1*
   affiliations 24, 90
   Benevolent Asylum 82
   boomerang throwing 48
   Borton and 43, 59
   Rose Bay settlement 69–70, 91
   souvenir medallions *5.4*, 90, 91, 93
   statues by Hogarth *5.2*
   Thornton and 103
   as tribal celebrity 88–89
Water Police *6.3*, 36, 37
Watson, Jean *7.2*, 127–128
Watsons Bay 36, 69, 126–127
Waverley 67
Webb family 140
Wellington mission 60, 135
Wells, Charley 121, 123
Wentworth, Billy 146–147
Wentworth, D'Arcy 55
Wentworth, John 53, 55
Wentworth, Laura 80
Wentworth, William Charles 54–55, 70–71, 104–105
Wentworth family holdings 70, 94–95, 146 *see also* Vaucluse Estate
Werriberri (William Russell) 45, 83
western Sydney people *see under* Aboriginal clans and bands
whaling 74
White, John 52
White, Major 52
William and Ann 62
William IV, King 60
Williams, Iris (Boronia) 140, 146–147
Williams, Dr Shayne 3–4, 5
Williams, Tom, OBE 146–147
Windsor 22
Wingle 70, 90, 103
Wollongong 115, 132
Wollongong tribe 34, 102
women
   domestic service 79–81, 136–138
   economy 12, 16, 35
   marriage and abduction 22
   pregnancies 136–137
   shortage of 24
Wong-ko-bi-kan (Jackey) 100

Index

Woollahra House 66, 71
Woolloomooloo *2.8*, 44, 80
Woolloomooloo settlement 45, 48–49
Worgan, George 52

Worgan, Major 52

Y
Yass 135

www.ingramcontent.com/pod-product-compliance
Ingram Content Group UK Ltd.
Pitfield, Milton Keynes, MK11 3LW, UK
UKHW061224180426
11947UKWH00027B/2002